Frederick Uttley Laycock

Economics and socialism

A demonstration of the cause and cure of trade depressions and national poverty

Frederick Uttley Laycock

Economics and socialism
A demonstration of the cause and cure of trade depressions and national poverty

ISBN/EAN: 9783744723411

Printed in Europe, USA, Canada, Australia, Japan

Cover: Foto ©Suzi / pixelio.de

More available books at **www.hansebooks.com**

ECONOMICS AND SOCIALISM

*A DEMONSTRATION OF THE CAUSE AND
CURE OF TRADE DEPRESSIONS
AND NATIONAL POVERTY*

BY

F. U. LAYCOCK LL.B.

"I cannot play upon any stringed instrument, but I can tell you how of a little village to make a great and glorious city."
THEMISTOCLES

London
SWAN SONNENSCHEIN & CO
PATERNOSTER SQUARE
1895

PREFACE

THE discovery of the truth endeavoured to be set forth in the following pages is the outcome of a project which, in one aspect, was an attempt to show the absurdity of the socialism which is at present exerting so great an influence for evil. This fact has doubtless affected the contents of these pages, although the original plan was practically abandoned.

My first idea, briefly expressed, was to discountenance socialism, but on the other hand to advocate the method of taxation suggested by Mr. Henry George.

The arguments against socialism, it appeared to me, included not only its interference with liberty, which is the plea generally urged against it, but also its tendency to a reduction of the whole nation, and particularly of the poorest, to greater poverty; and furthermore, its antagonism, in effect, to the very equality its supporters profess to advocate. On the other hand, taxation of ground values I conceived to be a just and natural system of taxation, and its adoption a beneficial measure of reform striking at the very roots of an undoubted evil. I proposed to show, more perhaps in detail than in these pages I have done, that this method of taxation was quite opposite in principle and method to socialism. I saw that it was not, as is generally imagined by front-rank Socialists, merely a less efficacious remedy than their own. Still less was it, as thought by more obscure Socialists, the practical recognition of an evil, the demonstration of which was a proof of the correctness of their own teaching.

But although I had realized so much which did not appear to be generally known and admitted, I was, as I afterwards found, still very far from the truth. It was easy to show that socialism fully developed was the reduction of economic error to an absurdity. I might at once have seen that injury to a smaller extent was already being done by the error in its milder form, and could only be avoided by the entire uprooting of the doctrine from its first beginnings. Yet although the coal war of 1893 had strongly impressed itself upon my mind as a gigantic mistake on the part of the men, it had only appeared mistaken in that the state of trade was so utterly disregarded and the laws of supply and demand so visibly set at defiance. For awhile the truth only slowly dawned on me that the error was still deeper, and a principle once started into operation must work itself out to its logical conclusion, and must result in good or evil proportionate to the extent it is followed. It then appeared to me that such was the case, and that Mr. Henry George's teaching in "Progress and Poverty" had lacked greater success for the very same reason as he himself called attention to with regard to free trade in his "Protection or Free Trade," namely, that he stopped short of the whole truth. It is beyond doubt that some good might be accomplished by the adoption of his method of taxation, but that it is not an all-sufficient remedy New Zealand furnishes some evidence, and I hope these pages will show the reason of its failure. The evil of trade combinations may, however, be averted by showing, as I have attempted to show, that in the matter of real wages, as opposed to money wages, the combination method is entirely powerless to increase them.

But there was still something wanting for a complete solution of the problem. So far I had been content with what I thought to be my discovery with regard to the Labour question. As to taxation, I knew I had no claim to originality, except, perhaps, in the method of treatment of the subject. But in view of the benefits to accrue from the system of taxation proposed, and also in view of the truth with regard to labour, I imagined that the whole problem of poverty was solved. I was at that time inclined altogether to disregard the currency question as a matter of indifference, although I knew that there were existing arrangements which were by no means perfect. What I conceive to be my discovery in that respect is rather an indication of the importance of strict method. With regard to the labour question, I had for, at any rate, some days been expecting to reach the conclusion indicated, before, in fact, I did reach it. As to the currency, the idea of charging for coining and its full importance came upon me quite suddenly when I was endeavouring to find a natural system of coinage. And although it has since given me greater difficulty in being sure of the exact results, and of the necessity of putting a limit to the amount of metal coined, than has the Labour question, yet I have never had any doubt of the advisability of adopting the consistently natural system.

The examination of the whole subject has been made as brief as seemed consistent with clear explanation. The appeal for evidence to historical events or tendencies has been avoided, because such evidence is too uncertain to be relied upon, except, perhaps, as negative evidence. It is obviously impossible to postulate of historical tendencies that a given result was due to a particular cause, without having the most reliable and minute knowledge of other possible causes, together with some proof that the circumstance alleged could have the supposed tendency, and not an opposite one. All this would imply such an examination as is now offered before the evidence of the experience could be accepted at all. Any experience may, however, be properly used in illustration, and further verification of theories the correctness of which is otherwise established. And the theories cannot be considered established unless they will explain the experience.

The subject is possibly a difficult one to make simple enough for popular reading. But it is, of course, essential that the mass of the people be taught if advantage is to accrue from any demonstration of the truth in this matter. Indeed, amongst the schemes I first thought of for making clear the important difference between Henry Georgism and Socialism, was the formation of a society for which "Land and Liberty League" seemed a desirable designation. I conceived that such a society should have for its objects the securing of the imposition of the single tax on land values, with a view to making land more accessible on the one hand, and on the other hand the avoidance and discouragement of what at present is known as socialistic legislation, as also of any undoubted attempts to disregard the laws of supply and demand, or to raise prices by diminishing supply. That scheme is still open, and the discovery of the fact that, carried to their logical conclusion, the League's principles must compel it to teach more than I at first anticipated, will not detract from its usefulness or success. It will rather, by offering a more harmonious doctrine, and consequently a better hope of strong conviction, give increased power to convince others. At the same time there will be no lack of moral force when once inquiry has been aroused and conviction secured.

Throughout the civilized world there seems abundant need for the better application of the truths of economic science. For some time poverty and trade depression have been subjects constantly demanding attention. The condition of political parties is an indication of this fact. Politics, in the strict sense of that word, have become much less important in most countries than economics. And I venture to hope that a return to first principles will result, not only in the amelioration of poverty, but in the clearer definition of the policy of parties.

For to my mind party government, in one form or another, is the only reliable guarantee of constant progress. I need hardly add that such progress is essential to the well-being of a people in other respects than the mere supply of the necessaries of life.

The literature of the subject I have attempted to deal with has grown to such proportions that I can scarcely hope to have mentioned every instance on which I have been anticipated. But I am not without confidence that I have contributed something new to the discussion of the subject, and consequently to mankind's knowledge of truths which have the most important bearing on human life, and which have too long remained hidden from human view.

F. U. LAYCOCK.

SHEFFIELD, *February*, 1895.

CONTENTS

CHAPTER		PAGE
	PREFACE	iii
I	INTRODUCTION	1
II	POSTULATES	20
III	DEFINITION OF WEALTH	29
IV	ELEMENTS OF PRODUCTION	40
V	EXCHANGE AND DISTRIBUTION	59
VI	MONEY	76
VII	DIVISION OF WEALTH	97
VIII	RENT OF LAND	113
IX	TAXATION	131
X	INTEREST ON CAPITAL	154
XI	WAGES OF LABOUR	167
XII	WAGES OF SUBSISTENCE	181
XIII	TRADE COMBINATIONS	202
XIV	COMPETITION AND CO-OPERATION	223
XV	POLITICS	246
XVI	COST OF PRODUCTION	265
XVII	COINAGE AND CURRENCY	288
XVIII	COLLECTION OF RESULTS	320
XIX	APPLICATION	348
XX	ETHICS AND PHILOSOPHY	370

ECONOMICS AND SOCIALISM

CHAPTER I

INTRODUCTION

It may be that in some communities a knowledge of the natural laws which influence and more or less control the production and distribution of the wealth essential to human existence and comfort is not of great importance. At any rate it is clear that the fullest command of the science of economics would be of little avail to any people who had not the political power to secure the conditions which a study of the laws of the science proves to be favourable. And in a period of war and turbulence, when the most perfect division and distribution of wealth amongst its producers would be constantly liable to be entirely set aside by the forays of war, or the unjust exactions of some powerful soldier, little benefit could accrue from theoretically exact knowledge of what ought to be. But when a nation emerges from its early state and begins to enjoy settled peace internally, together with political freedom; when the only war in which the nation engages is carried on abroad, and by mercenary troops, who adopt soldiering as a profession, or even under a conscription, in which each must take his turn; then it is likely that the mass of the people will betake themselves to the production and consumption of wealth. The necessity will, therefore, more evidently arise for conditions favourable to its proper division and perfect distribution. Moreover, in an age of political freedom and activity those conditions are likely to be the result of artificial arrangements of one kind or another, over which the people themselves have, and exercise, considerable power. So that a fairly general knowledge of the laws which regulate the various operations implied becomes essential, if artificial arrangements are to accord in any degree approximately with abstract justice or even expediency. Indeed, most will admit that justice is always the highest expediency, and the fact that, in special instances, it may advantageously be tempered with mercy does not detract from the truth of the general rule.

The science which deals with this subject is not only little understood by the great bulk of those who ought to regard a knowledge of it as essential to the performance of their duties, but it is as yet imperfectly explained by all the ability which has so far been brought to bear upon it. Some even of those truths which have received the fullest demonstration have not yet obtained the general assent of those who have made a study of the science. There are still wide divergencies of opinion on questions the settlement of which is of the utmost importance to human welfare. This state of affairs is not the result of any want of study of the subject by men of undoubted learning and ability. But the reading of the views and statements of various authors, together with the arguments those authors give in support of them, has a tendency to make them part of the reader's habit of thought, and prevent him discovering for himself what fallacies have crept into the arguments. This probably accounts for the slow progress of the discovery of the principles and explanations underlying observed facts, and not any deficiency even in original powers of thought—certainly not in reading and research. In face of the great mass of what has been written on the subject by able and learned men, all that can be attempted here, even with regard to the principles with which alone this book must be occupied, is to point out the chief landmarks of the progress hitherto made, with such reference as may be absolutely necessary to the errors or confusions which have prevented further progress.

Exactly at what point such an inquiry should commence is, perhaps, a subject which affords considerable free play to private opinion without in any way doing great violence to the truth. The literature of Greece might conceivably claim an examination in this connection. But the real rise of the science of economics is much more recent than the age of Greek literature, and it is undesirable here to go into a study so purely academical. Nor will Rome furnish any matter for present discussion. The teachers and scholars of Rome were lawyers. They touched this science less than the philosophers who occupied a parallel position in Greece. The truth is that there was little need or scope for the science until men had learnt that slavery was an institution contrary to nature and justice. Nor could there be much hope of the subject receiving practical attention until commerce had made considerable headway.

The first name, therefore, which will be mentioned is that of Antonio Serra, an Italian who wrote in 1613. In his time wealth was so much confused with the precious metals that it has since been imagined the people of the period generally considered wealth to consist of treasure in the way of gold and silver. That such confusion should exist is not difficult to understand in the light of what will be found in the subsequent chapter on money. Particularly is this the case when it is reflected that there was more need then to store up treasure in the form of a generally acceptable commodity than in more recent times. It cannot be too well remembered that it is a mark of the imperfectly developed mind of the human race to do and desire many things without any adequate reflection on the reason why these things are done or desired. By far the greater portion of the most advanced nation now on the face of the earth (whichever nation it may be) have not realized the difference between wealth and money. Moreover, the economic error which still remains even amongst writers on the science is founded on this confusion to a greater extent than can be easily believed. So that there is little room to wonder that a similar confusion was made when money was much more in the form of a tangible commodity than it is at present.

Now, although Serra did not definitely dispute the notion that money in the shape of gold and silver was wealth, he nevertheless showed himself in advance of his time. An attempt was being made and advocated to obtain a plentiful supply of treasure by the artificial expedient of forcibly lowering the high rate of exchange, which resulted from scarcity, and which was in fact the natural inducement to increase the supply. Serra showed that money was likely to be abundant from the same causes that any one might readily see would tend to make wealth abundant. Fertility of soil and convenience of situation (matters which no Government or people could control) were likely to attract abundance of treasure. Beyond these natural advantages, skilful and industrious artizans, an extensive trade, and the order and security which could only be had under a Government based on principles of justice, were the available means of attaining the same object. There could be no better doctrine than this even in the present time, after centuries of study of the subject. Whatever wealth consisted of, there could be no denying that these means would be advantageous in rendering it more abundant. And it is a doctrine worthy of consideration in these days also that even supposing money to be properly an object of desire, the most efficacious means of increasing its supply is to give every facility and encouragement for an abundant production of useful commodities. Serra's teaching in this respect was greatly in advance of much which now receives favour, and ought alone to rebut the error on which many vaunted economic institutions are based.

A dialogue published in England even before Serra's time, under the initials W. S. (William Stafford), contained interesting matter favouring trade in at any rate the more substantial wares, but it cannot receive any considerable notice here. Serra's name has been mentioned because, whether or not he fully realized the true nature of wealth, he seems at least to have mastered the foundation principle that a nation would be most likely to become rich by trade and industry, and not by artificial contrivances of Governments.

The age was, however, an age of restrictions, and such progress as has been made has necessarily been from restriction to freedom. Venice had grown rich by free trade. Being rich, she had imposed restrictions, in spite of which she had remained still wealthy. Charles V. of Spain, full of confidence in the silver to be had by him from America, retaliated on Venice. His example was followed on every hand. Nowhere were such stringent restrictions imposed as in Spain. But other countries were only less unwise in the matter. In France, however, a modification was made when the Duc de Sully gave a measure of freedom to export produce. This freedom benefited the agriculture of his country, and he rightly calculated that a king might more easily obtain taxes from a people who were thriving than from a nation bound down in poverty.

From the policy of absolute restriction two or three chief steps may be noticed as tending towards freedom. Of these the first is the system known as the Mercantile system. The expression is here used in a comprehensive sense. Dr. Friedrich List, who was a great admirer and advocate of the system even after other writers had passed beyond it, preferred to call it the Industrial system, a name which has, however, been applied to the subsequent teaching of Adam Smith, shortly to be noticed.

There is no great author or even school of authors who can be said to be responsible for the Mercantile system. It simply grew. The name most connected with it is that of Colbert, a French minister, who for the encouragement of manufactures prohibited the export of corn, with the result, which he could hardly have anticipated, of causing land to go out of cultivation. He furthermore placed a tax on the importation of manufactured goods. It was to this Colbertism that List was anxious to apply the expression Industrial system. But the doctrine to which the term Mercantile system is more properly applied is somewhat different.

Bearing in mind the importance which was attached to the acquisition of the precious metals, gold and silver, it is easy to understand that their export was regarded with considerable disfavour. The East India Company found it necessary to pay for their imports from India in silver. For this they had to defend themselves, notably against the Turkey Company, whose trade suffered by the competition, and who endeavoured to make out that the East India Company would ruin England by importing manufactured goods cheaper than the Turkey Company could import them. The gist of the East India Company's defence of their export of treasure was that the goods imported were resold to other nations so as to produce at least as much treasure as had been exported. With this notion of the balance of trade is connected the name of Thomas Mun. Sir Josiah Child had after him to defend the Company against the Turkey Company.

The next system demanding notice is what has been called the Agricultural system, proposed as a substitute for the system of Colbert. In this we come upon the rise of Political Economy in the proper sense. Professor Jevons made himself responsible for attributing its suggestion to Cantillon, whom he therefore called the father of the science. But this view is not commonly adopted. The names generally associated with the teaching are those of Quesnay, Gournay and Turgot. This is the order of importance of the three names in connection with the system. Quesnay expounded the doctrine and was looked upon as its author. Gournay was, however, associated with him, and is responsible for the now famous phrase *Laissez faire laissez passer*. Turgot was the statesman of the school. They were called Les Economistes, but are better known by the other name they adopted— namely, the Physiocrats, because they advocated a natural system.

This was the middle of the eighteenth century. That the doctrines of this first attempt at a complete science were imperfect need hardly excite surprise. Its authors had not yet fully realized the nature of wealth. They confused wealth with matter. Value as an element of wealth was disregarded or misunderstood. They conceived that only agriculture and the raising of raw material produced wealth. That alone seemed to increase the quantity of matter available for human use, and that alone, they imagined, gave a surplus. The surplus we shall notice as rent. But although we shall see that all wealth must come from the earth, yet the raw produce of the soil is not the only form of wealth, nor is the raising of raw produce the only means of increasing wealth. The increase of utility in objects is the increase of wealth. The mere carrying of an object from a place where it is useless to one where it is required will be seen to be an addition to the means of human happiness and a production of wealth.

The distinguishing feature of this school was its great preference for agriculture. But it must be remembered that Quesnay, though Court physician, was the son of a farmer. It must also be remembered that under Colbertism agriculture had suffered heavily from the restrictions placed upon it. Hence it was not without reason that the cultivation of the soil found its champions. Besides which it must be conceded that the Physiocrats asked for no restrictions in favour of agriculture,—only that it should be set free. Their great remedy besides freedom for agriculturists was the imposition of the *impôt unique*—the single tax on the net produce of land, of which more must be said in its place. An important error of Quesnay's was that low prices were prejudicial to the lower orders of the people. It should be mentioned in passing that Bandini in Italy is said to have anticipated the Physiocrats in their doctrines, having written in 1737, although his treatise was not published until 1775.

Following the Physiocrats in point of time, we come upon the great Dr. Adam Smith. No man before or since has exercised anything approaching the influence that he did upon the science, though it must not be concluded that no improvements have been made upon his teaching, nor even that no one has shown as great ability to grasp the subject. There was, however, a completeness about his work which has compelled subsequent writers to go over the ground he had already covered. And it must be confessed that his errors have been to a large extent copied by his followers. On some points this will appear as we proceed.

Not only was his observation of facts wondrously complete, but he adopted his own method and exercised his own thought in dealing with them. The Physiocrats had realized the importance of land in the matter of wealth production. He gave great prominence to the importance of labour. So long before as 1667 Sir William Petty had referred to the influence of labour in the creation of value. He had even then said that "labour is the father and active principle of wealth, lands are the mother." Locke had said that differences of value were owing to differences of labour. But Smith was the first to take this as a basis of economic doctrine. It will be seen that the taking of labour as the basis of value was an error. But the great service Adam Smith rendered to mankind was to show what wealth really was.

The confusion between wealth and money has already been referred to. The prevalence of this error, with the great regard paid to the possession of treasure, was probably the cause of most of the restrictions placed upon trade. The underlying confusion is very difficult to eradicate from men's minds, even from those of great thinkers who treat of the science, and still more from those of clever speakers and writers of less clear perception. When the history of the nineteenth century is fully and faithfully written, it will be found recorded that, in the last decade of the century, a great deal of commotion was caused with regard to what was termed a living wage. Newspapers seriously reported the speeches of so-called Labour Leaders, in which it was stated that a new and valuable principle had been adopted in the relations of capital and labour. When inquiry is made as to what the living wage and the principle consisted of, it will transpire that it was a fixed minimum payment, calculated in money, without any ratio or regard to the prices of the wealth necessary for living, and that even as a minimum money wage it depended on a doubtful demand for coal (the commodity to be produced by the labourers concerned) at such a price as would secure an exchange. Thus it will appear that it was totally uncertain whether even the opportunity to earn the money would be available. And beyond that there was no connection between the quantity of money and any standard of living. Yet the historian must state that many apparently intelligent men were found to support this plan as that of a living wage, and of the remainder very few realized the absurdity even of the expression.

This, however, was not because no one had seen the difference. Hume had vigorously attacked the error before Smith. And Adam Smith fully realized that wealth was not money, but the useful things

which satisfy human desire. On the other hand, he showed clearly that the Physiocrats also were in error when they confused wealth with matter and force.

The second great service rendered by Adam Smith was to advocate free trade with all the world, the breaking down of the commercial barriers which had separated nations. In England, at any rate, that lesson has been learnt from him. And to him apparently belongs the credit of being the first to advocate it, though its adoption was a long way off when he wrote.

In Adam Smith's work we have the foundation of the greater part of the succeeding economic science. And only a very brief reference can be made to the writers who developed, qualified, or added to his doctrines.

First in point of time amongst those who materially influenced economic teaching was Malthus. His work is important rather on account of the influence it exerted than because of any truths he enunciated. His teaching is open to obvious and fatal objections, but it had the advantage of supporting existing institutions. He endeavoured to show that poverty was not the result of any imperfect distribution of wealth, but of the tendency of the human race to increase up to the limits of subsistence. Food and subsistence he conceived could only increase by arithmetical progression,—that is, by additions of further quantities,—while population would increase by geometrical progression,—that is, by multiplication. The absurdity of this method of argument is not difficult to perceive, even supposing that there is an indisputable truth underlying the whole. As a matter of fact, however, there is every indication that mankind find it easier as civilization advances to increase the earth's production beyond the needs of human existence. The professed object of Malthus, it ought to be mentioned, was to show what was the principle which prevented population increasing beyond the means of subsistence; for the tendency to do that was hardly doubted. The principle he at first found in the positive checks of misery, disease, etc. But he afterwards found also a preventive check in the prudential regard which men had to the need for subsistence, and the care accordingly exercised not to undertake the burden of a family without the prospect of being able to maintain it. When the doctrine had reached that point it did not amount to much. In truth there is no reason why the ideas should ever have affected economic science. But there is no denying or forgetting that they did. And the influence on the science was not good. It must, however, be conceded to Malthus that he helped to wean the notions of the time from the prevailing inclination to recklessly encourage increase of population.

The other writers who must be mentioned dealt more with economic science in the strict sense. J. B. Say in France urged Smith's free trade doctrines and made himself famous for his treatment of the subject of gluts in the market, showing that they were the result, not of over-production of commodities, but of under-production of other commodities to exchange for them. David Ricardo in England established the truth of the suggestions previously made (first by Anderson) as to the law of rent, thus making clear the proportionate share which, in a country where competition is free, the owners of the soil will take of its productions. When we deal with the subject of wages of subsistence, Ricardo must be severely criticised for the share he took in sending inquirers on the wrong track. But his ability as an economist, and particularly with regard to the currency, is undeniable, though it has perhaps been much over-rated. J. R. McCulloch is well known as an editor of Smith's great work, but there is nothing in his own original writings calling for special attention here. Nassau William Senior was an economist possessing powers of criticism and original thought. His name will be mentioned in connection with some of his views. James Mill, though less known than his son, nevertheless made some contribution to the discussion of the subject. To him apparently belongs the credit of pointing out that all man can do in the production of wealth is to move the objects of nature. The importance of this is to show that the production referred to when the restricted meaning of producing raw material is attached to the expression is not so distinguishable from other efforts as might be imagined. When reduced to the consideration of what exactly the various services of farmers, manufacturers, carriers and merchants consist of, the effect on external objects is the same. Other names might be mentioned, as Torrens, Wakefield, Babbage, Jones, Bastiat and Bagehot (who wrote after J. S. Mill), but it will be enough to refer here to John Stuart Mill, whose work marks an epoch in the study of the science.

It would probably be too much to say that the position occupied by J. S. Mill with regard to economics is entirely the result of his own labours. He had the good fortune to write just about the time when the labours of Smith and his school had culminated in the adoption by England of the free trade in commodities which they had advocated. The success of the measure was so much beyond dispute that an impression began to be felt that the last word had been said on the science, although events have shown that much remained to be done. Mill was the last important writer on the subject in England, and something like a feeling grew up that the science which it was half imagined had begun with Smith was now completed by Mill. Erroneous as this was, there can be no denying that Mill had striven to deserve the position. He prepared a comprehensive work dealing with the subject in detail, and embodying as far as he could the work of his predecessors from Smith onwards. He even included in his survey much of what has reference to schemes of social regeneration rather than of economic science. A full examination of the errors of his work would occupy much time and space, but a few points must be noticed in their place.

In passing John Stuart Mill the subject can no longer be treated as flowing in a single channel. In one direction there has been a great tendency (which indeed he also fell into in the course of his life) to re-involve the science. This involution has been an avowed one, in spite of the fact that the theory of evolution has been more and more generally accepted in almost all human thought.

The method which consists of re-involving the subject cannot but be described as entirely vicious. There is a very great difference—a difference as between good and evil—between, on the one hand, showing the relation of a science, and what it reveals, to other sciences and their teaching; and, on the other hand, confusing the proper subjects of one inquiry with those which belong to another. Generalization is not confusion; it implies specialization. To heap together physiology, morals, economics and the fine arts into one heterogeneous mass, as has become almost habitual in some quarters in these days, is certain to do harm, even though some good thoughts may be found by readers who have the skill to separate the various constituents of the motley collection. Although this is true, however, it is also quite true that the expounders of the science must have regard to its place as a study relating to human well-being. It cannot be said that economists have always brought their conclusions to this line. In short, it has not been kept well in mind that the sphere of economics is the satisfaction of human desires, not the determination of their quality, nor, on the other hand, the furthering of objects merely subsidiary to that satisfaction.

In another direction we have Professor J. E. Cairnes, who endeavoured to explain away Mill's errors and to put the teaching of the latter into an aspect which might receive acceptance. Professor Henry Fawcett was a great admirer of Mill, and followed him closely into his more important errors, though it must be confessed he also effected some improvement in certain directions. Dr.

Amassa Walker must also perhaps be placed in Mill's school. W. T. Thornton is chiefly noticeable as having controverted some of the doctrines of this school relating to wages.

In America a body of protectionist doctrine sprang up under the influence of List, who has already been mentioned. Following List, its first and chief exponent was Henry Charles Carey. The doctrine held and put forward with considerable subtlety of argument was that free trade might be advantageous for old countries, but a measure of protection was necessary for the establishment of manufactures in a new country.

Another school demanding passing notice is known as the historical school. It has its home chiefly in Germany. Not much importance can here be attached to its methods, although their evil is not confined to Germany. As a study there can be no harm in ascertaining various historical economic conditions. But it must be retained in its place as an historical study. When this method is put forward as a ground for advocating certain doctrines and institutions because of observed tendencies in that direction, much injury is capable of resulting. For instance, there are those who imagine they see by this method that Socialism is fast hastening into the region of practical application. They observe that industry is being gathered into large concerns preparatory to that consummation. And they look particularly for signs of it in the United States of America—a country with abundance of natural resources and a population of little over twenty to the square mile, but which with that sparse population has its people out of work and starving by the thousand. The wonder is that any one ventures to handle such an argument at that end.

A more important school must, however, be mentioned. Even before Mill's work was written Augustin Cournot, a Frenchman, had dealt with the science of economics in a strictly mathematical method. A famous follower of his in this respect was Professor W. S. Jevons, to whom a prominent place must be given. As belonging to a great extent to the same school, Professor Marshall should be mentioned; but he and Mrs. Marshall have done most service in the industrial department of the subject. The views and explanations of this school belong to a deeper study of the theory of the science than need enter the discussions which will follow, and which are of more immediate practical importance.

Two other names may be mentioned as not exactly belonging to the mathematical school and not to be classed under it. Professor Sidgwick is the author of a work remarkable chiefly for its criticism of various views which have obtained in the science. Professor F. A. Walker, an American, has done good and independent work relating to wages—a subject which in recent years has occupied much attention among economists.

Mr. Henry George, another American, occupies a different but by no means a less important position. He has demonstrated once more the benefits of free trade in commodities, and the futility of the so-called protection. This was rendered necessary by the fact that in the United States of America the protection fallacy had been both advocated and adopted. But his chief addition to the science has been in his book with regard to taxation. The single tax of the Physiocrats has been disregarded since their day. To him belongs the honour of reviving it. In a few places the principle has already been adopted. In coming to his conclusions, however, he had occasion to notice the current theories of wages and to controvert them. And some credit is perhaps due to him in this respect.

This rough survey will be enough to indicate that the subject has been a good deal discussed, and it would be impossible even to attempt to follow all these writers through even a portion of their views. The inquiry will proceed independently of them, and the theories previously put forward will only be mentioned when it seems necessary to adopt or to refute them.

CHAPTER II

POSTULATES

THE postulates of the science appear to be :—

1. Man, for his continued existence and the gratification of his desires, requires to be constantly provided with certain material commodities which are known as wealth. His necessities extend beyond those things of which the supply is free and unlimited.

2. Of some commodities nature makes plentiful and free provision, but the provision thus made has always to be gathered or dug for, and frequently to be carried to the place where it is required for man's subsistence and enjoyment. It has also in many instances to be adapted to man's wants; besides which, it is found that of many commodities human beings can assist to make nature even more productive.

3. Each man will seek to gratify his desires, including his necessary appetites, as easily as he can —that is, with the least possible expenditure of his labour and trouble.

These postulates stand related to each other as subject complement and copula respectively.

The first is man's desire for consumption—the demand, the struggle for existence, impelled by the instinct of self-preservation and the desire for happiness. It will be convenient to speak of this as the demand.

The second is man's ability to provide for his needs and desires, the supply, human capacity for increasing, adapting, and distributing nature's productions, and the competitive effort to do so. It will be convenient to speak of this as supply.

The third postulate is the connecting link of the other two—the law, *norma*, or rule, which lies at the root of the science, guiding every action of which the science takes note, and establishing a first principle to which all right conclusions must conform.

It may be convenient to say here with regard to both demand and supply that there is no evidence of any ultimate limit. Man's desires increase in variety as they are supplied. In this he differs from all plants and all other animals. So that, unlike them, he is not merely confined to his own reproduction as a means of increasing consumption. Although his physical appetite may not increase, his desires for gratification, if not infinite, may increase indefinitely. The mind, at any rate, refuses to be limited. The satisfaction of present desires impels a human being to seek fresh modes of enjoyment, and not merely cessation from effort. This fact will sufficiently account for the want of any general surplus of wealth, and for the continued desire for further productions requiring additional effort, however great the possibilities of wealth production may be.

On the other hand, it is acknowledged that in various parts of the earth the possibilities of present production are more than enough for the world's needs. A very little effort could vastly increase these possibilities. There is no lack of evidence, for instance, that of vegetable substances, even comparatively barren land, can by the application of more scientific and perfect cultivation be made much more prolific. This improvement is possible to an extent as yet unascertained. It appears, therefore, unnecessary to discuss at any length the doctrines taught by Malthus. There seems also no need for any of the artificial restraints on population which have frequently been advocated. Before their necessity could be admitted it would require to be shown that, in spite of the application of the labour available in all ranks of society, there was still a dearth of commodities. This seems to be nowhere shown even with regard to particular political divisions.

Nor does it seem likely that any possible restraints could be of service towards the end proposed. Certainly there can be no advantage in limiting the supply of wealth with a view of keeping down the population. It is noticed that plants in their natural state flower most profusely at the margin of their habitat—that is, under those conditions in which they can only just exist. It is as though nature would have them make up in the reproductive effort for the want of favourable conditions for vigorous growth. Such places and conditions would not be where we should look for the most perfect plants. And much the same considerations apply to mankind. The largest families are generally found amongst the poorest people. If any conclusion is to be drawn from experience on this point, it must be that in the long run the human race is more likely to keep its numbers within bounds by increased wealth than by diminished subsistence. Increased prosperity may increase population, but a prosperous person or nation will exercise greater foresight than a less prosperous one in securing a prospect of subsistence for the children to be born. Moreover, though it is true that the high birth-rate experienced in great poverty is somewhat compensated for by a high death-rate, yet on a comparison with lower rates in both respects the balance of desirability is entirely in favour of the latter.

At any rate, it is certain that any artificial restraints (unless literally in chains) would be more likely to be adopted by the best of the race than by the inferior types. If heredity has even the least modicum of truth and applicability to humanity, those restraints would operate to cause only such progress as is from better to worse. It is indeed probable that the imperfect conditions of wealth production and distribution have that tendency at present; facts and experience point to that conclusion. What is here desirable to be made clear, however, is that artificial restraints on population, which appear in the first place not likely to diminish want and suffering or to conduce to the desirable progress of the race, are in the second place not at all necessary. And there is no evidence that ever they will be necessary. The point does not in truth come within the present science. If after the economist has completed his work and the truths of his science have been applied to human life it is found that there is still insufficient wealth, it will be for some other science or department of social science to find means of increasing subsistence or diminishing population.

The question of whether or not the wealth available for man's use which is to be found in distant regions is or is not applicable to his needs will not be discussed here. It is a question for settlement by considerations of industrial science and the possibilities of transit. But that there is now no difficulty in that respect is amply proved by the observations very frequently made by men whose thinking powers are altogether untrained. Such men frequently say that the cause of poverty and distress is over-production or under-consumption, and never by any chance do they speak of under-production. This is evidently inconsistent with over-population. It is true that wealth does not always reach the people who need it, but the cause of that is exactly what the science now under consideration sets itself to discover.

It is important, however, to make quite clear what the economist may safely take as his data, to what particular domain his inquiries must be directed, and how far, if at all, other considerations should cause him to hesitate about drawing the conclusions to which his inquiries lead him.

And, first, he may surely take the demand as proved without his arguments. The physiologist tells him that besides air man must have food and drink. The air may be free and frequently the water, but the food is seldom accessible without considerable effort of some kind, and that by or on behalf of every individual. Beyond this clothing may be considered necessary and beneficial; shelter in the way of houses will be required by most of the human race, not to mention the endless variety of comforts and luxuries which in the progress of the race are invented.

The question may be asked whether the economist may treat all these desires as legitimate, or whether he should attempt to find means of preventing their gratification to the full extent; and if so, to what extent the supply should be limited. If this question appear too absurd to be worth stating, the objection can only be met by saying that in effect it frequently finds place in the writings of some who attempt to treat of the science. But, in answer to the question, it must be replied that the economist, as such, has nothing to do with the consumption of wealth considered merely as the satisfaction of human desire. So far as it may have an effect on future production he may consider it; but as to whether certain kinds or quantities of wealth are beneficial to humanity he can take no notice. That is a question for the physiologist, the moralist, or it may be the artist or the general biologist. But as an economist he must rigorously confine himself to his own science if the issue is to be clear.

Were the fact otherwise, the study of the subject must at once cease, and the whole of the conditions be left to mere haphazard. For if an individual cannot choose the kind and quantity of wealth required for his own consumption, who is to choose it for him? What means can be found for discovering a person more fit than himself to exercise this discretion? and how will such a person exert his authority? It may be that some kinds of wealth are wholly deleterious, and a wise Government will prohibit their use, but that is beyond the province of the economist. It is equally impossible for him to consider the quantity of wealth to be provided for each individual except by reference to that individual's desires.

Fortunately, no such fetters are put on the inquiry. Nowhere is there any evidence of any injury likely to be caused by a constant and plentiful supply of wealth to every human being. Alternate fasting and feasting may be injurious, but such a condition could not be the result of a perfect supply, for perfection in that respect would imply constancy. Whether the race, or the nation, or the individual be considered, no good can come of attempts to starve either the weak or the strong. The life of the individual will be fuller and more perfect for an ample and easily attainable supply of subsistence. Any artificial attempt to secure the survival of the fittest will be to hinder nature in the work which she alone can, and in the long run will, do of herself. And the obstruction will cause pain and injury.

In the second place, a question may be asked on the subject of supply. Need the inquiry be hampered by considerations as to whether man should be prevented from obtaining *easily* the wealth which it has just been seen he may without injury enjoy plentifully? Already men have shown great aptitude for making use of the forces of nature so as to save bodily labour. There are not wanting those who look upon this as a lamentable fact. But Professor Marshall has shown that the use of machinery is not injurious to the human being. Man, he shows, is better for the work he can have done by steam and electric power, not only in the increased production, but in his own physical and mental constitution. What workmen lose in mere manual dexterity they gain in enlarged perception and judgment. The physical frame can be thereby saved from injury, which it would otherwise have suffered. With a view to mere development, it is evident that exercise of body or mind can be obtained better and more beneficially without its being compulsory for wealth production.

By these considerations the scope of the inquiry is limited and more clearly defined. The economist has only to suggest conditions for the efficient supply of wealth constantly and abundantly to every individual. He may disregard the so-called social organon, which is in fact a mere mental creation. Society is an aggregation of individuals: the individual is not an organ of society. It is only by analogy that society can be said to be organized at all. The unit is the individual: he has wants and desires of his own, and the economist must consider him as an individual in studying the supply of those wants and desires.

Something ought perhaps to be said with regard to the third postulate, and the subject in hand will then be defined. The inquiry starts without any apparent necessity for poverty. Poverty is unsupplied need. The need is the subject of the science, but the complement spoken of in the second postulate is amply sufficient for the present (and, so far as can be seen, for the indefinite future), if it can be properly applied. The one link by which it must be applied is laid down in the third postulate. Each individual will satisfy his desires as easily as he can. The truth of this postulate is not taken for granted, as in the case of the other two; it is self-evident, and, in fact, an axiom. For it is inconceivable that a person could desire anything and wilfully spend unnecessary trouble in obtaining it; unless, indeed, he had another object in the expenditure of the trouble, which would be another desire to be satisfied and a further instance of the truth of the proposition. It is not a truth which requires qualification. In itself it affords the fullest scope for the most self-denying altruism. It, moreover, leaves ample room for the fact that men are not always perfect in their judgment or vigorous in their actions. Their desires may be weak, or their lethargy may be strong. As to man's altruism, it is a form of desire or nothing at all. The demonstration of the science does not require a non-existent, perfect economic man. It takes man as it finds him, and assumes nothing concerning him except what is universally true. Each man is a more or less perfect business man; how much less perfect it is impossible to estimate and unnecessary to know. Nor is the motive or object of the man's desire a disturbing element in the inquiry. The desire in its relative intensity, not in any way its perfection, is to be measured, in order that it may be supplied. This only is within the province of the economist.

CHAPTER III

DEFINITION OF WEALTH

IF any true conclusions are to be reached with regard to the subject now entered upon, it will be necessary first to have clear definitions of the terms to be used. The meaning of the word wealth in its general acceptation is not by any means as precise as is required for scientific demonstration. The objects of which wealth consists cannot well be enumerated, but the expression must be sufficiently defined to make clear what is referred to, and to make it possible, when the character and circumstances of an object are known, to say whether or not it is included in the total sum of wealth.

In the first place, it should be noted that, for the purpose of this inquiry, wealth consists of material objects. To speak strictly, it should be stated that the quality of wealth inheres in those objects according to certain ascertainable circumstances, as, for instance, situation. So that the same objects are wealth at one place and at another not wealth. But for practical purposes it is enough to say that the wealth consists of the objects. And these are material objects. This at once distinguishes wealth from personal services—that is, from labour. Wealth may render service, but it cannot be said that whatever renders service is wealth. Labour renders service, it may produce wealth, but it is not itself wealth. And although such wealth, when transferred, includes, or is the result of, human labour, the labour is one thing, the wealth is another. By the labour the material objects have been moved, and by various considerations the quality of wealth is now found to be in those objects.

In the second place, the objects referred to must be necessary or desirable to human beings for their maintenance or gratification. This quality is spoken of as utility. The expression value in use referred to by Adam Smith should be entirely discarded from this connection. For the word value has now, and without doubt had then, a different meaning from utility. Professor Jevons spoke of disutility. This might be a convenient expression for his then present purpose, in order to give him the sign minus for his mathematical demonstrations. But disutility must be because of the situation of the liquid or solid matter referred to, as, for instance, water in a mine or solid earth which must be removed to make way for the foundation of a building. Moreover, such disutility of matter is invariably owing to the difficulty it causes in obtaining, adapting, or using other material wealth. It will, therefore, be sufficient to disregard this negative wealth as though simply valueless material, making other wealth more difficult of access. We thus treat only of positive wealth, all of which must have utility—that is, it must be useful to mankind, either in the sense of being really beneficial or, at least, desired.

A third limitation is that nothing can be considered wealth if and where it can be freely taken in unlimited quantities, or in quantities which so far exceed the demand as to be practically unlimited. Nothing is more essential or desirable to human beings than atmospheric air. But on the earth's surface it cannot be considered wealth, for the reason which underlies the common expression "free as the air we breathe." When, however, the air has by some means been conveyed into deep mines, it there has all the qualities of wealth. Water is not wealth where every one may take as much as he requires without payment or permission. But in the middle of a large city only that water can be had which has become wealth. The quality of wealth now referred to may be described as scarcity.

The union of the two qualities last mentioned—namely, utility (in the sense explained) and scarcity—is what is really meant by the expression value. It is a quality which combines the other two. Nothing has value except what is desired, nor has anything value, even though desired and useful, unless it is more or less scarce. If these two qualities are united there is value without further qualities. It is not necessary that any object should be exchangeable or transferable in order that it may have value. This will immediately be seen in the case of skill, which is valuable and frequently costly, but not exchangeable. The determining influences of value in exchange open out a wider inquiry, which will be noticed in another chapter.

A fourth limitation is that wealth must be such as can be exchanged. It is not essential that it be transportable, but at least the right to its use and the power of enjoyment of it must be transferable. Thus the skill of labourers, of whatever grade, is not wealth. For although a physician may sell his services, he cannot sell his skill, and accordingly it is not wealth. Nor is the skill of any other person, though it be such as will directly assist him to produce wealth. The skill may be, and often is, valuable to the individual, and in the probability of its exercise valuable to the nation, but it cannot be transferred or exchanged. Even though it be considered to be a quality inhering in a material object, and consequently not offending against the first limitation, yet it is eliminated from the subject of wealth by the impossibility of its exchange. It must be confessed that did the skill or other good quality belong to one of the lower animals it would indeed be wealth. For it would be a quality inhering in a material though living object. And it is in the qualities of objects that wealth is really found. But such skill or good quality in the animal would be wealth only in that it could be transferred. The whole animal with its attributes could be sold from hand to hand.

In the fifth and last place is a limitation which has frequently been overlooked, but which for a proper understanding of the subject must be made and kept quite clear. The expression wealth ought not to, and in this book will not, include that which has not been adapted by man to his use. Nor does adaptation as here used mean appropriation. Unexplored land has already been eliminated from the total sum of wealth. For as yet it cannot be said to possess value, except it may be to a nation as territory, and not to an individual as useful land. Even though there may be gold or diamonds lying on its surface, these precious things are still not wealth. They can perhaps hardly be called valuable before their existence is known of. But it is certain they have not been adapted for man's use, although in their case the mere carrying of them away would be sufficient adaptation to constitute them wealth. Even after appropriation, as in the case of gold reefs and diamond mines, care must be taken that the reefs and mines with their ungotten gold and diamonds are not looked upon as wealth in the scientific sense. They are still land, and must be kept distinct in the mind from wealth, though their products are certainly wealth. In the same way all land must be clearly distinguished. In so far as it has been adapted by human labour, the fertility or other usefulness inhering in the land is wealth. But the extension or space, the situation, and the natural fertility of the land are all independent of man's adaptation. He cannot carry away or otherwise adapt, although he may appropriate, the situation or extension of the land. And, although also he may increase or diminish natural fertility, yet so far as it is natural it must not be considered wealth. This extends to all that is usually spoken of as natural wealth, such as rivers, virgin forests, and ungotten minerals. Occasionally all the utility of land is the result of man's adaptation, and is therefore wealth—sometimes only a portion is wealth. But as in this science we deal always with values, no difficulty arises in the separation of wealth from land. The value of the one and of the other is a question of fact to be ascertained in each case—and that without great difficulty.

There seems to be no English word which exactly expresses the condition of artificial fitness for man's use now under consideration. The words adaptation and preparation both refer to the act rather than the condition. The word adapted when used to describe the condition of any object refers as much to a natural condition as to an artificial one. The word prepared is not open to the latter objection. So that in coining a word to express the fifth quality the better plan seems to be to take prepared as the basis, and, for want of a better expression, to describe the quality as preparedness—the condition of having been artificially adapted.

These limitations will determine what is included in the expression wealth as it will be used. The five qualities which must be combined in the quality of wealth are materiality, utility, scarcity, exchangeability, and preparedness.

Substituting for utility and scarcity their equivalent, the one word value, we have as a definition of wealth—

The valuable and exchangeable material objects prepared by human effort for human use—that is, by the efforts of man for the satisfaction of his needs and desires.

With this may be compared the portion of a sentence of Mr. Henry George's which appears to contain his definition of wealth—a definition in one aspect better than that just suggested: "The natural substances or products which have been adapted by human labour to human use or gratification."

In both cases, however, it must be borne in mind that the objects which are not yet finished products, in being directly applicable to human satisfaction, use, or gratification, may, nevertheless, be wealth. They are in the course of adaptation, or are assisting man to obtain other requisite wealth. The utility required by the definition may be direct or indirect.

Professor Nassau Senior's definition is clear and excellent so far as it goes. He says of wealth: "Under that term we comprehend all those things, and those things only, which are transferable, are limited in supply, and are directly or indirectly productive of pleasure or preventive of pain." The definition includes the second, third and fourth qualities mentioned, but does not make clear the need for the first and fifth, unless perhaps the first is to be implied from the use of the word things. That, however, is not clearly evident.

In order to make quite clear what wealth consists of, it may be advisable to mention or recapitulate what the definition excludes.

The first limitation, as was pointed out, excluded labour—that is, personal services—as not being material or tangible substances. Nor are such services qualities inhering in such objects, which might perhaps be said of skill. Even the services of an animal, a cart-horse, for instance, are not wealth, though directly productive of wealth, and though the strength by which the cart-horse renders those services may be considered as wealth, because it inheres in a material and transferable object.

The same limitation will apply to mere rights. If a right is to a material object as against all the world, the person having the right may be said to own the object, and consequently to possess wealth. But if the right is against a person who is merely under obligation to render wealth, the right cannot be called wealth. If wealth exists on which some mortgage is held, it must be counted only in the hands of the person actually in possession of it.

A national debt must not be considered as wealth. To the nation it is, it need hardly be said, not even valuable. But, beyond that, even to the individual it is not wealth, although commanding wealth. It is merely a right to future taxes, created by the authoritative power in the state for the benefit of the individual on grounds not now under discussion. Similar remarks would apply to monopolies. Some monopolies, such, for instance, as those granted to inventors, appear wholly beneficial in encouraging invention, as well as just in securing to each the result of his labours. But though the article produced under a monopoly may be wealth, the monopoly itself is not wealth.

The objects above mentioned would not offend against the second, third and fourth limitations, and would consequently satisfy Nassau Senior's definition so far as it is clearly expressed. But to admit them as wealth would cause obvious confusion. For to admit labour might lead to the conclusion that a vigorous man could satisfy his need for wealth by his own exertions, without natural objects on which to exert them. Further, if rights were admitted as wealth, the same wealth might be counted as belonging both to the possessor of it and also to the man to whom he owed a debt, which would obviously be confusing the subject. So that labour and mere rights must be excluded; although by labour wealth may be produced, and by a right it may be commanded.

The second limitation excludes all those objects, even though material, which a man who possesses is willing to freely part with. The third excludes those which he would not willingly be entirely without, but which under his present circumstances are so plentiful to him that he does not consider them to possess any value; and he desires no more of them. An instance is atmospheric air on the earth's surface. In the remainder of the inquiry these two qualities will always be taken together and spoken of as value.

The fourth limitation excludes qualities of persons, as natural or acquired skill, strength, learning, good health, affections, personal reputation, and many valuable possessions which cannot be transferred.

The fifth limitation excludes what will hereafter be spoken of as land—nature's free gift. It is either unadaptable, as the extension of the earth's surface with its material foundation, and the course of a stream with its constant supply of water, or it is, at least, unadapted, as minerals still ungotten, and virgin forests still uncut.

This should make clear the objects to be treated of; but one important distinction is still undealt with. Value and the possibility of exchange naturally call for some measure of value. If value alone existed there would be no need to measure it. It is true that law courts attempt to estimate the value of that which is not transferable. This occurs when they pronounce judgments for damages as a solace for wounded affections, compensation for injured health or limbs, or amends for detrimented reputation. But, apart from the question of whether or not the value of these things can ever be satisfactorily estimated, it is evident that no recompense could be afforded for their loss were it not for the fact that other things are transferable. The idea is to give something which is valuable and transferable in place of that which was of value, but could not be transferred, although it could be lost or destroyed. The possibility and frequency of exchange call for the use of a medium, and this medium of exchange (known as money) naturally becomes a measure of value. Money frequently consists of a valuable commodity or portion of wealth. But it is not essential that the medium used be intrinsically valuable or possess even ornamental worth for its own sake. It is merely a representative of value. Paper with certain authenticating marks is frequently made legal tender money. Such money does not derive its value from its intrinsic worth in even the least degree. The nature of the money commonly used by civilized communities will, however, be more properly dealt with after the subject of exchange. The object at present is to distinguish wealth from money. The important distinction is found in the different purposes to which wealth and money are respectively applied, the one being for use, the other for exchange. Some money consists of what is really wealth. But it does not derive its value from that fact. For indeed it is not intended to be used as wealth. Its use is in being passed on by way of exchange. When metallic coins are melted for use in the arts, the metal ceases to be used as money, and becomes really wealth, possessing a value for its own sake. But in the usually known instances the coins passing between two persons are not intended to be used as wealth, but merely as money. For that purpose a piece of paper bearing the proper marks, and not in itself worth a farthing, is in England quite as valuable as five gold sovereigns. Indeed, it is more valuable for the purpose than a hundred silver shillings. Similar statements would generally apply to other nations.

The two things, wealth and money, are thus clearly separated. Wealth is valued and acquired for its own sake. Money may or may not possess value in itself. That is a matter of indifference. But it possesses value by representation, and is sought after as a means of commanding wealth or services. If, as in the case of corn (which has been used as money), it will probably soon be consumed, its use is not purely as money, although it does duty for money. The true use of money is merely to be passed on during the whole course of its existence as money. Money is used by being transferred; wealth is used by being retained or consumed. It will be necessary to bear in mind the various distinctions here mentioned if true conclusions are to be arrived at.

CHAPTER IV

ELEMENTS OF PRODUCTION

THE scope of the inquiry has now been further defined. It will, therefore, be more possible to reach definite and clear conclusions than it otherwise would have been. For instance, if land in any sense had not been rigorously excluded from the term wealth, it would have appeared that the inquiry was in part how to increase the amount of land in a country. If labour or skill had not been excluded, the question might have seemed how to add to the total sum of labour available in any community, or how to improve technical education. It is needless to say that such questions are simply absurd from the economist's point of view. But by the process of delimitation we ascertain once for all what it is we seek, and consequently obtain a better chance of reaching the object desired. Having stated what we mean by wealth, we can at once inquire how, if at all, it may be created or increased, and man's requirements thus satisfied.

In the first place, it is obvious that land—the earth on which we live—is a necessary element in the production of wealth. Wealth consists of material substances which must inevitably be obtained from the solid globe on which man exists. Land is essential to him, even though no such thing as wealth were necessary. On it he must find support for his material body. There are means of floating in the atmosphere, but it is only by the use of materials taken from the more solid earth, and only for short periods at a time. In a somewhat less degree the same is true of the sea. Beyond this support, however, if man must have wealth, he must obtain it from the earth.

It is quite true that some wealth is obtained from the portion of the earth which is covered with water. Not only does the ocean supply man with a way which is more easy to traverse than a desert land of similar area would be, but it supplies him with many useful commodities, and particularly with fish for use as food. Even the atmosphere is material, though gaseous, and it also has some share in wealth production. But what will occupy more of the attention of the student of economics is the land strictly so called. It is capable of monopolization in a way in which the sea and atmosphere are not. On it also the homes of mankind are found. Men and women, for the most part, are born, live and die on it. From it the greater part of the wealth is obtained. Nations fix their boundaries on it. Besides which, it would be impossible to use even the sea without certain help to be had from the land.

Land being so important a part of them, it will be convenient to speak of the whole of nature's free gifts as land. That is the term which (partly from their associations, no doubt) has been generally adopted by writers on political economy. No confusion is likely to occur from this use, and it would be more difficult to convey a true meaning by means of any other term than by continuing the use of that already adopted. Meantime it may be borne in mind that what is meant by the expression is the earth : that which exists independently of man, and would have existed had he not lived, or even had he lived as a plant only. Indeed, we may go further, and say that which would have existed if he had had the power to move himself, but no power to move external objects. Once grant him the power of moving external objects, and there is a possibility that he will begin to create wealth by adapting external objects to his use.

Here, then, is the first element of the production of wealth — an ultimate element not capable of further subdivision for the purpose of the science. It is true that it includes organic and inorganic substances, objects which have life and those which have not. But although there is a gulf such as the chemist would recognise between these two kinds of objects, and although the biologist has to admit man cannot bridge over that gulf by his own efforts, yet, and for the very reason last mentioned, the distinction is one which the economist has not to deal with. He must take nature as he finds it, organic and inorganic; for his business relates only to what man has to do with nature.

The next and only other ultimate element to be noticed as an agent in the production of wealth is labour. As already pointed out (in the first chapter), this consists of moving the objects of nature. All that labour accomplishes consists only of this moving. It must also be remembered that all useful human effort must be under the guidance of human mind, even though the mind only guides certain muscles, and does no planning or thinking, as thinking is generally understood. When this is kept in view it can be seen that all human effort, the effect of which is so exerted as to influence other persons or things, is essentially the same. It is the internal act of the mind directing the muscles of the body, and their movement causing movement in external objects. This is so whether those objects consist of the solid substances of which the earth and its strata are composed, or the atmospheric air by the vibration of which the human voice transmits thought by the sound of speech. The same truth appears whether the implement used be a plough or a pen.

The difference between physical exertion and mental labour is thus only one of degree—the relative extent to which the' brain or the muscles enter into the effort. Now, seeing how inseparably connected and inter-dependent are the body and mind in their animate existence, it is evidently impossible to entirely separate into two distinct classes avocations in which mind and body respectively predominate. Whether the effort or the effect be considered, the result is the same. The difference is only one of degree. Such a division as is suggested must, therefore, be an artificial one.

This will explain how it is that those who attempt to set up distinctions and avowedly legislate for certain classes find such difficulty, or rather impossibility, in drawing a line of demarcation about which they can agree even amongst themselves. The truth is no such distinction exists in the nature of things. A comparatively small section carrying on, for instance, a particular department of a certain industry may separate themselves into a class having characteristics common to themselves and to no others. They do a known kind of work to a specially named material. But if they once admit even those most nearly approaching them in the nature of their work, they can never afterwards consistently stop until they have admitted every individual of the community who receives rewards for his personal services. There may be occupations mental, more or less, in degree, and there may be grades of society. But in all cases of large communities the gradation is insensible, and the relative degrees of physical and mental activity cannot be measured with such exactness as to give a satisfactory line of division.

Nor can any distinction between productive and unproductive labour be at all conclusive. Supposing that services are useful, or thought to be useful (and the test of that is whether they will be paid for and to what extent), then it is impossible to say that some are productive and others not so. All that man can produce is utility; he cannot create a particle of matter. Nor can he convert a particle of inorganic matter into organic matter, as would be the case if he could entirely by his own efforts produce corn or vegetables. He can move the objects of nature; that is all he can do: nature herself must do the rest. In this respect the farmer and the miner, the manufacturer and the merchant, are alike.

Moreover, the series does not stop there. The services of some professional men, such as engineers, are called into requisition directly to give advice to persons as to processes of wealth production. A little more indirectly perhaps, but none the less truly than in the case of the persons they advise, their services are productive. Some teach by means of lectures those who are to produce. Others again give them the foundation of knowledge on which they will build their future powers of industry. Still others, like the last, giving services purely personal, give entertainment and amusement, or it may be incitement to good deeds. But it is impossible to say to what extent this is also instructive and inspiring, and therefore to what extent indirectly productive. He would be a bold man who should dare to draw hard and fast rules and act on distinctions where in the nature of things none exist.

Nor, as already intimated, is it possible to draw a line of delimitation between grades of evidently productive employments. Economists have frequently recognised as a distinct class that of employers or *entrepreneurs* as distinguished from the employed. But there is no essential difference. And no particular purpose is served, at any rate, in a broad inquiry into the subject by adopting the method. It could only be useful in answering on their own ground the arguments of those who have adopted the method. Those who wish to see the plan followed will find it worked out by Professor F. A. Walker. The results are practically the same in the end. In the absence of fallacies, this must be the case. It will, therefore, not be necessary to refer to the method in detail in this inquiry. No distinctions will be drawn but those which can be clearly defined. This is partly in order that the greater definiteness and simplicity may afford the better opportunity to the reader of criticising the arguments and discovering fallacies. Fallacies are frequently hidden in what appears to be subtle reasoning; and when subtilty means mystification, the less subtilty the better.

It is evident that there is no real and essential difference between the employer and the employed. Both must labour, and their labour is in its essence the same. It includes the same internal effort of brain and muscle, of mind and body. It includes also the same external moving of material objects only differing in relative degree. Moreover, a man who has the necessary internal qualities may pass from one grade to the other. Such transitions are so frequent and infinite in their variety that they cannot be fully enumerated. Even in those employments in which it is most difficult to pass from a lower grade to a higher one it depends much more on the qualities of the individual than on the difficulty of the transition. It is true that some employments offer much greater difficulties in this respect than others. But these difficulties vary so much in different employments that no conclusions could be drawn from them. They are, in fact, another argument against the artificial distinction. Nay, frequently the very same grade in one establishment is occupied by a person who is employed which in another and exactly similar establishment is occupied by an employer.

Still further, the distinction is inexpedient, in that it neglects to take note or must make special exception of those occupations in which a man is, so to speak, his own employer. Such are those who come directly into contact with their customers, the consumers of wealth. The gradations from one degree to another are so infinite and insensible that it is impossible to draw a clear line of distinction. Evidently all human effort must be included in the one word labour, just as all nature's gifts are included in the one word land.

It is thus seen that there are two distinct and ultimate elements in the production of wealth. And of ultimate elements there are only two. For granted land and labour wealth to some extent can be produced. But the extent of such production would be very small. A naked savage without a hut or a stick might by his labour prepare himself wealth in the way of roots and berries. He might even save it for future use. But no one would expect a nation of such savages to become very wealthy or even to lead desirable lives. It will need no argument to prove that there is an advantage for mere wealth production in having wealth prepared beforehand, instead of consuming all productions as soon as acquired.

Discarding the further use of the illustration from savage life, it is evident that it is a distinct gain in the matter of wealth production to sow a portion of the crop of corn in prepared ground, instead of consuming the whole of previous gatherings and trusting to the unaided bounty of nature. Animals which have been caught and possibly tamed, domesticated or trained become wealth. Their usefulness in further production of wealth is readily seen either in their mere growth and reproduction, or in their actually assisting man to move objects. The same is true with regard to inorganic substances prepared for man's use. The tools which he uses, from the smallest and simplest instruments to the most costly machinery, are an assistance to his labours. It is also of great advantage to have such a store of subsistence that he is not hindered by the necessity of gathering food and other necessaries for his immediate maintenance. All which amounts to this, that the store of previously produced wealth of various kinds is useful as an aid to production. Wealth considered in this aspect is called capital. It may, however, be necessary to further make clear what capital really is.

The meaning of capital, in spite of some good definitions, is in a most desperate state of confusion. Even economic writers have betrayed great confusion of mind between capital properly so called and capital improperly so called. Socialist writers are particularly noticeable for their inability clearly to distinguish between capital and land. Still more frequently amongst writers of various shades of opinion and in ordinary language capital is confused with money. It is true that the ordinary use of a word is the true index to its meaning. But when persons discuss a science in which a word has a precise meaning they should observe that meaning. This rule is not respected as it ought to be with regard to capital. Nor are the more prominent writers on the subject free from the error, even when they have stated the precise meaning they intend to attach to the word.

John Stuart Mill showed great confusion between

wealth and money in his chapters on capital. At the commencement of those chapters it is stated that money is not capital. But the writer made the fatal mistake of confusing the two together, because, forsooth, money could be converted, as he thought, into capital; or, rather, was susceptible of such conversion. Money in itself could not perform any part of the office of capital, but, said Mill, "anything which is susceptible of being exchanged for other things is capable of contributing to production in the same degree." For example he might have added, "A sieve bottomed with brass wire gauze is susceptible of being exchanged for a cheap tin pail, so that such a sieve is capable of being used to carry water, which when carried generally becomes wealth." It is a similar argument. Truly the latter depends on the accidental possibility of effecting an exchange of a sieve for a pail. But the former depends on a similar accidental possibility of exchanging something which will not answer the purpose required for something which will do so.

Such statements lack the exactness required for scientific demonstrations. Mill amply showed this to the confusion of the subject. Amongst several instances of the borrowing of ten thousand pounds, and a painful labouring to show the result of the borrower's different modes of spending it, the author speaks of the national capital being reduced by ten thousand pounds. Such an expression is about as full of meaning as if he had said the national capital was reduced by ten thousand yards. The capital of the nation knows nothing of a monetary pound or ten thousand pounds. It consists of so many houses, a certain length of road, canal, or railway, a number of coal-pit shafts, with the necessary engines and plant, some mills and machinery, a quantity of raw material, or material in course of adaptation, a supply of food, clothing, and other necessaries, with so many ounces of gold, silver, etc. That such a thing as a pound sterling exists, and that an ounce of gold is worth at the mint £3 17s. 10½d., is merely and entirely an artificial arrangement. It is an arrangement which the nation could alter at its will without by the alteration itself increasing or diminishing in any degree the national capital. It must not be concluded that the price of an article is merely its value in gold. Yet if there could be such a thing as the nation's capital being reduced by ten thousand pounds, all the nation would have to do to increase it to that or any other extent would be to declare that an ounce of gold should be worth more than £3 17s. 10½d. That would tend to diminish the value of the pound, and the capital would tend to increase in price to a commensurate extent. So that Mill was under the most evident confusion between capital and money. Other instances are easy to be found in his writings. Several passages in his chapters on capital might be adduced. He speaks of the capital of the nation being reduced when money is spent, whereas it is only reduced when wealth is consumed.

It may be objected that he referred to that which the ten thousand pounds would buy. The answer to that is that he did not say so, and did not argue as if he attached that meaning to the expression. There seems no other way of drawing conclusions as to what he really did mean than by noticing these two things. But for this confusion he could never have reached the conclusion he did, that wages were lent by capitalists, an idea which must be referred to in another chapter. The detailed examination of his writings on the subject would be out of the purview of this book, but the confusion may be readily traced by those who can follow the thread of his intricate arguments.

Mill did not, however, wrongly define capital. He only failed to observe his own definition, and allowed himself to confuse the object with something which did not answer the definition. Mr. Henry George examined the definitions of McCulloch, Ricardo, and Mill, with the result stated by him that "the great defect that these definitions have in common is that they include what clearly cannot be accounted capital, if any distinction is to be made between labourer and capitalist." But is the drawing of that distinction by means of a definition any necessary part of the inquiry? It surely is no part of the office of the scientist to find or support distinctions which do not exist. It is true that a custom has grown up of speaking as though there were really a distinction between capitalists and labourers. But the seeker after truth cannot trim and shape his definitions to suit the ideas of those who may or may not be in the right in their contentions, and who consequently may or may not be correct in the expressions they get into the habit of using. The scientist must be a student of nature. He must, to speak figuratively, stalk over the subject he has in hand with long, slow step, and restless, searching eyes, trusting nothing, fearing nothing, seeking truth. Now, there is no real distinction between the capitalist and the labourer, though there is a distinction between capital and labour. At any rate, no distinction has been by any one pointed out. When any one finds such a distinction he should apply it carefully to the case of a hawker of fish or vegetables, who buys his stock in the wholesale market, and then trudges his round with basket or wheelbarrow (or it may be with a horse or donkey) to sell that stock, and who lives on the profits. The distinction should determine whether the man is a capitalist or a labourer. No attempt will be made to answer such a question in this book; and it is believed that the question cannot be answered except by saying that the man is both capitalist and labourer. That is the truth concerning every man who has an occupation, whether as employer or employed, unless in the most exceptional circumstances. The difference between men in this respect is one of degree only.

There is, however, a distinction between capital and labour. For capital is at least a portion of wealth, and the whole of wealth has already been clearly separated from labour; as it was also distinguished from land. Mr. George has perhaps recognised the truth of the matter sufficiently for practical purposes, in spite of his attempting to set up differences which do not exist. But his definition is open to some objections. He holds that capital is only part of wealth—that part, namely, which is devoted to the aid of production. He quotes with approval the words of Adam Smith, "that part of a man's stock which he expects to afford him revenue." But the truth is that even to satisfy Mr. George's definition the man need not have any clear thought about the matter at all. Everything depends on the object he has in view in using it. His expecting a revenue from the stock is unnecessary. He may imagine his labour did everything, but if it was helped by a portion of wealth that wealth would be capital, were it but a joiner's plane or a shoemaker's awl. If money, which will usually command wealth, may be used as an illustration, it may be made clear in this way. Suppose a man to have money with which he proposes to enjoy a holiday; that, according to Mr. George, will not be capital to him, it will produce him nothing. But if he takes a business journey with it to produce him wealth he will use it as capital even in Mr. George's sense, although he has imagined he was only using his labour.

Looked at in this way, wealth may be capital to one man and not to another, though actually used for the same purpose. A hunter used by a gentleman for his pleasure is no part of his capital if the expression is used in the sense indicated. But if a livery stable keeper had the horse it would be his capital. Again taking this view, pleasure grounds laid out to be used for public resort at a charge are capital to the individual (so far as the adaptation or preparedness is concerned), but not to the nation.

Now with Mr. George's definition as stated above, in spite of his criticisms, the definition of Ricardo sufficiently agrees. Ricardo says:—

"Capital is that part of the wealth of a country

which is employed in production, and consists of food, clothing, tools, raw materials, machinery, etc., necessary to give effect to labour."

Mill says :—

"What capital does for labour is to afford the shelter, protection, tools and materials which the work requires, and to feed and otherwise maintain the labourers during the process. Whatever things are destined for this use are capital."

This definition also agrees with the statement, clearly expressed by Mr. George, that capital is the portion of wealth devoted to aid production. But it varies by a shade from that of Ricardo in the direction Mr. George would not have it vary. His idea is that capital is only that which is actually paid for as capital. In the hands of the consumer wealth with him is not capital. If a jeweller takes diamonds from his shop for his wife to wear, they cease to be capital. If he brings them back to offer for sale, they become capital again.

By this means he attempts to get a distinction between those who live on the reward paid for the use of capital and those who live on the wages paid for their labour. Such a distinction, however, can never be perfect or useful. Apart from those who use their capital in their own business, like the hawker already referred to, there are many who own capital for which others pay them interest, whilst they also receive wages for personal labour in other employments. This latter class includes most of those known as thrifty working men. They are at one and the same time both capitalists and labourers.

McCulloch's definition departs a shade of meaning further from Mr. George's ideal in this respect, and offends also in other respects. McCulloch says :—

"The capital of a nation really comprises all those portions of the produce of industry existing in it that may be directly employed either to support human existence or to facilitate production."

One of Mr. George's objections to this definition is that it does not include many valuable things which are really capital, but which may not be directly employed either to support human existence or to facilitate production. Such he considers to be the stocks that consist of articles of luxury. Here again is the setting up of a distinction which does not exist. It is not for the economist or any one else to decide for a nation what are articles of luxury and what are necessaries. If the articles may be used for the purpose of gratifying human desire they must be considered as capable of direct employment to support human existence. And this is so even though they may be more than is absolutely essential to preserve life. Human existence is more or less ample, but whatever the human being uses for its support must be considered capable of employment for that purpose.

The same objection is raised to the definition of Ricardo. Mill's definition Mr. George considers too vague, because it remits the distinction between capital and not-capital to the mind of the capitalist. That is to say, the distinction consists in his will to employ it for one purpose rather than another. It is difficult to get out of that vagueness if any portion of wealth is to be excluded from the total sum of capital.

A further objection made to McCulloch's definition is that it includes products of industry which, though they are not necessarily luxuries, are yet used as such. They are capable of supporting human existence or facilitating production, but are being consumed in ostentation or useless luxury. This is, as may be seen, really another form of the previous objection. It attempts to determine what are luxuries and what are not. The same reply is accordingly open to it as to the other. There is no determining for this purpose whether hats and boots are necessaries or not. They are not essential to support life. And yet most people would now regard them as necessaries. The same might be said of many other things. Clearly there is no distinction here except such as is a matter of opinion.

Mr. George's great object, however, with regard to all the definitions is to exclude the wealth which is in the hands of the labourer himself. Such an exclusion serves no useful purpose. Nor does Mr. George succeed in his attempt. The wealth, in whatsoever hands, is useful in aiding production, if it is so used. The labourer may, in fact, benefit himself by means of it. Even a week's subsistence beforehand will enable the labourer to obtain better wages than if he were without any means of subsistence.

The only possible line of distinction to be drawn between wealth, as a whole, and capital, a portion of wealth, is that which is obtained by saying that capital is wealth devoted to production of further wealth, and not the wealth used in mere pleasure. Such a line of distinction is, however, problematical and very unsatisfactory. It is impossible to say what is mere pleasure, and what is recreation of mental and physical powers. If used for the latter purpose, with a view to further labour, it is directly devoted to the production of wealth.

Another reason for avoiding any such distinction as attempted by Mr. George is that already mentioned; namely, that the same wealth would be capital in the hands of one person and not in those of another. A house or mansion would be capital if let out on hire, and not capital if the owner lived in it and saved paying rent to another. This is clearly a distinction arising purely from the different ways in which the same commodity is regarded.

It appears, therefore, better to say at once that capital is wealth regarded in the special sense of an element of production. McCulloch's definition is the one which most clearly meets this view. According to it capital is the produce of industry; as all wealth is. It is, moreover, such as may be directly employed, either to facilitate production, as mills, mines, and tools, or to support human existence, which will include the whole remainder of wealth—necessaries and luxuries.

We have to deal with the capital of a nation. Clearly that must include all the wealth that is directly or indirectly used to aid production. In view of the impossibility of ascertaining clearly what is productive and what is not productive, we can only treat capital as labour was treated. That is, we must conclude that if the use of wealth is paid for it is productive wealth. The test is whether it will be paid for or not. If paid for, it must be concluded that it found its uses as an aid to the production of that out of which it was paid. And, moreover, if it saves the owner from having to pay for other wealth, it is sufficiently remunerative to be considered as paid for to him. If it contributes to his support it is an aid to his further production.

We thus, therefore, arrive at our third element. We had, first, land—the earth apart from man's efforts; secondly, labour—man's personal efforts devoted directly or indirectly to the adaptation of natural substances and consequent production of wealth; thirdly, we have capital—namely, previously prepared wealth used or regarded as an aid to the production of further wealth. This compound of the two ultimate elements enters as a distinct agent and acquires the character of an element of production. We thus distinguish three elements, land, labour, and capital, having their distinct offices in production.

CHAPTER V

EXCHANGE AND DISTRIBUTION

THE three agents in the production of wealth have been noticed, and taken together they completely account for the production of wealth and its reaching the consumer. But the method requires a more detailed consideration. If every man or every family produced directly from the earth all the wealth required, even with the aid of implements previously prepared, the human race would still remain in a condition of comparative poverty and live a life of a very low standard. Different places, however, offer facilities for the production of different kinds of wealth. As only a limited number can be at each of those different places, it is very evident that benefits may accrue from an exchange of wealth between the various districts. For human happiness and wellbeing is generally increased by variety, and the demand frequently takes the form of a desire for something different, instead of for more of the same kind.

Moreover, labour becomes more efficient by being specialized. The man who has confined his attention chiefly to a certain industry is more likely to be proficient in that industry than he would be in another. He will also excel another individual who has equal abilities and general training, but has never devoted himself to that particular occupation, though the latter may excel in another occupation. Besides which, men have often special aptitudes for different kinds of work.

From these facts arise the necessity and advantage of exchange of wealth and of services. The objects of human desire are so various in their character that it would be difficult for any one to catalogue his requirements and desires for a year or even a much less period. And with regard to both land and labour, there may be almost infinite variety in both natural and acquired adaptation for the satisfaction of those requirements and desires. By means of exchange, however, the various objects of desire may be passed from producer to consumer to their mutual advantage.

It was pointed out that value and exchangeability were necessary ingredients of wealth. Value was stated to be a compound of the two qualities utility and scarcity. So that from the very definition of value it may be seen that it is fixed by the state of demand and supply. The utility in the sense it is here used exactly corresponds to the demand. It is, in fact, that which causes the expression of desire. The scarcity is the limitation of supply. Thus value rises with increased demand or diminished supply. It falls with diminished demand or increased supply. Now price is value calculated in money. It is the expression of the measure of value. That is to say, money is the instrument, price is the extent of measurement. Fixing the price is the balancing or measuring of the value with money. And seeing that value is itself fixed by the state of demand and supply, its measure, price, must be fixed in like manner. Price also will rise with increased demand or diminished supply, and fall with diminished demand or increased supply. And only in this way can value and price be affected.

It is true that an alteration in the proportionate quantity of money with which the wealth is to be measured may influence prices, but any such variation will be an alteration in the measure itself. The apparent alteration in price will be merely a variation in the standard.

"The law of supply and demand" is an expression frequently made use of, and the idea represented is often vigorously attacked as an iniquitous law made by men. It need hardly be said that those who take up such a position are not much addicted to clear thinking. It perhaps cannot be said that there is any one law which may be called the law of supply and demand. If any such one law may be spoken of it will be expressed in this way: no sale (or exchange for money) will take place except at the price which one party is able and willing to give, and the other able and willing to accept, for the commodity or service. That law which shall be called the first law of supply and demand seems very truthful and very innocent. It is not, however, a mere truism, as it may seem. It means that the demand and supply must at least meet in price, and that if they fail to meet by ever so small a measure it will be exactly as if they had been separated by a more appreciable difference. If the prices overlap, so that the seller is willing to take much less than the buyer is willing to give, and the buyer consequently willing to give more than the seller is willing to take, not only will there be an exchange, but it is probable that a larger quantity will be exchanged. Stated in that way, however, it depends entirely on the particular circumstances of the case, and to get at the truth it will be necessary to return to the consideration of the nature of value.

Of even useful objects the quantity which can be used has some limit, and when that limit is reached the objects cease to have the quality of scarcity. Consequently, though useful, they are not valuable. Of many objects of which wealth consists that limit of utility is scarcely ever reached in the condition of supply of any one. But some things are much more essential than others; they are more useful, more desired. Each person (though perhaps unconsciously) puts these first in his mind, and the object most desired will vary greatly with different individuals. As each, however, obtains a supply of the objects most desired, his mind will naturally turn to other objects of which the supply is now relatively smaller. Those objects, though less useful to him if he had no supply of the others, have now become more valuable. For they have always had greater scarcity, and are, now that other wants are supplied, more desired—that is, possess greater utility for the satisfaction of desire.

In the most absolute necessaries of life a very little scarcity will cause an increased value. And the value will continue to increase rapidly in proportion to the increase of scarcity. For these things must be had at all cost. When once, however, the full supply is reached their value rapidly falls off with an increase in supply. For of those necessaries there is by no means an unlimited demand. The quantity which can be used has a limit, and when that limit is reached no further supply has value. If the supply is much increased the scarcity is less felt, and value rapidly falls in proportion. It is important to bear in mind that the value of the whole is fixed by the greater or less desire expressed for more. This proportionate scarcity has been expressed by economists as the final or marginal utility. However they may be regarded, the determining influences of value include a combination of utility and scarcity. If of those desiring a commodity no one possessed any of it already, the value might be exceedingly high. But when what they now have is taken out of the market, and they begin to be satisfied to some extent if it still appears that there is much to sell, the prices will fall. This fall in price may perhaps be below what they have given. On the other hand, if it begins to appear that more will be wanted than can be supplied, the prices will go up, although many are already satisfied. The value of the whole is ascertained by the price of that which is in the market.

But some other facts must be noticed. In the first place, even with regard to necessaries, it is clear that there are possibilities of substitution. If, for instance, one kind be very scarce and the price very high, and if another kind be substituted for it, the other kind will be bought in place of the first. The value of the first kind will thus be hindered from rising, as it otherwise would have done. The substituted kind will then tend to become more scarce, and consequently more valuable. Moreover, with regard to less necessary objects of desire, there will be less fluctuation, with a small variation in supply. Necessities will be supplied first with one thing or another. But beyond those commodities required for that purpose there will be many which will partake more or less of the nature of luxuries. For several reasons these will generally remain more constant in value. They can more easily be altogether spared. A larger quantity of them can be used without reaching the limit of their utility, for of luxuries human beings seem never to have had all they desire. Luxuries taken together are more various in form, and the law of substitution, as it is called, is likely to have more effect.

In all cases it must be remembered, in the second place, that the value of the total quantity of any commodity is regulated by the proportionate scarcity of what is in the market—that is to say, the less there is in the market in proportion to what is desired the higher the price will be, and *vice versâ*. The price, therefore, may become so high that some stock of that commodity which is not really in the market has become much more valuable than when its owners bought it; or, as the case may be, has exceeded the value they have previously put upon it in deciding not to bring it into market. It is clear that in such cases the owners will reconsider their attitude. Some will be induced to bring their saleable objects into the market, and either spare them altogether or substitute some other object of desire. Whilst on the other hand, as already mentioned, those also who thought to buy will reconsider; some will decide on abstinence or substitution. Thus the rising of prices through increased demand or diminished supply will tend to induce supply and discourage demand, and consequently to bring back the prices to the same level. This may be called the second law of supply and demand.

Similar reasoning will make it clear that a fall of prices will have a tendency to cause sellers to prefer what they had put in the market to anything for which the money realized by it would exchange; and, consequently, to stop supply. On the other hand, as to those who intended to abstain from purchasing, the fall in price will incline them to give money to satisfy the desires which, in fact, did exist, but were relatively weaker than other desires. Or if they had intended to buy something else, the fall will induce them to substitute that of which the price has fallen for what they proposed to buy. Thus the fall in prices through decreased demand or increased supply tends to decrease supply and increase demand, and consequently to advance the prices again to the same point. This may be called the third law, and is the converse of the second.

These two are, therefore, further laws of supply and demand. It might be better to speak of demand and supply, for the demand is the subject, the cause of the supply, while the supply is the complement. The order in which the words are uttered is not of great moment, but the proper realization of the order of the ideas is of the utmost importance. Much confusion would have been saved if it had always been borne in mind that supply existed for demand, and not demand for supply.

With regard to these laws, it must be noted that in each case what is spoken of is a tendency. It is true that sellers occasionally hold for a rise and buyers wait for a fall. And if they have rightly interpreted the market their thus acting will probably accelerate and increase what would have taken place. The tendencies indicated are not interfered with by the temporary suspension of their action, or the tacit or expressed combination. On the other hand, it may be the market has been miscalculated. If so those who attempted to turn it more quickly, or to a greater extent, in their favour find that they are in a worse condition than they would have been. Their holding has lowered prices, for there is still more in the market. Or their waiting has raised prices, for now they must have the commodities almost at any cost, and the sellers know it. The schemers find that there was a greater or less supply in proportion to the demand than they imagined, and they have defeated their own purpose.

All these considerations with regard to value and exchange will apply not only to wealth and commodities, but also to land and labour, which are exchangeable. There are other considerations, however, which do not apply equally to land, wealth, and labour. For the total supply of wealth can be increased, while the supply of land cannot be so increased, although more may be brought into the market. The total supply of land being thus limited, the value is ultimately fixed entirely by demand.

The importance of this will be seen in its place. On the other hand, it is the labourer for whom the whole proceeding takes place. If, therefore, a rise of price occurs with regard to a particular kind of labour, although it will tend to bring others into the trade, it will probably not induce a greater amount from the individuals already in the trade; rather the reverse.

Moreover, while land obtains its total value entirely from the need for it—the supply being limited—labour as a whole tends to be withdrawn from the market as the supply of wealth reaches more nearly to the satisfaction of the desires of labourers. This increased supply of wealth reduces the value of land, because it tends to decrease the demand for its services as wealth producer. The same increased supply of wealth increases the value of labour, because the desire, for the satisfaction of which the labour was called forth, is more nearly balanced, and the supply consequently tends to decrease.

If the desire spoken of in the first postulate were already entirely balanced the need for the supply spoken of in the second would no longer exist, and the third would be beside the question. The nearer, therefore, that condition is approached the less is the demand for another's labour, but (and this is the important point to be borne in mind) the less the supply of one's own. There is very great danger of confusion here, and perhaps it is difficult to clearly express the meaning intended. The demand which raises prices is the demand by one for another's land, wealth, or labour. If the desire, by any person, be for his own land, wealth, or labour, the price he will give for another's may be low, but the price he will require for his own will be high. Now every man's labour is his own, only he can give it. And he only parts with it in exchange for something he prefers. If, therefore, wealth is so plentiful and cheap that he can easily satisfy his desires, he will keep his labour, unless he is tempted with a higher price. For he only offers his labour to obtain the satisfaction of those desires.

Let the attention be strictly confined to one individual. He has desires for, say, wealth. His first step towards satisfaction is an offer to supply labour—the greater his desire the greater his offer of supply of labour. That supply is to be balanced by money in the first instance, and the greater the supply of labour the lower the price. That is to say, the greater the unsupplied demand for wealth the lower the price of labour. But let it be well remembered the demand referred to here is each man's own demand for wealth, and not another's demand for the wealth he supplies. On the other hand, the less the unsupplied demand for wealth the less labour will be offered and the higher the price of it. In short, the more difficult the access to wealth the lower the price of labour. The easier that access is the higher the price of labour. Or, still more briefly, the cheaper the commodities the dearer the labour.

If it be preferred to trace the first method further, we have, in the first instance (as the price of labour), money which is to be exchanged for wealth. On account of the great unsupplied demand for wealth in the individual having exchanged labour, the labour was so freely offered that the money is small in quantity. If the wealth be high in price money will buy little. The individual will be left with a large demand unsupplied. The labour, which is what he attempts to balance it with, continues to be offered at low rates. And thus the process continues. Dear goods mean poor wages. If the wealth be low in price – or cheap, as it is expressed, —his desire will be more nearly balanced. His demand will be less, his supply of labour consequently less, and the price he will require consequently higher. Which is the result reached in the previous paragraph.

It must, of course, be borne in mind that all this arises from the consideration of the labourer's own demand for wealth. And in truth it applies chiefly with regard to the reward of labour relatively to that of land and capital. But the consideration of the demand for another's labour which is caused by the demand for wealth just referred to does not introduce any real modification of these conclusions, whatever modification may be apparent. Because such a demand can only make itself felt when it is accompanied by a supply of what is valuable. This consideration, rightly understood, bears out the previous one, that an abundant supply of cheap commodities raises the price of labour, while a mere unsupplied demand lowers wages.

These, however, are perhaps wider considerations than properly belong to this chapter. If not fully grasped they may be left to a later stage, for they open out on the final results. All that need be grasped here is that, while in the market the same laws of supply and demand rule prices with regard to land, labour, and wealth, the considerations which affect the supply outside the market are different in each case. The ultimate or total values, if it may be so expressed, of the three objects are settled by widely varying considerations. In the market there is no difference in the method of their treatment.

What in the long run determines value is not at present under consideration, but the reader must be warned against hastily concluding that it is the cost of labour. It is true the cost of bringing wealth to market ultimately, though indirectly, determines the prices of what can be produced as required. But what that cost is must be inquired into, and not rashly put down as this or that without further investigation. One thing may be concluded as certain, that if labour must be specially directed to the production of any commodity the commodity will have value or cease to be produced. For labour is always more or less scarce. It cannot be had without some reward.

Many objects, however, have value not depending on the cost of production. A much-appreciated picture by a dead artist, an article desired for its historic associations, a rare and beautiful gem accidentally found, are instances in which commodities are valued entirely by the demand, as land is. The supply is fixed. But in most instances the cost of production, howsoever that may be fixed, eventually tends to fix the price.

Once again, although in the market increased demand raises prices, it frequently occurs that the increased demand in the end lowers the price of a commodity. For the larger quantity which can be sold affords opportunity for better methods of production. And thus it appears in a variety of ways that the laws of supply and demand are but the natural laws of the market, and even with regard to wealth they must not be carried outside their proper sphere. The market, it need hardly be said, however, includes potentially, not only what is already on sale, but what may become so.

Exchange is really the means of distribution of wealth in the sense in which the word distribution will be here used. That sense is the natural and true one—namely, distribution in kind to those who require it of the wealth produced. What has been generally called distribution, meaning proportionate division of mixed wealth between rich and poor for their shares in production, will in its place be called division. There is a danger of confusion in using the same word for both ideas, and fortunately the language furnishes two distinct words, each well fitted for a different one of the ideas. The confusion has probably much to do with the suggestion of socialists and kindred teachers that producers should be considered first and distribution "wisely and equitably regulated." Such a notion would imply that the communal authorities are to determine, not only whether people are to have beef or mutton when they desire meat, but also whether they should have fruit or flesh, and, indeed, whether they may be given coal or bread, besides implying other things if possible more absurd.

A few words may be of use with regard to inducements to exchange. A person or a locality producing a particular kind of wealth and comparatively or absolutely not producing other kinds will naturally be able to supply that kind of wealth much more easily than other kinds, and will also be willing to part with it to obtain those other kinds. The commodity produced will be less valuable to the producers than will the commodities required for consumption. This is because of its smaller relative scarcity. Such wealth will be cheaper than it would be in the hands of a person or in a locality where it was not produced. In the latter case it is not less useful, but more scarce, and therefore dearer.

The business of exchanging and conveying goods between the producers and consumers (that is, of distribution) is carried on by merchants and carriers. They engage in the work for profit. As between merchants and carriers no strict distinction exists, some being more exclusively merchants and others more distinctly carriers. Still others are between the two descriptions. The descriptions themselves are only descriptions of degree. Both merchants and carriers are frequently also producers. It will be convenient to speak of all those engaged in distribution as traders. Seeing that they engage in the business for profit, it is evident by the third postulate that there will be a natural tendency on the part of each of them to buy in the cheapest market and sell in the dearest. This tendency is independent of what social reformers may say, and is a tendency in the nature of things. It is not one which can be altered by maxims and precepts. But while the tendency is natural, it is also beneficial, and should be encouraged rather than discouraged. Every man ought to buy in the cheapest market, and sell in the dearest. For in those markets is the greatest relative desire expressed to sell or to buy. The trader, while answering his own purposes, is best answering the purposes of his fellow-men by adopting that natural maxim. The attacks which have been made on the maxim can only be attributed to a mode of thought betokening the last extremity of mental inversion.

The practical result of the consideration of this natural tendency is not less important. It is to indicate that, so far as those are concerned who wish to exchange their productions with others, the method to be adopted is as far as possible to reduce their cost, and sell them cheaper. The trader for his own sake will be continually on the alert to find where he can buy most cheaply, and also where he can sell at the highest price. Some profit he must have or cease distributing. Moreover, he cannot convey any goods from place to place free of cost. Consequently, in addition to his own profit, he must have cost of carriage. This cost will vary with the commodity in the proportion it bears to the total value. A variety of considerations must be taken into account in settling whether the exchange and carrying will be a profitable employment. The more or less perishable nature of an article must be considered, as well as its bulk and weight, in proportion to value. But it may be laid down as a natural law that the greater the difference in price of any commodity at two different places, or in the hands of two different sets of individuals, the more exchange is likely to take place between them. For the greater is the inducement offered for the exchange.

Naturally the tendency to produce cheaply (known as competition), and the tendency by purchase to raise the prices of the productions of others (which should be known as the struggle for existence), goes on, as it should, up to the limit of individual desire. It is only artificially that the tendency to exchange is checked, so as to leave human desires with less satisfaction than the individuals would be willing by their labour to attain. In plain language, when men are out of work and "trade is bad" it is the result of some artificial interference with the free play of supply and demand. This is not generally admitted, but it is proposed to demonstrate it.

Some Governments avowedly attempt to prevent other nations selling in their markets—that is, to prevent their own people buying from other nations the things they desire. From some humour this is termed protection. The whole subject has been so thoroughly dealt with by economic writers that no attempt will be made here to set out at length the absurdity of the expression or of the idea expressed. Protection presumes the possibility of oppression. It is evident that no people can be oppressed by having their wants supplied. It is also evident that unless the people want or desire the commodities the foreigners will invade their markets in vain. Nor can the term protection be properly applied to those who are by it enabled to greatly increase their profits. Protection only extends to securing justice. Justice can never require or permit that a man be hindered from buying from one in order that he may be compelled to buy from another.

The idea expressed by the term is, if possible, less defensible. That men should have their lawful desires for subsistence thwarted is no benefit to them. That their wealth should be made more expensive is in itself an immediate injury. Moreover, it has been pointed out that such a proceeding cheapens their labour, though some have pretended that "protection" was for the raising of wages. Still further, badly paid labour is less efficient, and the commodities of those who get themselves "protected" are apt to be more costly in production. They thus keep themselves out of the markets because of the higher prices. While if they were to attempt to ensure that their workmen should have as much wealth at the higher prices as at the lower ones, the additional cost of their maintenance must be added to the cost of the commodities, and the same effect produced. This takes no account of the waste of irregular work. But this protection is not the only interference with wealth production under the mask of protection. The evils of it will accordingly have to be noticed in various aspects.

CHAPTER VI

MONEY

IN dealing with exchange and distribution it seemed advisable that consideration should be given to value in its simplest aspect, and merely to state that price was value measured in money. That was quite true so far as it went, and it was the simplest, and, perhaps, on account of its simplicity the only, means of getting at the truth. A complicated machine must be considered in detail as well as in the whole, if it is to be understood. In the same way the complicated conditions of wealth supply must be examined in detail, or the subject must ever remain the bewildering maze that to most persons it is at present.

The conclusions of the last chapter, however, though true in respect of value, must be taken, when considered with respect to price, with this qualification: that the standard of measure is a perfect one, and does not vary. It will, however, be seen that, for one reason or another, prices do not always seem to follow the conclusions arrived at. Those conclusions are not for that reason untrue. The movements examined were, as would be noticed, perfectly explained. If the appearances do not agree with them, there must be other movements affecting them. The truth is that there are several such movements.

One fact to be taken into account is that as wages rise more wealth is demanded, and thus it occurs that statistics of prices only occasionally furnish instances of labour at naturally high prices side by side with low prices of wealth. Human beings, if not engaged in producing wealth, will consume it unproductively, and thereby raise its value. Another very important consideration, however, is that the standard is not perfectly invariable, and what appears to be a general change is often an alteration in the standard.

These and other considerations show that from price considered generally it is practically impossible to reach true economic conclusions. The conditions are so complicated, the varying causes so numerous and difficult to understand, that to take observed prices as data from which to argue is, to say the least, little better than tossing up a coin and observing on which side it falls, as a means of ascertaining whether a certain artificial arrangement is good or evil. Prices generally are matters to be explained, and not to argue from, while to purposely interfere with them is like altering a steam gauge as a means of getting up the steam. It is even worse, for the price gauge is part of the machinery, and to tamper with it is to throw the whole out of order.

The subject of money has occupied much attention, and is badly understood even yet. It is desirable to ascertain the truth about it. As with other objects, the understanding of its origin will help to make clear its nature. It will need no argument to prove that the first attempts at exchange must take the form of barter. Barter is the giving of one object desired for its own sake for another object also useful in itself, without any further exchange. The most untutored savage has, without doubt, his rudimentary notions of equivalence, and that even in the cases of barter pure and simple. But it must be noted at the outset that cases of barter pure and simple are much rarer than appears to be imagined. As soon as exchanges begin to take place with any considerable frequency, there arises the necessity for some medium by means of which the trade may be carried on. This becomes the standard with which each compares what he has to sell or buy. Such a standard arises very early in the commercial history of a people. In its earlier period, before credit has begun to take much part in transactions, and while the essential notion of money as a counter is not well understood, the standard is invariably something which is in itself valuable in the eyes of those who use it. This must be so from the nature of things. Otherwise the transactions would probably remain simple barter. Because unless the things which the parties to any transaction had to exchange were so related to each other in value that each individual exactly preferred what the other had to offer, no exchange could take place. But, by the aid of something which is generally esteemed, an exchange can take place in which the articles to be transferred are unequal in value. The difference is made up by means of the generally esteemed commodity. Frequently also an article may be sold entirely for that commodity.

Corn is obviously something which may be used as money, and it has been so used. It is valuable in every man's judgment, and is easily divisible for the purposes of exchange. The same may be said of cattle. They are less easy to divide with exactness. But as the pastoral state, in which cattle are likely to be used as money, is an earlier one than the agricultural stage when corn is used, the transition is a natural one. It is quite sufficient, however, for the purposes of money, that the commodity used be esteemed without any real and beneficial usefulness. Consequently shells and other merely ornamental articles have answered and still answer the purpose.

But although these commodities are esteemed for their own sake, they very quickly become unconsciously recognised as the medium of exchange. And whilst the value of other things is measured according to the standard they furnish, they themselves gain a value from their common use as money. In the community where they pass current they are therefore the most advantageous commodities to be used in the purchase of any article. The different tribes of Africa have already taken to different currencies, and the traveller must provide himself with the proper description of cloth, beads, wire, etc. (the money there current), according to the tribe he purposes to visit. Such transactions cannot, however, be properly described as purely money transactions. The civilized trader doubtless values both objects in his own currency; the savage values them in his currency such as it is. But there is no common currency. The savage may have sold an article for what is to him money, but the civilized trader has not given what is money to him. Still the notion of money is not altogether absent, as a little consideration will show.

As already mentioned, some commodities are generally esteemed. That, with the scarcity, is what is really meant by intrinsic value as applied to a money material. Many things are valuable to certain people. Some things are valuable in all eyes. Now as soon, as, in any exchange, one of the parties accepts something which he does not desire for his own use, or as stock in trade, but because he knows it is so generally acceptable that he can readily get what he desires with it, the notion of money has arisen. The money material may possess intrinsic value. It may acquire value from the prestige it gives to its owner. But these are not monetary notions. The monetary notion is that the object received is not what is itself required, but it is what will buy something which is required.

The first notion of money is, however, a long way from the complete establishment of a currency. The corn, cattle, or shells, cloth or beads, gold, silver, or bronze, will have at the very beginning their inherent attractions. At first the possibility of their use as money will only add a little value to them in the judgment of him who receives them. This may perhaps amount to just enough to induce him to conclude a bargain with the feeling that he can at any time get so much value for the commodity he accepts. A few such exchanges will tend to give to the commodity the quality of currency. Still the idea of money is not fully developed. The commodity is taken to be used (either consumed or retained as stock or ornament), or, if need be, to be spent. It is not intended merely to be spent. When the idea of money has reached its full development the object received as money is accepted for the express purpose of being passed on. It is not valued as a commodity, though it may have inherent qualities which would render it valuable even as a commodity. It is regarded purely as money. It is an object, distinguishable from wealth, which has come into existence. The person who receives it would not accept it at all but for the known possibility of transferring it to another for value. It is of no use to him until he parts with it. Until then he retains it for use when required. To get more of it is of no advantage to him whatever, unless by means of it he can get a proportionately greater quantity of wealth or services.

It was pointed out that the use of any object as a medium of exchange naturally established it as a measure of value. Persons trading are so used to measuring the value of articles in terms of that object that it becomes much the most convenient measure. From the necessity of measuring value in order to arrive at any transfer or exchange arises the fact that as a measure money, or its equivalent, though it be but a mental equivalent, must be present in every commercial transaction. As Adam Smith pointed out (in words which he evidently realized did not clearly express the meaning he intended to convey), the total sum of exchanges which have taken place in any period, if each man counts all he has bought and all he has sold, must be divided by two in order to ascertain the actual exchanges that have taken place. For in each case of exchange one side of the bargain has been money, and only the other actual wealth. But it is not necessary that there should be as much money in a country as will amount in value to all the exchanges which take place in a year, or even in a month or a week. Apart from questions of credit or promises taking the place of money (which must shortly be noticed), the legal tender money itself, whether it be coined metal or authorized paper, is capable of acting as money to a greater or less extent, according to the rapidity of its transfer from hand to hand. Like the yard-stick in a linen draper's establishment, it runs along with the commodity to be measured and traverses the whole distance. But to double the rapidity of the one measure will answer the same purpose as using an additional yard stick at the original rate of work.

Moreover, the possibility of the entire absence of the actual medium follows from what has already been said. It is useless to give a man money for goods if he must simply keep it for a little time, and then hand it back to the same person for goods which he will require. If the vendor of the first goods can trust his purchaser, it is just as convenient that the two lots of commodities measured in money be balanced against each other without the medium itself ever passing between them. Hence arise mutual debits and credits. Even if the two sides do not exactly balance, it is only necessary to pay the difference in money. And for that money it will be seen also that paper can be substituted.

From the same considerations as show the possibility of dispensing with the medium follows the possibility of using as money paper, not in itself of appreciable value, but bearing marks authenticating promises of reliable persons to pay value. It is a matter of indifference to any man whether he receive the actual bulky and heavy object which he accepts as money or whether he receive a paper which will enable him to obtain the object at any time he may desire it. The latter method is often the preferable one. Such papers will, therefore, pass from hand to hand, sustaining all the functions of money. In one aspect they may be called money. In another aspect they are but proofs of promises to pay money, though this proof passes current as money. Such are bank-notes. Such also are bills of exchange given by one individual to another, though they occupy an intermediate position between bank-notes and pure credit. They are only current to a limited extent. Paper money may indeed assume very various forms.

It must not, however, be concluded from these considerations that the functions of money can be neglected as easily as a substitute can be found for the actual medium. Putting aside mere barter, which seldom occurs amongst commercial peoples, every sale is made by means of money, at least as a measure. If the money is not actually present, it is in the minds of the traders. Moreover, even when for the time a promise to pay is accepted in lieu of money, the promiser must be prepared to pay at the time fixed. So that although by means of promises the functions of money can be performed in its absence, yet this is subject to an important qualification not previously mentioned. Every promise must eventually be followed by performance to complete the functions of money—that is, by payment or delivery of money or money's worth.

In the case of mutual credits and debits wealth is by this means exchanged for wealth. The promise is performed by delivery of money's worth for like value. But when money is passed from one to another, or the promise of one person is passed by his promisee to a third person, the money or promise must in itself or its representative come back to the person who first delivered it. As already intimated, money in the proper sense of money is never consumed. It is not intended to be consumed, but to be transferred. A very few take metal money and melt it for other uses. But a great part of the money used is not at all useful for that purpose. Silver money, for instance, in England would be very unprofitable to be used in that way, for silver can be obtained much cheaper than by melting coin. With the trifling exception of using money in this way, it is altogether useless except as a measure to be transferred.

When a promise properly evidenced reaches the person who gave the promise, and he gets command of it by giving value, he may annihilate it, and by that means a portion of the nation's money ceases to exist. On the other hand, he may issue fresh promises if other persons will accept them as money, as they usually will on being satisfied that the promises will command wealth. In this way virtual money can be created and destroyed. Actual metal money can only be created by bringing it into circulation from stocks of gold and silver not previously circulating, or from what may be obtained by mining. As money it is destroyed by being taken out of circulation and used for ornamental or other purposes.

Subject to these possibilities of creation and destruction of money, it can be used by constant circulation, and by that means only. Now the ratio of the money to the wealth or other object to be measured by it is the price. The total quantity of virtual money in circulation multiplied by its average rapidity is the total price of everything which is sold in the given time, whether that time is long or short. Supposing wealth the object to be sold, if more wealth is brought into the market and sold in a like time, either, on the one hand, more money must be created (that is, put in circulation), or the average rapidity must be increased, or, on the other hand, the prices must fall. If less is brought into the market, either, on the one hand, money must be taken out of circulation, or the average rapidity decreased, or, on the other hand, the prices must rise. Again, if more money is brought into circulation or its rapidity increased and no more wealth is offered, prices must rise. If money is taken out of circulation and no increase of rapidity takes place, either wealth must also be taken out or prices must fall. It will be observed that the possible contingencies are very varied. Money may vary either in volume, or rapidity of circulation, or both. The objects to be measured with it include wealth, land, and labour, and are all subject to the laws of the market noticed in the last chapter. These in themselves, it will be remembered, gave scope for very varied contingencies affecting value. It cannot be too well borne in mind that a variety of circumstances may influence prices. For there are those who, confusing money with wealth, cannot help thinking they will do themselves good if they can by any means raise the price of what they have to sell. And it is only by fully realizing the nature of money and the causes modifying prices that these errors can be avoided.

Here may be noted the nature of a panic. Suppose that on account of prospects of increased trade and higher prices merchants have been buying largely and circulating their promises to pay. The result has been a great increase in the amount of virtual money in circulation and constantly rising prices. Now let something occur which gives the impression that prices are about to fall and that the promises of some money may not be performed. The very fear that prices will fall will cause some to sell at once, and thus hasten the result. The very danger that some may have difficulty in keeping their promises will cause people who hold those promises to insist on their fulfilment at the earliest possible date, lest the loss should fall on them by delaying. Hence arises the panic. Merchants who relied on selling their commodities as a means of fulfilling their promises must then either sell at lower prices, and lose by it, or fail to keep their promises. In either case promises which have circulated to some extent as money are annihilated on their falling due. This decrease in volume must, if possible, be made up by increased rapidity of circulation. For a time there is great demand for money or such credit as will pass as money. The discount rate for it is accordingly very high. But the volume of money is decreased, and after the first panic its rapidity of circulation is also decreased. So that there is quite sufficient to account for not only lower prices afterwards, but also (and probably because of the lower prices) fewer transactions at even the lower prices. Doubtless much of the evil of these panics would be avoided were it not for the contagion of fear. But it is as useless to advise men not to be afraid under those circumstances as to counsel a timid or over-nervous person to be brave and keep cool when danger is apparent. The evil is before and beneath the panic, but how to avoid it is a question for later chapters.

From the fact that money is not produced or consumed, but circulates, another result follows. Money may be said to be valued in terms of wealth, as wealth is valued in terms of money. If, then, the money which any person transfers represents in his hands little wealth (that is, prices are high), he may expect when it comes back to him that it will still represent little wealth, and *vice versâ*. That or other portion of the same circulating medium must come back to him if he would have money again. In the main (that is, beyond a very small proportion) it will not be created or destroyed. Whatever it represents, therefore, of wealth parted with by him he must expect it to represent when it reaches him again. It will consequently be useless for him to attempt to alter the natural value of his money by artificial contrivances to get the money without giving the wealth. Moreover, such attempts are apt to cause a decrease in the rapidity of circulation (if not of the volume of money), which in itself will reduce the price of what he will have to sell in a short time afterwards. This point will be made clearer in a later chapter, when, however, the circulation of the wealth itself will be observed.

These considerations should make clear the essential nature of money. How little it has in common with that of wealth, and how clearly the two ideas should be distinguished, is readily seen. There appear to be two reasons why they have been so much confused together. One of them is that, although money is essentially but a measure, yet the possession of the money measure usually gives command of that which is intended to be measured by it, to a greater or less extent, according to prices. Apparently men from this argue that because one man can get wealth for money all can do so. They forget that men only get wealth from each other by means of money. Even if the money could be indefinitely increased the increase would be of no advantage to them. They, moreover, do not trouble to think where eventually the wealth must come from if their money is to purchase it.

The other reason is that although to the whole community money is but a measure, and the nation can be no more enriched by increasing its money than it can be clothed with yard sticks, fed with metal weights, or have its thirst quenched with pint measures, yet money is a measure of a mental desire, while the other measures relate to physical properties. And it is more difficult for human beings to analyse the operations of their own minds than to understand the extension, weight, capacity, and other qualities of the material world around them. One man may with advantage work for money, for it is a means of obtaining wealth from another. And it does not at all matter whether he has realized the function of money in society or not. But when any one undertakes to make laws or arrangements for a number of persons he must realize what it is they really require. He must not arrange to give them money when they require wealth without making sure that the money will command the wealth desired.

Yet by statesmen and others responsible for interference between buyers and sellers this confusion has been and still is very rife. Nations and combinations have thought and still think they can better their conditions by increasing the stock of money or raising the prices of what they may have to sell. But it is evidently futile to increase the stock of money if wealth is the object to be aimed at. For the money is not so much as desired for its own sake, and it is a singular instance of the limitation of mental powers that it should be treated as if it were so desired. Moreover, this raising of prices is exactly what is likely to hinder their obtaining the very money they desire by hindering trade with other communities. And the fact that for the moment the money is drawn to the nation or combination attempting the interference is exactly what causes the hindrance.

We may now pass from the consideration of the general nature of money and observe what is actually used. Whether or not the monetary arrangements of civilized nations are perfect is a matter for consideration in a later chapter.

The materials commonly used amongst civilized peoples as money are the precious metals, gold and silver, and paper representing fixed sums of money. The paper, it need hardly be said, must bear recognisable marks; in no respect is it accepted for its intrinsic value. It is, moreover, always supposed to represent the precious metals. No paper can pass current with savage tribes. Nor are the precious metals profitable for use in trading with such tribes. They have not learnt to appreciate those metals at the value they bear amongst civilized and even semi-civilized nations. And they do not understand the uses of a currency.

Amongst civilized and semi-civilized nations the precious metals are used as money. In most, if not all, of them there is a system of coinage in which certain weights of metal when coined bear certain monetary denominations. It is these coins which form the basis of the monetary systems of the different nations, and paper money is made to refer to them.

In international transactions the money used is somewhat different. In fact it was at one time thought that nations did not use money for international transactions, but bartered the precious metals as commodities. This notion probably obtains largely at present, but, with the exception of those nations who mine the metals, and to that extent, the idea is quite erroneous. When it first obtained it was an improvement on previously held ideas. For those who held it did at any rate advocate a free trade in treasure, on the ground that the treasure was a commodity, and it was, therefore, advantageous to trade it away. When, however, it is fully realized that wealth is more to be sought after than money, there is no reason for pretending that nations trade in the precious metals as commodities. To a very great extent the trade between nations is exactly like that between individuals, except with regard to the kind of money used. It is purely a trade of buying and selling—not of barter. The money passing between them is gold or silver by weight. It is exported or imported as money, and not as wealth. It is not intended to be used for the purposes available to the precious metals, but merely to be used or retained as money for internal circulation or re-exported for commodities. Moreover, to only a very small extent is it exported or imported. The greater part of the commodities are paid for with bills of exchange, which are balanced against each other by bankers and their agents. Only the balance is transmitted in gold or silver, and that only takes place when the balance due from one nation to another is such that the rate of exchange will afford a profit on the carrying of the gold or silver.

The details of the process of the settlement of balances belong rather to a treatise on banking than to this work. But it may be stated generally that even with regard to inland transactions a great proportion of the larger transactions in a mercantile country are settled by a process of balancing at a clearing house. To this clearing house cheques and bills are sent to be credited and debited to and against their holders and payers.

In international transactions accounts are balanced in a somewhat different method. The bills of exchange or cheques are made out in the denomination of the coinage of one of the countries concerned. In the case of two countries in both of which the price of gold per unit of weight is fixed at the mint, and there is unlimited coinage at that price, comparison of the money of the two countries is easy. The weight of gold in the coin of each country is known. There is nothing to be done but to ascertain how many of each of the coins is contained in a given weight of metal. This fixes a ratio between them. In strict theory that ratio should be invariable. But it is evident that if a person has to send gold from London to Paris it will be worth his while to give the money to some one in London to whom the same amount of money is owing from a person in Paris; by that means obtaining a bill on the Paris debtor ordering that debtor to pay the Paris creditor of the London debtor. By that means the two creditors get their money and the two debtors pay their debts. But instead of gold being carried from London to Paris, and other gold from Paris to London, a paper is sent from London to Paris and back. The Paris debtor pays the Paris creditor, and the London debtor pays the London creditor, only the paper crossing the channel. Now if more has to be sent to Paris from London than to London from Paris actual metal must be sent in any case. It will, therefore, be worth while for any one of the London debtors to give a London creditor, not only the amount of the bill, but also a small addition to it for a bill ordering some person in Paris to pay the debt. He thus avoids having to send the money. In such a case the exchange is said to be against London.

Stated in this way, however, it would appear that some debtors must seek out creditors in their place, and pay them the additional rate of exchange, whilst the creditors must send the metal. But in actual practice the bills of exchange are sent in payment. They are paid into banks, and from banks handed to brokers, who buy the bills from each other. In Paris, if it appears that money will have to be sent from London to Paris, there is a proportionately greater demand for bills drawn by London creditors ordering Paris debtors to pay money to persons in Paris. The exchange is thus in favour of the Paris debtors, who accept these orders and promise to carry them out, for they have but to pay some one in their own city. In London, on the same fact appearing, there is great demand for the same bills; the London debtors are anxious to pay merely by paper, instead of sending metal. There is less demand for bills drawn by Paris creditors ordering London debtors to pay money to London creditors. Of the latter sort of bills there is a surplus. So that the exchange is against the London debtors, who cannot, it appears, pay all they owe to Paris by handing it to persons in

London. It need hardly be said that the brokers must, in addition to the exchange, have some commission to pay them for their trouble.

If there is no ratio of value with regard to one metal fixed in the two countries, other considerations have to be taken into account, as also when it occurs that a currency is debased so that it does not represent its nominal amount of metal. But even after allowing for this it is important to remark that the rate of exchange does not depend merely on the question of which country has sold the greater value of commodities to the other. Remittances may be made by means of paper, not only for goods sold, but also occasionally for personal services rendered, or as gifts, loans, or interest on loans. And these remittances will pass into the ordinary channels, and affect the rate of exchange accordingly.

Still another consideration must be taken into account. The people who carry on this international trade in money do it for profit. As they are in communication with the various places between which the exchange takes place, it is obvious that they will take care to have their money in the place where it will earn them most. If, therefore, the rate of discount is higher at one of the places than the other, that will have a tendency to induce a supply of money to that place, whether or not there is money due from it. If money is much in demand the discount rate will be high, even though the bills should indicate that place to owe to another place. The bills ordering persons there to pay money will probably be balanced by bills or cheques ordering persons at the place where discount is lower to pay the money. By this means the person giving the bill gets the benefit of the exchange, which was against him and his place, if money must be sent, but is in his favour when he to some extent reverses that condition of affairs by selling his own paper to transmit. In short, a creditor will only have his money sent to him in face of an adverse exchange if he has use for it. But if he really wants it to make use of, he will have it even though it is costly to get it. For it must be remembered that the rate of exchange can never exceed the cost of transmitting the actual coin. As soon as it reaches that point some one will be willing to ship the metal required, and exchange will be influenced accordingly. The rate of exchange is eventually fixed, therefore, by the rate of discount—that is to say, money is subject to the same laws of the market as were noticed with regard to wealth. Higher discount rates or prices induce supply, whilst obviously they will discourage demand. Lower prices discourage supply, whilst they tend to induce demand. It thus appears how erroneous was the idea at one time held that money should be retained in a country by artificial means. The most efficacious method of retaining it is to allow free play to commerce, and the very need for it will cause it to come into the country for the purposes of exchange.

From the fact that the rate of exchange cannot exceed the cost of transmission it follows that as money is carried for a very small sum in proportion to its value, the value of money strongly tends to retain the same level throughout the area in which it circulates. This is what enables traders in commodities to carry on their transactions as though it maintained an absolutely perfect level. Bankers and money brokers undertake the transmission of the money without the special interference of the traders in wealth. Traders in commodities consequently have little to do in their actual dealings with rate of exchange, and carry on their transactions as though money absolutely retained the same level. In those instances in which there is such a considerable variation in the rate of exchange as to compel their attention to it, it becomes a serious misfortune and hindrance to trade. For it is obvious that trade must be hindered if merchants and others are seriously affected by contingencies which are entirely outside the business they devote themselves to. In the ordinary instances, however, the rate of exchange, although it fluctuates from one side to the other, does so to only a small extent, and that about equally on each side; so that it presents no serious obstacles to trading, and money flows between nations as between individuals.

CHAPTER VII

DIVISION OF WEALTH

THE distribution already referred to—namely, distribution in kind—is that for which alone the word can most conveniently be used. The expression has always been used by economists to denote the division of mixed wealth between landlord capitalist and labourer. It will, however, be expedient to use the word division for this purpose. The word expresses the idea quite as well as, or better than, the other. For this is evidently a question of dividing a bulk. It is a question of size of pieces, of quantity or unclassified number. Whilst the word distribution, which is the only one fairly applicable to the other purpose, is one which (in spite of its near relationship to the word division) carries with it more of the idea of classification. The word division will, therefore, be used in every instance in which the separation into shares between the different productive agents is referred to. Distribution will refer always to distribution in kind by merchants and carriers.

It has been tacitly assumed in the consideration of exchange and of the economic laws which relate to buying and selling that the persons engaging in these transactions recognised the right of private property. The basis on which the right to property rests will receive notice hereafter. For the present it will continue to be assumed that the owners who have a right to the control and enjoyment of wealth and the elements of its production are at any rate ascertainable. It is for the moment unnecessary to state whether they consist of individuals or communities.

The right of property in wealth must be conceded if the right of enjoying it is to be established. An ownership by some right is essential to its consumption. Now it has been seen that there are certain requisites to the production of wealth. It will hardly be disputed that the rightful ownership of these elements of production will give a right to the wealth they produce. It seems impossible to conceive that any one can be entitled to wealth in the production of which he had no share. There is an apparent exception in favour of one to whom another who had a share in its production is under obligation. In this case, however, the right is against the person who is under the obligation. It is not an independent right to the wealth itself, though the person having the right may acquire the benefit of the wealth by right of the person through whom he claims. In the nature of things the rightful owners of the elements of production (whoever they may be) will in the first instance be entitled to the wealth produced.

These elements of production have been seen to be separate and distinct in their nature. They are also capable of separate ownership. The question then arises how, if at all, the separate shares of their owners can be ascertained. In a country where each is free to make the best bargain he can for himself the exact payment will be determined by the contract. But can any law or laws be found which will indicate how the terms of the contract as to price are likely to be fixed? If contracts are not free then regard must be had to that which interferes with the freedom. It is difficult to see how general economic laws can be discovered which determine the various shares in such cases. Where, however, free contract obtains it is possible to lay down laws which will indicate the relative shares of the owners of land, labour, and capital in the wealth produced. In many cases the division takes place by means of the sale and conversion of the wealth into money.

The respective shares of land, capital, and labour are usually spoken of as rent, interest, and wages. But care must be taken in using these terms not to give them the meaning generally attached in ordinary language. Rent in the common acceptation includes payment for the use, not only of land, but of houses and buildings. But although the ground on which they stand is land, the houses and buildings are clearly capital. They are the result of adaptation by means of labour. On the other hand, the dividends on a railway company's shares or stock are spoken of as interest; indeed, the whole is included as capital. But this revenue includes the advantage from the possession of land, much of which has become very valuable. Again the expression wages usually refers only to the wages of those who receive weekly payments from employers. It does not in ordinary language include payments made to those who carry on business independently of *entrepreneurs*, and deal directly with their customers. It frequently excludes the higher grades of employment, or those employments in which the expression salary is used instead of wages. In the economic sense, however, rent must include all benefit from what has been described as land; all advantage accruing from the use of capital must be spoken of as interest; and the reward of all labour, from the lowest grade to the highest, including that of managers and employers, must be regarded as wages.

Rent in the economic sense must be understood as payment for the use of that which by nature was given free. It will include the annual value of the land in the centre of a town, for instance, but not the value of the buildings put upon it. It will include also mine rents and royalties, with payment for the use of the surface land used in connection with the mine, but not interest on the outlay for sinking a shaft or preparing necessary plant. It will include the value of fertile agricultural land, but not the improvements effected by the outlay of capital and labour. That there is such a value belonging to the land in its original state will readily be seen. The law of rent is called Ricardo's law of rent, because apparently the truth of it was first established by him, although he was not the first to suggest the law, nor even the first to publish a statement of it. It is, in fact, very difficult to ascertain when an idea first took root in the mind of either individual or community. It is only when the individual or community first realizes its truth and import that it is found a scientific discovery has been made.

The definition of rent being borne in mind, land being considered as that which has not been produced by human labour, and all value which owes itself to the latter source being excluded from consideration :—

The rent of land is determined by the excess of its produce over that which the same application can secure from the least productive land in use.

From the fact that land varies in its utility it is easy to understand that some land will generally be left uncultivated and unused because much better land is available. Some will just be worth using or cultivating. Other land will be worth cultivating even on condition of paying a rent for the opportunity of doing so. The land which will just pay for cultivation if no rent has to be paid is said to be at the margin of cultivation. That which will afford a rent is above the margin. That which will not pay for cultivation at all is below it.

What is below the margin of cultivation will evidently not be cultivated. It is not worth while to cultivate it. It will not afford a profit. Those who might possibly cultivate it if a demand existed find, or think they find, it better to engage in some other employment. In a word, it awaits an increase of population. At any rate, no demand is shown for its products at present. If there are any who lack what it would supply, it is either because some one holds it and will not permit it to be used by others at any price, or it is because those who would be willing to take and use it find that the land is not such as to afford them as good a return after payment of expenses as they can obtain elsewhere from some other employment. In either case it will be seen that the evil is artificial.

The first case is not one which will extend over very large areas. But it is not unknown. So far as it exists, however, it is by the authority of some government, which enables the owner to exert rights over the land he does not use. Possibly he could not retain without that authority the land he really does use. And no complaint is made as to the exertion of the government's authority on his behalf in respect of the land he uses. Certain conditions may possibly have to be suggested hereafter, but not in this chapter. No complaint is at present made with reference even to his retaining land which he does not use. The contention at this point is that his retaining it is only possible by the aid of a government, and that a government is an artificial arrangement. Government is not undesirable or even of necessity contrary to nature. But as it is a contrivance capable of human modification, it is possible that care should be taken by those responsible for government that when the products of certain land are required for the nation's subsistence the government's authority should not be exerted to enable persons to retain the land unused.

The second cause of land not being used, although its productions are needed, is want of adequate return for its use. This will be due either to the owners requiring a value exceeding that of the actual usefulness of the land as a wealth producer (a sense in which the phrase value in use might be appropriate), or to some hindrance which prevents the money or other value necessary to induce its cultivation from flowing to those who would cultivate it.

We may neglect for the present purpose those who lack the productions of the land in question for other than strictly economic causes. Instances of this are found when they or those on whom they depend are unable or unwilling to expend the labour necessary to obtain those productions; or, whilst they actually labour, yet waste the proceeds of their labour without supplying what they more properly require. These are considerations with regard to the impotent, idle, and prodigal which will be neglected throughout this inquiry. There is scope for their special treatment in another work.

The case of the owners requiring a value exceeding its usefulness is similar to that which was just previously referred to as due to artificial causes. There is no difference except in degree between holding land at a prohibitive price and refusing to let it be used at any price; the effect is the same.

The hindrance unduly reducing the price offered to possible cultivators must clearly arise from some artificial interference. For it was seen that under the free play of supply and demand, if the supply of a commodity was reduced, the price would tend to rise until the demand was again supplied. And there is nothing to indicate that the rise would stop until such a price was reached that there was no further need for advancing the price. At any rate, the supply would reach the point at which buyers preferred something else.

It is useless to argue that the persons requiring

the production of the land in question have not the money with which to buy. That is conceded. They have, however, the labour; and though it may be admitted that they are possibly not competent, through lack of training or of capital, to exercise their labour on the land, they may still offer their labour to others. And they may with advantage to themselves offer it at such a price that the others can make for themselves a profit out of it sufficient to induce them to supervise and employ it. There is thus no need for their lacking the wealth whilst this land remains below the margin of cultivation and their labour is unemployed. But if by some means the flow of currency is, so to speak, dammed up, then, while they may be attracted towards it in the trade in which it happens to be, it will not reach those who would cultivate this land. The land consequently will not come within the margin of cultivation. These means of damming up will evidently be artificial means.

So that both the forms of hindrance to the cultivation of land the produce of which is needed are artificial. Remedies for these evils will be suggested in succeeding chapters. For the present purpose, what is important to note is that the land which is uncultivated or otherwise unused for wealth production is below the margin of cultivation. The word cultivation is used in this sense as including use of any kind in deference to established usage. Margin of use is a phrase which might be used without fear of confusion, even in view of the expression marginal utility, which refers to an entirely different matter.

The land which is used is either at or above the margin of cultivation. As examples of that which is at the margin of cultivation, we may take land which is worth cultivating by its owners, but for which no person will pay a rent. Many such cases might be found in countries where it is the rule for farmers to own the land they cultivate. It is also seen in some instances where a rent is paid for a whole farm but some of the land is so poor that it is only in the times of greater demand for its produce that it is worth the cost of cultivation.

All other land is above the margin of cultivation or use. Now, it is evidently as profitable to any one proposing to use land to pay the excess value of the latter kind of land as to cultivate the worst. That excess is rent in the economic sense.

We thus find proportionately the first share in the total produce of the land. It is fixed by the margin of cultivation. As the margin of cultivation falls through increased demand for the products of land rent must rise proportionately. For it is now evident that worse land must be cultivated, and the land which was at the margin is now somewhat above it. Rent must be paid for this land, and the value of other land which was already above the margin is proportionately increased. If by any means, as by the introduction of produce from elsewhere, some of the land can be spared, the margin of cultivation will rise, and rent will accordingly be proportionately reduced.

Having a law which determines the share of rent, we may proceed to ascertain the relative shares of interest and capital. In this connection Mr. George has afforded considerable light. In the first place, it is evident that of the total products rent is the first definite and ascertainable share. The balance of the total proceeds must be divided in some proportion or other into the shares of capital and labour. Other things being equal the sum of the latter shares must, therefore, fall (since rent rises) as the margin of cultivation falls, and rise (since rent falls) as the margin of cultivation rises. That is to say, the relative shares remaining for capital and labour will be increased as it is found that land can be spared, and decreased as worse and worse land must be taken into cultivation or use.

For the moment we must part company with Mr. George, and mention a fact which does not accord with some of his views. It must be very distinctly borne in mind that the shares here spoken of are relative shares. The actual value or benefit of the share of rent may, in some cases, rise at the same time as the shares of capital and labour. This would happen if by means of improved machinery or increased trade facilities a much greater supply of wealth could be had in any place. In such a case the relative share of rent would decrease, whilst the shares of interest and wages would increase. For less land would now be necessary for the same supply of wealth. But the actual share of wealth devoted to payment of rent might be increased, because of the increased abundance of wealth. The change which would take place in the relative shares would consist of an increase in the value of land calculated in terms of wealth, but a still greater increase in the value of capital and labour. The relative share of rent has decreased, whilst the actual share has increased. The converse of this proposition would also be true. The same considerations might apply, even though the margin had actually fallen, and the rent consequently risen, if it were the result of a larger consumption by capitalists and labourers.

We may again pursue Mr. George's views. We have observed the relative shares of land on the one side and capital and labour taken together on the other. The fall of the margin of cultivation increases the former and reduces the latter. The qualifying sentence at the conclusion of the preceding paragraph may for the time be disregarded. We have now to find the shares of capital and labour as between themselves. So far as wealth can be produced by means of labour, without the aid of capital, it need hardly be said that labour takes all the remainder after rent is paid. It is evident, therefore, that wages may be said to be the produce which results from the application of labour to the best land, which it is free to use without the payment of rent. In other words, wages amount to the total result of labour at the margin of cultivation that is on the land last required for use as a wealth producer. It may be fertile or comparatively barren. It may, in fact, turn out to be better than some already used, but, on account of its situation or otherwise, it hitherto has been and is now treated as worse land than that cultivated.

The nature of the services rendered by capital in wealth production has already been indicated. The payment for these services must be considered more in detail in a later chapter, and Mr. George's errors pointed out. It is, however, clearly possible to determine by a scientific law the share of capital as against that of labour, assuming freedom of contract. Capital is not like land in being strictly limited in quantity and capable of monopolization. It can be indefinitely increased by the application of additional labour. Although, therefore, in the first instance, the use of capital may even double or otherwise multiply the productions which could have been obtained without its aid, yet it is unlikely it could long continue to obtain a reward commensurate with that result. Those who have to compete with the owner of this capital would readily discover the profitableness of its use, and devote their labour to the production of a similar species of capital. If, by the laws of supply and demand already noticed, another species of capital becomes more valuable by reason of its productions or use being more in demand, it is evident that labour will be directed to the production of that kind of capital. By this means the share taken for the use of capital will (neglecting special circumstances) constantly tend to the same level in all its modes of employment.

It is evident that capital will only be paid for because of the advantage it offers, and it will tend to find its most profitable employment. Capital cannot, it is true, increase the supply of wealth except in those employments where from its nature it can either make labour more efficient or by its reproduction increase its own quantity. But when capital exists in other forms it must evidently share in the proceeds of wealth production, or that kind of capital would cease to be stored or produced. As, however, its use offers advantages, it is paid for, and the payment for its use will, on the average, be similar to that for the use of other kinds of capital. Now the whole advantage resulting from the use of capital has special relation to the time of its use. The advantage consists in the increase of wealth arising from having it now rather than at a future time. The increase arising from productive capital must, however, be spread over all capital; and, in fact, over some so-called capital which must, hereafter, be noticed, but which is really spurious capital. Whatever will command wealth, although it may give no assistance in its production, will, nevertheless, be valuable. If, therefore, a person can buy something which will give him an income, such as government stock, he may profitably purchase it as if it were capital. It is not capital, and may be of no benefit to the nation which pays for it. But a portion of wealth must be devoted to it, for it is treated as capital, and commands wealth. Interest on capital, therefore, will be limited to the total increase of wealth arising from its use and spread over capital in all its forms.

But there is a further limitation to be noticed. The greater supply of capital will, it is evident, tend to reduce the amount which will be paid for the use of any given quantity of it. The capital may double itself, or increase itself manifold during the period. But as it cannot in any case do so without some labour (in the way of attention, at least) the amount which will be paid for its present possession will be further influenced. It will vary, not only with the actual advantage it will confer (which it can never exceed), but also with the amount of capital available. It may, therefore, fall much below the actual advantage it confers, although it can never rise above that advantage. The possession of a certain quantity of capital may enable a man to double his income compared with what it would have been had he been entirely without the capital. But if he already has as much as he needs, or can use, he will not pay anything for more of it; and if there is much capital seeking employment, its owners will be willing to accept much less in payment for it than the advantage it confers. In fact, the whole advantage will never be paid for its use. Why should a man trouble to employ capital at all, if he must pay away all the benefit it confers? It would be better to use only his own labour.

Interest on capital, therefore, will amount to that portion of the increase of productions arising from its use which, from its relative scarcity, those who employ it will be willing to pay for its use. Of real and spurious capital, real capital alone produces increase, but spurious capital shares the benefit.

The remainder is for labour. No actual limit can be put to what labour will take except by considering what must first be taken for the use of land and capital. The labourer is also a consumer. He works for the satisfaction of his desires. It is for him to consider whether he will labour further, or rest content with the consumption of what his present labour brings him. The exact division between the various labourers of different grades and employments will be noticed in a separate chapter. Briefly, it may be stated that the wages are fixed by competition for places. The result of this is, as far as possible, to equalize the wages of the same ability, training, and exertion in the various employments. In this respect labour resembles capital. It is free to pass from one employment to another. But, on the other hand, competition cannot equalize ability, nor will it equalize exertion. So that in this respect labour resembles also land. As land is subject to natural differences of situation and fertility, occasioning differences in value, so labour varies in value on account of inherent differences of ability and energy. From this has arisen the phrase " rent of ability."

Wages, then, it will be seen, may be expressed in two ways. They amount either to the produce of the labour expended on the land at the margin of cultivation, or to the remainder which is left from the use of that land after payment has been made for the use of capital. This latter payment will amount to that share of the advantage of the capital which, from its greater or less scarcity, labourers are willing to pay for its use.

These results will require a more detailed consideration. It has been assumed that land was held under free contracts for its use, the owner of land taking only the economic rent, the true owner of capital taking the advantage accruing from its use, and competition being entirely free. The effect of the absence of any of these conditions must be noticed. Land is held on various tenures and contracts, some of which demand consideration. The subject of interest on capital offers some problems worthy of explanation. The subject of wages also is one on which the utmost confusion is apparent on every hand. Labourers of all grades suffer loss from this confusion, and it is important that the subject should be made clear.

CHAPTER VIII

RENT OF LAND

THE share of productions which constitutes rent in the economic sense has already been indicated. There is perhaps no perfect example to be found of the separation of rent, in this sense, from the shares due to the use of capital and labour. Rent is, nevertheless, paid or enjoyed in various forms. And to a large extent, by means of different kinds of tenancies, this rent is enjoyed by others than those who actually use the land. It is proposed to notice in this chapter a few of these forms of tenancy, so as to make clear the nature of economic rent, and how it enters into the payments which, according to the common acceptation, are known as rent.

We may take, as the first instance, rent paid for land let for the purposes of cultivation. This would include not only agricultural land strictly so called—that is, so called in the sense of arable land—but also garden ground on a large or small scale, land used for pasturing purposes, and, finally, land used for growth by cultivation of timber. In all these cases the gift of nature consists of the extension or space, the natural fertility of the soil, such as it is, including the benefits of natural watercourses, and the atmosphere, with its various influences, summed up in the one word climate. All of which are more or less modified by the *contour* of the land.

In all the land comprised within this class it seldom occurs that the rent paid includes only the value of the natural agents. It usually includes payment for the use of erections, such as farmhouses and their buildings, as well as for fences and fertility acquired through artificial works or long cultivation by one person or another. These additional advantages are capital, and are not included in the economic meaning of land. Payment for them is, therefore, included in interest on capital, and not in rent of land.

There are, however, cases in which the capital last mentioned does not owe its existence to the persons who receive payment for its use, nor to any one from whom they have acquired it by purchase. This consideration opens out the question of the various terms on which land is held. To find a clearly defined instance of the payment of economic rent, together with an additional sum for interest on the capital expended by the landlord in the improvement of the land, it is necessary to find a tenancy in which the tenant receives full compensation for the improvements made by him. It is not, perhaps, too much to say that this is the exception and not the rule in the tenancies which have hitherto obtained. In those newer countries, where improvements have generally been made by those who held the land as their own freehold, the capital has usually been put upon the land by those who afterwards reaped the benefit of it.

But in the older countries the case is different. In England, in various parts, a system of tenant-right customs has arisen, under which allowance was made for improvements effected by the tenant on the land of another. In a portion of Ireland also a custom of tenant-right has obtained. The copyhold land to be found in some parts of England is an example of another mode by which the tenants have acquired the benefit of their improvements. In the latter case, however, a considerable portion of the rent, in the economic sense, has also been acquired by the holder of the land. But these are special instances. So far as England is concerned, the various customs have had to be supplemented by Act of Parliament, and the arrangements are still imperfect. There seems scarcely any instance of a clear arrangement giving to the holder of land the full value of his improvements.

The difference between rent in the economic sense and rent as commonly understood has already been referred to. But a greater difficulty is presented in those systems of land tenure which do not clearly distinguish between improvements effected by the landlord and those which are in natural justice tenants' capital. No plan can be suggested of dealing with such land so as to raise the condition of its cultivators, and to get the greatest possible benefit to the nation, except that of altering the system of tenure so as to secure to the tenant the full value of his improvements. Without this it is impossible that men should be induced to put forth their efforts to make their land more productive. With it scarcely any difficulty will prevent their doing so, although in this case, as in every other matter, one man's efforts will greatly differ from those of another.

Even a high rent (in the common acceptation) is much less of an evil than insecurity with regard to improvements. But it must be clearly understood that the rent must not exceed what the tenant can pay. Very great injury has been wrought in Ireland by the rents being fixed higher than the tenants could by any means pay, and allowing them to get continually into arrear. Under these circumstances they were constantly in the position of insolvent debtors, or perhaps even of slaves, who could not hope to have property of their own. Their only plan was so to cultivate their land as to appear poor, and thus be allowed to remain on the farm, paying what they could afford. The principle is the same in both cases. The conditions of tenure are not such that the holder of the land can have any reasonable hope of enjoying for himself the improvements he may make to the land and the additional produce which may result from the greater application of capital and labour.

Men will accomplish great tasks if the inducement is sufficient and there is hope of success, but if they have no hope of success they will make no effort. On the other hand, it has sometimes been remarked with what poor rewards men would be content if they were sure of that little. This tendency has been called the magic of property. But there appears no ground for the use of the expression magic. It is a natural tendency. There would be more need for the art of the necromancer to induce men to put forth additional efforts the benefit of which was to go to others, and not to themselves. It is especially so in this case, seeing that those who would obtain the benefits of their labour need those benefits less than the labourers themselves do. There is no question here of self-denying effort for the wretched and suffering.

It need hardly be stated that the economist can have nothing to say in favour of any arrangement which fails to secure to each the result of his own labour. The mischief from his point of view is not so much that it enables the landowner to take for his own benefit the value which justly belongs to the tenant, but that it prevents the tenant creating the value. It is not that the tenant is robbed of his improvements, but that he is robbed of the incentive to make them. It may readily be conceded that few cases of actual forfeiture of such improvements exist, but few opportunities are offered. The nation is the poorer for the inefficient occupation of the land. This result follows from all systems which are inconsistent with a definite contract rigorously carried out and giving to each party to it an enforceable right to his own creation of value. Not to give a tenant a right to the full value of his improvements is to prevent his making those improvements. To permit him to continue occupying land at a nominal rent, which, on account of his poverty, he does not pay, is to encourage him in that poverty as a means of avoiding payment. It is, moreover, to keep out of occupation some one who would make better use of the land. These evils have existed in England

and particularly so in Ireland amongst agriculturalists.

Closely connected with the evils already mentioned, and coming under a similar condemnation, differing only in degree, are some older customs. One of these is the metayer system, under which the tenant pays by way of rent a fixed proportion of the produce of his farm. It is true that under this system he has a perpetual holding of the land, but it is evident that of any improvement he may make or of any additional industry he may exert a portion must go to the landowner. So that the difference is only one of degree between this tenancy and that which gives the landowner the right to all the tenant's improvements.

Once more, and for a similar reason, the economist cannot commend communal holding of land in any of the various forms which have obtained in the earlier stages of civilization. They were doubtless enough for the times in which they obtained, but they fail to enable each one to enjoy his own improvements.

These various defects in land tenures have the one feature in common that, by failing to offer an inducement to it, they do not tend to the improvement of land as a wealth producer. It may be laid down as an axiom that any perfect system of land tenure must secure to each the benefit of his own capital and labour. And something will have to be said in another place as to how this is to be done. Speaking generally, all these defective tenures belong to the era of civilization to which, as will hereafter be pointed out, socialism belongs. The rule of persons is apparent in each of them. They are survivals of the notion that certain persons have by nature, or rather by conquest, a pre-eminent right to own and enjoy the land. In the worst of them it would seem that all not so favoured should be thankful for the opportunity of cultivating the land, paying the landowner a portion of its productions for the privilege. Indeed, there is in these customs a flavour of personal servitude.

Even with regard to the communal form of holding there seems to be the absence of any provision for permitting the introduction of new members, as though those already in the place had an exclusive right to that land.

A use of land differing in its nature from the various forms of cultivation is that which includes mining, quarrying, and other forms of taking the actual substance of the land. In this connection some views of Ricardo's may be noticed. He states that "rent is that portion of the produce of the earth which is paid to the landlord for the use of the original and indestructible powers of the soil." In many cases the rent is not paid to any landlord. For economic rent exists even when the land is in the hands of the freeholder. And in other cases, such as those of long leases, the lessee enjoys a portion of the true economic rent. An objection more to the present purpose, however, refers to that part of the definition which speaks of the rent being for the original and indestructible powers of the soil. It will readily be seen that the soil is only a portion of what is paid for. But we need not lay stress on merely verbal incompleteness. This Ricardo would perhaps have admitted. He realized that agricultural land (even in its wider sense) was not the only land for which rent was paid. He spoke of the rent of mines.

There is still another objection to the definition, and that is found in the word indestructible. It is submitted that the word is misleading, and vitiates the definition. There is no need that the qualities for which rent is paid should be indestructible. Indeed, it is difficult to say what powers or qualities are indestructible. Most qualities of land are destructible if means of destruction be taken. A stream may be diverted; the land may be flooded; even the constant cropping of virgin soil will destroy its original fertility; to say nothing of the breaking up of fertile land for mining or building. And yet these powers are natural and inherent in the soil, and are, therefore, the proper subjects of rent.

Now Ricardo used this expression advisedly. He proceeds to enforce it. He objects to the use by Adam Smith of the term rent in its economic sense for natural forest lands. Because, says he, the benefit of holding them is to take away the timber, and not to use the soil. He also objects to the use of the term rent as applied to coal mines and stone quarries. It is a compensation paid for the value of the coal or stone which can be removed, and has no connection with the original and indestructible powers of the soil. This objection does not seem capable of being sustained. These payments are payments for the use of land in any reasonable meaning of that expression. They are subject to the same law of rent as payments for land of the previously mentioned class. Whether with mines, quarries, or forests, the most profitable will be used first, the less profitable afterwards. And a rent will be obtainable for the best when a worse must be taken into use. As with other land it may occur that a more fertile mine or forest is left until after a less fertile mine has been worked, because of the greater convenience of access of the latter. In all cases of economic division of wealth we have to do with relative shares as shown by value, and not with actual quantities of the commodity available. If this objection of Ricardo's were allowed, the science would have no place for the payment of mine and similar rents. It certainly is not interest on capital or wages of labour. And all payment for the use of land in its natural condition must be included in rent of land, or endless confusion will ensue. With regard to forests as included in this class of land, it must be borne in mind that only timber lands remaining in their original condition are included. If the timber has been planted and otherwise cared for, the land is included under the first class mentioned in this chapter.

As to the land included in this class, none of the difficulties mentioned with regard to the previous class seem to exist. The whole matter belongs more to modern days. The holder of the land generally expends all the capital which is expended in preparing the land for profitable working of the substance to be taken from it. The payment to the landowner is purely economic rent. All interest on capital is included in the tenant's profits. Where, however, the landowner is the actual holder the rent is not already separated. None the less, however, it is generally easy in the matter of value to separate land from capital. It may also occur in a few instances that on account of the existence of a long lease the actual payment made for rent is greater or less than the value of the mine. The true economic rent of that mine or forest may have varied by the opening of better mines or forests, or by the increased demand for its products. But this is not a matter which need be discussed here at any length. The true economic rent is sufficiently ascertainable, although the party gaining by the change would scarcely be willing needlessly to reopen the contract.

The use of land for building purposes is a third distinguishable form of occupation. In this instance the natural elements of utility are the space, the solid foundation, and the light and air. The light and air are, of course, closely connected with climate, but climate does not as a rule enter into the advantages in the same way as in the case of the land used for cultivation. An exception occurs in the case of some manufactures in which certain atmospheric influences are important for the proper working of the material. In the case of houses for habitation the climate is also a consideration of comfort. But the class will include, not only sites of dwelling-houses and of mills and works for manufacturing purposes, but also such land as is required for shafts and head-gear of coal mines, and other similar forms of capital. It should, moreover, include sites of railways, docks, and markets. In this class the chief point considered is situation; as in the second class desirability and accessibility of natural substances to be carried away, and in the first class soil and climate, are considered in choosing land. Not that these are the only considerations taken into account. In the last case, for instance, it is of importance that even with a good soil and climate the market should not be too distant. But the essential qualifications for the production of the wealth are those stated. Other considerations show that the requirements of the other classes must not be entirely absent. This applies to each of the classes.

With regard to the third class of occupation, the division into rent of land and interest on capital is not particularly difficult. But it must not be concluded that the ground-rent fixed by contract between two parties is invariably the true economic rent. In numerous instances the land and the buildings are held as the property of the same person. In these instances it seldom or never occurs that there is any difficulty in ascertaining the relative values of the buildings and the site on which they stand. This would be so, not only in the case of actual erections, but also of such works as railways, docks, wharfs, shafts, and all artificial ways.

In other cases, however, leases have been made for longer or shorter periods at fixed rents. The lessees usually covenant to erect certain buildings, and to hand them over in good repair to the landowner at the expiration of the term for which the lease is granted. This is an arrangement which merits to the full the condemnation already passed on the various systems which fail to secure to each the result of his labour. In the case of building leases for short terms much hardship exists in this respect. It is not here complained that the lessee is in any way defrauded. He makes the arrangement in full view of the consequences. It must be confessed that frequently he must make the arrangement or suffer loss in another direction. But the complaint is chiefly that these conditions defer persons from building or using the land. The consequence of this is the nation's poverty. Particularly it may be mentioned that the poor are wretchedly housed. It would be altogether contrary to the spirit of this book to say a word against freedom of contract. But there can be no denying that the conditions which compel such leases are amongst the evils to be removed by the right understanding and proper observation of economic laws. And there is every possibility of removing these evils by obvious and just methods, which shall be suggested.

The rent fixed by these leases cannot always, it is evident, be the true economic rent. It must be more or less invariable. So that when the margin of use rises or falls, decreasing or increasing economic rent, the result must be that the fixed rent is above or below the economic rent. This is so even if the rent fixed in the first instance was as nearly as possible the true rent in the economic sense, which is not always the case. Economic rent will accordingly often be found partly in the hands of the lessor and partly in those of the lessee. But there can be little or no difficulty in any of the cases included in this class in ascertaining what it is and who is in enjoyment of it.

Reference was made in the previous chapter to the difference between absolute and relative shares. It was stated that the absolute or actual share did not necessarily follow the rise and fall of the relative share with which this science has to do. This may be further illustrated and enforced in the case of rent. To adopt Ricardo's favourite method of argument, suppose a district or country in which land is cultivated of five different degrees of fertility. Suppose that on the worst (on which no rent is paid) capital and labour produce for themselves four; and that on the other portions five, six, seven and eight respectively are produced. Of these quantities naturally rent will take one, two, three and four respectively. Total for rent, ten. Total for capital and labour, twenty. The share of rent is one third of the whole. Now suppose that by better facilities for cultivation or trade the produce is exactly doubled without any increase of population. This will give sixty, instead of thirty. But, for convenience of illustration, let it be supposed that only fifty-two are required for the maintenance of the population. This is a sufficiently considerable increase on thirty to give to consumption of wealth. We then have each of the different portions of land producing double its former amount. But the portion formerly producing four can be spared altogether, although it now produces eight. Rent will accordingly cease to be paid on the portion producing five, which now produces ten. The other three produce, respectively, twelve, fourteen and sixteen, of which two, four and six are rent. Total rent now, twelve, an actual increase of two on the former rent. Total for capital and labour, forty, double the former amount. The share of rent is less than one-fourth of the whole, a decrease relatively on the former share of one-third.

What, then, does Ricardo mean when he says: "It is obvious that the landlord is doubly benefitted by difficulty of production. First, he obtains a greater share; and, secondly, the commodity in which he is paid is of greater value"? As stated and argued by him this statement is very plausible. But it requires careful examination. First, we are told the landlord obtains a greater share by the difficulty of production. This is true; but it is a greater share in a smaller total. And one half of five is less than one fourth of eleven. That is, to double his share will give him actually less, if the total produced is reduced more than one half. Always it must be considered whether the greater relative share is in a greater or less total, so that the landlord may possibly not be benefitted by the greater share.

Secondly, we are told the commodity in which the landlord is paid is of greater value. We should naturally expect so from the fact that scarcity is one of the elements of value; though, doubtless, the notion of value never occurred to Ricardo in this way. Perhaps, for the moment, Ricardo confused value with utility. But he knew the difference, and could never have thought that the corn or other commodity possessed greater utility because of its difficulty of production and scarcity. He, however, seems to show that he meant value calculated in money. But value in money may or may not be a benefit, according as the money will exchange for commodities. In the true notion of it money, as already seen, is only valuable as a means of obtaining other commodities. If, then, the landlord obtains a share more valuable in money, he will have to consider whether the money will produce more of other commodities. If it will not, he will not be benefitted ; and if other commodities have been subject to the same increased difficulty of production, evidently it will not command more of those commodities, and, therefore, if in the matter of other productions the same has occurred as in those produced on his land, he will not be benefitted at all in the way of value by the reduced production.

His greater share may amount to less because, as we saw, the whole of which it is a part is proportionately more diminished. The greater value is of no benefit to him unless it will command, not merely more money, but more commodities. So that Ricardo seems to have been in a state of confusion in making this assertion. There is just one thing more possibly in his favour. He evidently intended to treat money as a commodity. This is not strictly allowable, but suppose it be conceded for this instance. The necessary inference is that the commodity money has not increased in difficulty of production. Otherwise the commodity of the landlord in question would not have been increased in value compared with it. So that, even allowing this strained interpretation of what Ricardo meant, it does not amount to much. It supposes only land producing a particular commodity. All the land producing other commodities must continue to bring forth as much as before. The particular commodity in question must not be otherwise producible, or the scarcity and high value will not be felt. Even with this monopoly the landlord only gets a larger share in a smaller quantity. It is lamentable consolation for making the actual producers poorer.

The practical bearing of the point is this. If the holders of the land which produces a certain commodity can prevent that commodity from being imported from elsewhere, they will keep for themselves a larger proportionate share of it, and also make it more valuable compared with other commodities. They will benefit themselves at the expense of the community. But the holders of all the land in a place cannot obtain more wealth by taking care to reduce supply, with a view to obtaining a greater share. The increased value in money would be spent in a higher value of other things.

It would be unfortunate if it could be shown that difficulty of production would absolutely benefit a whole class of people. Happily it cannot be so shown, whatever may be true with regard to single individuals. It is true that this does not disprove the fact that greater scarcity causes greater dependence of the poor on the rich. It will not be even disputed that the difficulty of production, and consequent poverty, is a barrier to independence. Those who wish to see this personal servitude, as it may without impropriety be called, must be left to advocate at their will the restrictions which tend to the poverty which supports it. Even more than this may be admitted to those whose desires lead them in the direction indicated. The relative share of rent is capable of being increased by reducing supply. And men often count themselves rich by comparison with those around them, rather than by their actual advantages. So that there is some reason to account for the owners of the soil opposing free trade.

As to the effect of free trade in commodities on rent, it may be expressed as a letting in of the margin of cultivation of the whole world. If the importation of a particular commodity can be prohibited or made costly, worse land for its cultivation must be used than would be if trade were free. The margin of cultivation is artificially depressed to the advantage of rent and the disadvantage of wages and interest. If trade be again set free, the land of that country is treated as that of other countries, and the margin of cultivation rises to the natural level at which it stands in the whole world. In the case of an artificial depression of the margin for one commodity, it must follow that a corresponding artificial rise will take place with regard to another, and, even to the landowners, the country, as a whole, will give less wealth for the interference and consequent difficulty of supply; while to capitalists and labourers the difference will be even more material.

It was pointed out that the laws of supply and demand considered as economic laws of the market applied to land in the same way as to wealth. But beyond the market they do not apply in the same way. Land is not capable of increase as wealth is. It is the gift of the Creator of the earth. The supply of it, though enough to all appearance for man's needs, is not capable of increase by man. Land in the economic sense refers only to nature's free gift. So that ultimately, and outside the market, land is not subject to the influence of further supply and consequent fall of price. Its value depends entirely on the demand for it. In the market there may be rises and falls of price caused by and affecting supply and demand. But if the demand continues to increase, as with increased population it must, there are no means of meeting the greater demand by a correspondingly greater supply. The price must rise. In other words, the value of land depends entirely on the needs of the people. It does not depend on any difficulty overcome or labour necessarily exerted by individuals. The land was once free and valueless, although potentially useful. Now it is valuable because scarce, and the greater the scarcity of wealth, and the consequent need for it, the greater its value.

Hitherto the value and other incidents of land have been discussed without any reference to the question of who in natural justice was entitled to that value. The point must receive consideration in the next chapter.

CHAPTER IX

TAXATION

ALTHOUGH taxation in its origin usually owes its existence to might rather than to right, it does not follow that there is no justice in it. But even when the right to tax is fully established, it has still to be considered that there may be a right way and several wrong ways of carrying out that which in itself is by nature lawful and expedient. Nor does the justice of the claim of the community on the individual, any more than that of any other claim, cure the injustice of the mode of obtaining its satisfaction.

Yet, taking England, even in recent years, for instance, careful consideration will convince any one with the ability to grasp the subject that no proper principle of taxation has hitherto been adopted in this country. And he will look in vain for any appreciable measure of justice or true expediency in any one of the methods in which taxation is carried out. To examine each one in detail is beyond the scope of this book, and not necessary for the present purpose.

The modes of taxation adopted in most other countries are even worse than those of England. For in them appears the still generally received idea that various industries should be protected.

This is done by as far as possible preventing those who carry on these industries from having what they desire, unless what they desire is produced in their own country. It will, of course, be remembered that some persons having considerable governing power there own the soil of the country. They do not own the soil of other countries. They would, therefore, be unable to make good any claim for rent on the goods imported from abroad. The effect of this protection on landowners has been sufficiently noticed. What was said applied even to a country where a class exists subsisting on the share of rent. But where land is owned in smaller portions by persons who must also labour the evil is much more contrary to the interests of all classes.

The question of a government's right in the abstract to demand taxes from the people under its rule need not be discussed. It belongs more to political philosophy than to economics. So that the right of taxation will be conceded to every properly constituted government without further consideration. Nor will the expenditure of the taxes raised be dealt with at any great length in this book.

The only question arising, therefore, is: granted the right of taxation, how shall it be carried out? We require a principle of taxation. Economists have usually offered only maxims. Some others have endeavoured to abstract and point out principles of taxation. But, as will be seen, the proper principle of taxation is a question for the economist. The philosopher who deals only with principles of legislation or of morals, even including the institution of property and its regulation, can have no particular concern with the principle of taxation. He may say that it should be fair, just, equitable, and in those senses equal to all. The economist will concede that, and observe it. But this taxation is a question of the production and supply of wealth in the economic sense, and not merely a question of property. To deal with the subject as it should be dealt with requires a knowledge of the conditions of the supply of wealth, its production, distribution and division. Clearly no principle beyond the obvious ethical principle that taxation should be according to natural justice can be reached without such knowledge and its application.

It is true that even such an ethical principle carries with it the conclusion that taxation should be compulsory. Were it not so, were every man permitted to contribute as he would, the exchequer would be filled according to the consciences of individuals, which are not equally enlightened or active. To admit the principle that men may contribute according to their liberality or selfishness would be a sure means of injustice. To permit a person to withhold his contribution to the revenue on the ground of his disapproval of the government expenditure would be equally inexpedient. It is much better to leave to private benevolence all supposed government duties, on the importance of which there is not sufficient concensus of opinion.

But the duty of the economist is not so much with the ethical principles as with other considerations, whilst not neglecting principles of justice.

The various maxims of taxation only touch the fringe of the subject. Taxation should certainly be equal, if equality here means justice. It should be certain, and conveniently and economically imposed. These are the leading ideas of Smith's maxims of taxation. But there is nothing in them or in his application of them which goes to the root of the subject, and applies the science of economics to the subject of taxation. Mr. Henry George adopts as his first maxim that taxation should bear as lightly as possible upon production. Which is certainly what would be expected from an economist who puts before him the task of finding the most perfect conditions of wealth supply. But we are still without a principle of application. It is proposed to reach one by proceeding from first principles and the foundation facts of the science, and not by stating maxims, as Adam Smith did, or by enquiring for the cause of poverty, as Mr. George did. Neither of these methods would produce a true principle. Smith's lacked application. Mr. George happened to hit the right method, but did not reach the true principle. And the conclusion to which he had come before, and on which, he stated this maxim of taxation, was, as will be shown, incorrect. The maxim was but a maxim, and not a foundation principle.

It may be stated as a preliminary principle that justice demands the rendering to every man of his own. That is a truism. For the sense in which the expression "his own" is here used is that of strict natural justice. What the more or less imperfect laws of any state may accord to the man is another question. In the first place, natural justice would certainly accord his own self to any man. The inherent powers of his body and mind are his own. He may owe a debt of gratitude to his Creator, to the race of men who have gone before, to the nation who gave him his existence. But gratitude is not a debt which is capable of exact estimation. It is even a matter of opinion for every man whether his existence is a blessing to be grateful for or not. Certainly no one outside himself has the right of determining to what extent he should show his gratitude for bare existence. This applies in his relations to the vague set of individuals known as the race, nation, or community, with all its force. It would even seem to apply to those who are the direct ancestors of any individual, to whom alone he can be considered indebted for existence. His nearest collateral relatives have no claim on him for his existence. And the remarks just made seem to apply even to those who have actually conferred an existence which may seem to any one a blessing or a curse, according to its nature and circumstances.

The considerations, however, apply only to the individual's own self. He may, nevertheless, be under obligation to others on account of contracts he has made with them. And certainly he is under obligation to those for whose existence in the world he is responsible. The extent of these latter obligations is made to vary according to the different laws of various states. But a natural instinct exists in the average person, which goes a considerable way towards causing him to meet them.

Moreover, it must be understood that this right of the individual does not apply to anything outside himself. Particularly, as will shortly be pointed out, it does not apply to the land. That is a portion of the earth, and must receive different treatment. It does, however, apply to his own labour; a right to that must be conceded to every one. It may be objected that the hopelessly invalid and helplessly deformed must on this argument be left uncared for. So far as the community is concerned, that is the case. Those who cause their existence are in strictness responsible for their care. But it may possibly be found that there is no need to carry this point to its final logical conclusion.

That the community should undertake the protection of its members implies that the strict right now under consideration is likely to be invaded. Such an undertaking by the community does not militate against the principle now contended for. Even a tax levied for this protection, if justly applied, cannot be called an invasion of the rights of the subject. The small injustice it inflicts is more than compensated for by the protection it affords against a greater injustice such as is likely to be suffered from the most dishonest of the community. On abstract principle each has a right to justice from the rest of the community free of cost to himself. But, as some are far from being honest, it is not inequitable that all should be compelled to contribute, if contribution must be had, towards restraining all possible injustice. Those who attempt the injustice will rightly be caused to suffer punishment.

There is no question here as to whether men

should stand on their just rights in selfish indifference to those less fortunate by nature or circumstances. They may, of course, give voluntarily more than is just. But if they are compelled to do more than is just it becomes unjust. Still, the right here contended for does not extend to any right beyond that of mere existence and the use of inherent powers. The additional advantages offered by a civilized community are often such that a person enjoying them may be called upon to contribute in proportion to what he receives of them. That, however, is a question which scarcely arises at present. Every individual man or woman having a separate existence has a right to himself or herself and the exercise of his or her powers. This naturally supposes that the rights of others are not invaded. To suppose otherwise is to deny the right itself. And were this principle of individual right not admitted, it would amount to the assertion that some had a right to themselves and others. Whoever might attempt to interfere with the liberty of even one person would by that act be asserting more than an equal right. Though the persons interfering should amount to all save the one interfered with, they would be asserting a right to themselves together with rights over that person. Unless he had become, or was likely to become, aggressive on the rights of others the interference could not be justified.

This should surely be enough to show that taxation should not be based upon the exercise of the labour of the subject. It should not be proportioned to his natural abilities or the exertion put forth by him.

This appears to dispose of one element of production. But the subject may be taken in hand after other facts have been taken into account.

Another element of production is land. Its case is very different from that of labour. The human race claims to have a right to the enjoyment of the earth on which men find they have their existence. Man cannot properly be indifferent to the sufferings of the lower animals. At any rate, he has no right unnecessarily to inflict such sufferings. But it will scarcely need to be argued that so far as they militate against his enjoyment of the earth his right is paramount. As the highest of living creatures, it is but fitting that he should have as much of the earth as he requires. There may possibly be other reasons, as that the human race utilises the land better than other creatures. But since the invention of gunpowder there has been no great necessity for arguing this point at great length. Indeed, the right to use and own the lower animals has already been conceded in a former chapter.

But what as between members of the human species itself? The rights of the lower animals are admittedly subservient to those of the human race. But may any of the human race itself be excluded from an equal right to the earth? If so, on what ground? It is difficult, and it would seem impossible, to find any ground for the exclusion of any man or number of men from their natural right to enjoyment of the earth. To concede to any particular nation, race, or colour of mankind a pre-eminent right implies their superiority over others. That claim must be proved before it can be admitted. It can only be proved by events. The nation or race must exhibit and exert its superiority. That which ultimately survives will show that it was superior. There is no *a priori* method of ascertaining that any section of mankind should have an exclusive right to the earth. To say that the strongest should enjoy it is merely to contend that the present holders should retain it until others are strong enough to turn them out of possession. In abstract justice, assuming that the earth is for the human race, it must evidently be for the human race equally. If, then, a tax can be fairly applied to land in any way there will be no injustice in it.

We have in the two elements now mentioned the ultimate sources of all wealth. Capital is itself the union of the two. Land and labour are entirely distinct. Any tax on capital may fall on both land and labour, for both these elements are found in it. There might be a tax on land, excluding labour, or on labour, excluding land, but if on capital, it might include all three, or not, according to complex considerations of its incidence. The question of taxing capital, therefore, will be left until it is fully determined on which of the original sources of wealth taxation ought more properly to be placed.

We have here, then, the earth given to all, and labour in the just and true ownership of individuals. It was said at the outset that taxation must have special regard to wealth production. The struggle for existence is, to a considerable extent, the cause of the expenditure of taxation. The need for wealth which that struggle implies is still more certainly that which produces the need for taxation. Could men live without wealth government might be carried on without it. But it is impossible to do so. And the source or sources from which wealth is drawn must be carefully considered in fixing a basis of taxation. Shall the incidence of taxation be on the labour, or on the land entering into the production of that wealth?

The condition of the nation must be considered. In the case of a wandering tribe of people living on what they found growing naturally, it might be fair that all should contribute equally. The same opportunities would be open to all, and granted a right of taxation, there could be nothing unfair in such a tax. It might even occur that each should contribute in proportion to his revenue. Good fortune would have something to do with that revenue. The more fortunate would, under such an arrangement, keep at least a portion for themselves of their larger gettings. And if the revenue were through the keeping of cattle, it would have to be considered that those of the larger revenue had obtained a better share of the pastures. A more just arrangement still would be a tax in proportion to those cattle. But this only applies to such a wandering tribe. They need no exact scientific economics. Their government is not kept up by a payment of wealth, but by a rendering of unpaid services. Each is, moreover, free to take of the fruits of the earth at his will.

The governments for whom a system of taxation is required are very different. They are territorial, rather than personal. They have left the wandering condition, with its purely personal bond. The

King of the Angles becomes King of England. The King of the Franks becomes King of France. Colonists join themselves into territorial states. States federate themselves for united government of a larger tract of land. This is the condition in which we have to deal with nations in treating of taxation. There is nothing inconsistent with justice in this territorial sway. But it must be clearly understood that a nation which announces itself as the owner for all time of a tract of land must hold itself open to take in all comers. The earth is given to man. No section has a right to say that of some considerable portion of a continent they are the exclusive owners. Nations may claim to own continents whilst they retain the expansive principle of including all who may choose to become members of the nation. Only on this condition can they justly monopolize nature's free gift.

We have now, therefore, a government ruling over and demanding taxes from all the people dwelling in a given area. A further fact must be noted. Not only have the people ceased to wander, but they have ceased to depend on the unaided productions of nature. The soil has fallen under cultivation. The ground is monopolized for the various purposes which go to make up the sum total of wealth production. Much of the ground capable of producing wealth is eagerly sought after. For some of it a payment is willingly made in order to obtain its possession. That for which no one is willing to pay is comparatively useless. That which seems most desirable is taken up. On and from it, in fact, the wealth is at present produced. From the nature of things it must be monopolized for at least a period at a time if wealth is to be produced at all.

Now this is the land over which the government requiring taxes rules. It was given free for all. It is and must be monopolized for wealth production. Its value is unequal. So that some are put at a disadvantage compared with others in the matter of wealth production. Can there be a better principle of taxation, therefore, than this—namely, that taxation should be in proportion to the value of the monopoly held by the individual of that which by nature is given for the free use of all?

This alone is an equal tax. To tax that portion of the community's property which each retains for his own use is the only true mode of equalizing taxation. The statement of the principle is its own justification. The community may rightly base its claim on the individual upon his monopoly of what it has a right to by nature. The need for wealth with the struggle for existence renders the tax necessary. The community bases its claim on the value which, as mentioned in the previous chapter, arises from that need. Because the individual invades the equal rights of the whole community he is required to pay what he obtains beyond his true share.

The tax offers, moreover, great advantages in respect of its expediency. Reference was made to the holding of land by some at a prohibitive price, and to the consequent possibility of its being uncultivated, whilst its productions were needed for the maintenance of the nation. A tax on the monopoly each held would be the most efficient means of ensuring that he should use what he held and hold none besides what he used. Here is the solution of the problem, if the difficulty is in that direction.

This is the true principle of taxation. Not the taxation of what the individual gets, but the taxation of what he keeps from others, whereby alone he can injure them. It is the taxation of land as opposed to the taxation of labour. It is the community claiming its own, and not that to which it has no right. In view of it the taxation of capital need not be discussed. For to tax capital, which includes labour, is to tax labour, which should be left free. Land alone should be taxed. This conclusion is reached by an independent method. It is the remedy advocated by Mr. George. But it was advocated by him on the ground that land monopoly was the great and only cause of poverty. When it is shown, as it is proposed, that his argument was incorrect, there is a danger lest it be from that stated that the conclusion was necessarily incorrect. Many conclusions have been found true, although the reasons given for them have been false. This same tax was advocated by the Physiocrats in France. But their arguments were mixed with error, and for that reason the tax was stated by writers, who at least ought to have known better, to be entirely disposed of. Others have discussed and argued in favour of what were, in fact, modifications of the same principle, but have not boldly advocated the tax in its purity.

A few comparisons may serve to show more clearly the nature of this tax. At the very opposite end of the scale from it is communism, more recently advocated under the name of socialism. Those who have advocated socialism have frequently stated that they do not mean by it what communism means. They only desire the municipalization of the means of production. But for the present purposes this modification is of no moment. If the community should take to itself the instruments of production, it would of necessity also take the labour required for the use of them. Whatever means, therefore, were taken of paying the labourers, whether in wealth, or in money or counters representing wealth, the labour itself must first go to the community. There could be no free sale of it. There could be no market for it, because the community would have taken the instruments required for its exercise. This is but a means of appropriating all the labour of the community, the government in return undertaking to pay wages in one way or another. Whether the wages should be equal or unequal is for this purpose a matter of indifference. Indeed, more than that might be said with regard to how much of the subject is a matter of indifference. This taxation of land, then, is the opposite to socialism.

Between the two there are very various degrees. A tax on income is a near approach to socialism. Many incomes are entirely wages. A tax on them, therefore, is purely a tax on labour. Several arguments have been used in favour of an income tax. It is not proposed to deal with them specifically; but this will be a convenient place to mention Adam Smith's first maxim of taxation somewhat more in detail. He says, "The subjects of every state ought to contribute to the support of the government as nearly as possible in proportion to their respective abilities: that is, in proportion to the revenue which they respectively enjoy under the protection of the state."

The first clause of this sentence leaves the word abilities very vague in its meaning. If it means natural abilities, then the maxim is entirely contrary to the contentions previously put forth in this chapter. It seems, however, that the expression is to be interpreted by the latter clause as referring to the respective revenues of the subject. This is clearly an advocacy of income tax. It may be said at once that ability to pay is no just ground of taxation. Such ability may arise from additional industry, and surely a man must not be called upon to pay more because he has worked harder than another of equal powers and opportunities. The other had denied the ability, if he would have exercised it, and the maxim by referring to revenue makes no allowance for this.

Not much precise meaning, however, seems to have been attached to the maxim by its author. He likens the expenses of a government to the expense of management to the joint tenants of a great estate who are obliged to contribute in proportion to their respective interests in the estate. This would appear almost like the land tax; for, no doubt, the services rendered to the joint tenants would be paid for in those expenses. Surely one would not have to do all the work and another enjoy the proceeds without his being paid. Yet the author of the maxim goes on to say that every tax which falls exclusively on one of the three sorts of revenue above mentioned, is necessarily unequal. It therefore offends against his maxim.

The three sorts of revenue are, of course, rent, interest and wages. It is true that he had not mastered the division of wealth as it has now been explained. But in dealing with rent he had mentioned an interesting instance or two which ought to have been sufficient to cause him to avoid the statements of his maxim. He spoke, for example, of the kelp covered by the sea half the day and gathered in time of low water from the sea-shore. It owed no existence to human cultivation. But the owner of the adjoining land took a rent for the privilege he conceded of gathering it. Another instance mentioned is that of the habitations which some inhabitants of the Shetland Islands must have on the land in order to fish in the sea. It is stated that "the rent is in proportion, not to what the farmer can make by the land, but to what he can make both by the land and by the water." And then the great economist says that taxation should be in proportion to the revenues of these people, and of the landlord to whom they pay the rent. They produce the revenue of both themselves and the landlord. There is no pretence that he has done anything for it. They get much of the income from the sea, which surely he did nothing to make fruitful. But taxes are to be imposed equally on what these poorer men keep for themselves and what they pay him for being permitted to fish in the sea. There would be less mockery in saying that poor people who own no land should pay all the taxes, and also maintain themselves and landlords. Income tax and this maxim, on which it appears to be based, will not be further discussed.

Another principle of taxation has been advocated under the name of equality of sacrifice. It is a modification of Smith's equality. But it signally fails to meet the difficulty. It supposes accurate knowledge both of revenue and need. It would have to take note of the difficulty with which each secures his income; of the expenditure necessary for keeping the requisite establishment to secure that income, which, in the case of many professional men, is an absolute business expense; and of the conditions of himself and his family, so as to determine how much of his income he can properly spare. Such a principle is little less than absurd, because of the utter impossibility of applying it.

Taxes on capital, as already mentioned, are also a stage between taxes on labour and taxes on land. If the tax is paid only when capital has been put upon the land, then it acts as a deterrent on using the land. The income must be enough not only to pay interest on the outlay, but also the taxation which will result from making the outlay; whilst a tax placed on the land, whether used or not, tends rather to induce the holder to put capital upon it. Under the injurious class of taxes just referred to, will be included taxes on the occupation of better houses, which are clearly a tax on industry, and a premium on living in inferior dwellings. Taxes will, of course, include both local and imperial taxation.

Nothing can be more injurious than the imposition of a tax upon the occupation of land or capital. This is a method which greatly obtains in England. It is said that many farms may be had rent free, if the occupant will pay the local rates. But this is more than they are worth, and they consequently are out of cultivation, whilst men are out of work and needing their productions. The question arises, what security a possible holder would have for any improvements he might make. But it appears that the local taxes, known as rates, do have the effect of preventing the occupation of land. The idea seems to have recently obtained that economy in government is of no importance compared with the advantage of public bodies taking upon themselves more and more of the duties suggested for them. But in view of the deterring influence of the increased taxation required for the multiplied duties, there is something of irony in the fact that amongst the duties so advocated is that of taking land forcibly and putting men upon it for its cultivation. It need scarcely be pointed out that the taxation of land herein advocated would leave the land just mentioned entirely free of taxes, local and imperial. Only ground values would be subject to taxation, not ground areas.

Taxes on commodities are also more or less a tax on labour. They are amongst the most injurious of taxes, offending particularly against Smith's third maxim, that the tax should be so arranged as to take out of the pockets of the people as little as possible beyond the amount received by the government. The duty on commodities has to be paid whilst they are in considerable bulk. But they are ultimately paid by the consumer. The producer will only continue to produce the commodities if he can put the taxes on the commodities; otherwise it would be better to produce commodities on which no tax must be paid. The result of this is that profits must also be paid on the duty or tax before it reaches the consumer. These taxes also indirectly operate to the creation of monopolies.

Duties by way of stamps on documents are frequently collected. This system of taxation is said to have ease of collection to recommend it; but that does not justify an unjust demand. And it is difficult to see on what grounds the community steps between two persons, who would make a bargain, to levy blackmail on the transaction. It certainly is an express penalty on carrying on the business of exchange.

Death duties have frequently been suggested as equitable taxes. The community has, however, no more claim on the results of a person's labour at one time of his life than at another. If any person has property actually the result of his labour (as opposed to that which still remains land), he ought, in justice, to have a right to dispose of it as he will, either during his lifetime or at his death. The subject of limitations which are contrary to the policy of the law is not now under consideration. The question is, whether or not the community has a right to step in between a dying man and the person for whose benefit he has purposely been labouring and take a portion of what he has left. There seems no warrant, in justice, for such a proceeding.

Nor does there seem any justification for the graduated taxation which has frequently been advocated by economists. If a man has produced what he enjoys, the fact that it is more than another enjoys is no reason for taxing him at a higher rate. The community should be grateful that he has produced a larger total to be taxed at the same rate : it will produce a larger total of taxes. If it has become money by sale, it is evident that those who purchased it considered it more valuable to them than the money they gave for it. The community has already been benefited to the full extent of the money. If the tax be that upon land, which is now urged, it is evident that the person paying it, even at the same rate as another, is making better use of the land than any one else is prepared to do, or he would not retain it.

The tax should be collected year by year from the first takers of the benefits of the land. This would ensure that the tax would fall upon economic rent, a value which owes its existence not to any human labour, but, as already mentioned, to human needs. There could be no shifting of the tax from the owner, who did not use the land, to the actual occupier. For the occupier would in any case have to pay all the land was worth in the market. The price could not, therefore, be increased because of the tax so as to shift the burden from the person taxed.

The exact method of the imposition of the tax will not be discussed ; it is more important to establish the principle. It may be said, however, that the tax would be easier to accurately assess, and also to collect, than any (beyond the most trivial) now in existence. The owner of land would make his own return, kept correct by a penalty of being liable to be bought out at his own price. It would, moreover, offer at once a solution of the problems of leaseholds and land transfer. These matters have been much discussed in England, but no reasonable solution seems to have been suggested.

The tax would be entirely confined to rent in the economic sense, so that the holders of land might make improvements to any extent without any additional tax being laid on them. So far as the land might be occupied by the owner, this would be everything required to secure to him his own improvements. But the imposition of this tax would probably not only put land into the ownership of its actual occupiers, but even, when it was let by one to another, it would more probably ensure the making of fair contracts.

These benefits, then, would accrue from the imposition of what has been shown to be the only just tax. It would prevent land from being held in idleness when its productions were needed. It would offer every encouragement to the fullest use of land; it would tend to introduce contracts securing to each his own capital and labour. For it must not be forgotten that if any one monopolised the land he must either use it or pay for keeping it unused.

Nor could injustice follow from the imposition of the tax. It would, of course, be introduced gradually, so as to cause no more displacement of labour than could be immediately absorbed. But it might commence in any country as soon as a government sufficiently enlightened and patriotic could be put into power to introduce the reform. Those who already used their land would find that taxes were removed from the capital they had put upon it and placed on the ground which formed the foundation. Those who did not use their land would at once do so, or part with it to some one who would do so.

Nor could any one really escape taxation. Every one must have wealth; and as wealth cannot be produced without land, it would be impossible altogether to escape its influence. Those who hold land for which they must pay rent or taxes must necessarily make the wealth they produce repay them the cost. In this way rent enters into the cost of those commodities. With regard to the land at the margin of cultivation or use different considerations apply, since no tax would be paid on it. But those who hold this land find it more costly to produce wealth than those on better land. Being driven to the very margin of use, their natural difficulties are greater. In view of this they escape taxation. The need for taxes, however, which causes their neighbours to have to pay more than they pay, whilst it equalises their conditions as it should, also makes more costly the wealth which they at the margin, as well as others, must consume. And even with regard to what they themselves produce, it is quite enough of a tax by the community that they are driven to this inferior land.

The principle underlying the foregoing considerations amounts in the end to the same as that of Mr. George. He, however, for reasons which only apply to him, advocates taxing all the rent out of the land. Nothing is here suggested but that taxes for what may be required should be placed upon the land. It may possibly amount in the end to the same result; but it is suggested as the true method of taxation, and not as the great remedy for poverty. There are other causes of poverty which will have to be noted.

For the present it is enough to say that land is the inalienable heritage of the race. The community has an absolute right to it. It is inexpedient that the community should take the land from those who hold it; it could only do so equitably by paying for the improvements they have made. The value not owing to those improvements is, however, the proper fund for taxation. And though, through their own past injustice, the governments of various lands have put themselves under an obligation to those whom they have permitted to purchase the land, yet this only demands that they should proceed to introduce a more just method, in such a way as to regard the obligations they are under, and thus to do no unnecessary injury in the resumption of their rights.

CHAPTER X

INTEREST ON CAPITAL

THE relative share of wealth which constitutes rent has now been sufficiently noticed both in its nature and origin, and in the just and beneficial method of its disposal. We now pass to a fuller consideration of interest and wages, the two remaining shares of wealth. And first we have to consider interest on capital.

It must be clearly understood that only real capital is capable of producing interest. Money is frequently spoken of as if it were thought that money in itself would produce interest. But it need hardly be said that money can produce no interest whatever until invested. On that happening, it is the wealth in which the investment is made which produces the interest, and not the money itself. No one would think of paying interest on money for which he had no use, that is, for which he had not an investment. This needs to be borne in mind when reading the absurd theories which some writers have allowed themselves to fall into, through confusing money and capital. It is only capital which earns interest. Interest which is apparently paid on money is really paid on that which the money bought. The money had passed to the lender in respect of his land capital or labour by way of payment for services rendered. He was at liberty to buy wealth with it, or to lend it to another to buy wealth with; he chose to do the latter. The borrower, therefore, took the wealth which the lender might have had, and agreed to pay interest on the money. Strictly, he pays the interest out of the advantage the wealth gives to him.

If, therefore, the wealth in which the money is invested fails to produce a return, the borrowing has been unprofitable. There are cases of borrowing by individuals merely for unproductive expenditure, and this borrowing is, of course, unprofitable. But a more important instance of such borrowing is that of loans to governments. It is evident that the wealth bought with the money which remains on long-standing national loans has long ago ceased to exist; it cannot, therefore, produce any interest or advantage at present. The interest paid on it is really paid out of the productions of the nation, which gets no advantage for the payment.

One other species of property, it must here be noted, is excluded from capital in its proper sense. Monopolies are not capital. In the cases of licences granted to certain persons to carry on specified trades, there may or may not be justification. There can be no justification for granting licences for the special benefit of the individual; there may, however, be justification for protecting the public by permitting only certain qualified persons to carry on those trades. Monopolies intended to restrain trade are evidently mischievous. To ensure that only qualified persons shall carry on the business is another matter.

If, however, a person invents some useful article or mode of manufacture, it would be a loss to the nation and himself if he were not protected to some extent, so as to enable him to reap some benefit from his invention. While the invention is a secret he can keep it to himself, but neither he nor the nation is much the better for it. If, in such a case, the nation will grant to him a monopoly of its use or sale for a period, and he, in return, will make full disclosure of his secret, so that all the nation may use it after that period, both he and the nation will be benefited. Neither of them will lose: the individual will gain an exclusive right to make profit out of his secret for the period; the nation will gain a beneficial invention in return for permitting the individual who gives it to enjoy some of the fruit. And it is impossible he can have too much for his secret, because he can only get the profit which others are willing to pay rather than be without it. By that means he must justify his claim to having introduced a beneficial improvement.

All other monopolies, however, are to be condemned from an economic point of view, except so far as they ensure that only fit men shall carry on certain trades. Nor should the number of those men be restricted, so long as properly qualified men present themselves for the work. The qualifications may be more severely scrutinised up to any extent, but the test of whether or not enough men are already at the business is to be found in the relation of supply and demand.

To the nation, however, none of these monopolies are capital. Capital consists only of material wealth.

Interest on capital is the share of its productions given for the use of that material wealth. The justice of the payment of interest has often been questioned. But attempts to stop its payment have invariably failed, and rightly so. The capital renders assistance in the production of wealth, and the question why payment for its services should be denied admits of no reasonable answer. Still, the phrase wages of abstinence, by which it has been attempted to defend interest, is not a good expression. It is not enough that men should merely abstain from consuming their wealth; they must be willing to use it, or allow it to be used in the production of further wealth. And in speaking of interest, it must be understood that we refer to a payment for actual services rendered in that production. Every one has a right to the wealth he produces. Nor is there any justice in compelling him to give or lend it freely to others. But he will get no interest for it if he keeps it idle.

The payment of interest has been attempted to be justified in various ways. A true idea of the subject can perhaps best be obtained by noticing Mr. George's views on the methods suggested. Not that it is suggested his theories are perfect, but they will repay consideration and help to reach the truth. It ought at once to be said that to him belongs the credit of showing that wages are not lent by capital or capitalists. But he fell into the opposite error. From finding, contrary to generally received views, that wages were not drawn from capital by way of loan, he at once concluded they were not drawn from capital at all. It is evident, however, that most of the wealth consumed by all civilised peoples must have been prepared some time previously. Yet that the wages are paid out of such capital as a loan is quite erroneous.

It is obvious on the smallest consideration that the labourer of the grade, commonly known as wage earning, must earn his wages before he can receive them. The employer of labour advances nothing but that for which he has received value in labour and by which his own capital has been increased. Moreover, in the light of what has already been said, it is difficult to imagine how the error could ever arise. In fact it could not have done so except by means of the notion that capital employed labour, and the confusion between wealth and money. Capital is, however, a thing utterly unconscious of its office in wealth production. It is something which must be used by persons who in the using of it are labourers. It has been seen that all personal effort in wealth production must be included in the one expression labour if any clear notions are to be obtained. But some of the older economists looked upon the farmer and manufacturer merely as capitalists, and their personal efforts as counting for nothing, as though capital was a thing of life and managing intelligence. Adam Smith even treated it in that way after showing that he fully realized the effect of the personal services of the owner of stock—his expression for capital.

Capital, to be advantageous in wealth production, must be used. The capitalist must be a labourer also, or lend his capital to another labourer, not as wages but as a loan. It is the labourer who must employ the capital, for the capital can never employ the labourer. This agrees with Mr. George's views literally, but not perhaps actually. For he means the labourer who receives the wages. Here is meant the master labourer who owns the capital or is responsible for its return.

The showing that wages were not lent by capital is as much as can be attributed to Mr. George. He was in error in stating without qualification that they are not drawn from capital. He was thinking of money wages, and consequently landed himself in confusion. To a great extent real wages are drawn from capital by way of exchange for the capital, added by the labour for which the wages are paid. There is no loan; there is an exchange. The employer and his servants increase the capital on which they work. The employer gets for himself and his men some money as wages. They purchase their real wages from the various capitalists with that money, and it is passed on for other exchanges. Capital is added in one department and consumed in another. The identical capital produced is seldom consumed or paid as wages for its production. With a very few exceptions the wages do not come directly and at once from the produce of the labour for which they are paid, as Mr. George would have us imagine. It is apparent on every hand. In some instances it takes months to finish a single piece of work. Labourers are meanwhile fed and clothed : not out of that capital but out of the stock of capital. It is part of the office of capital to be drawn from, in order that labourers should not wait until that work is finished. The labourer consumes the accumulations of the previous period, while his efforts get ready a further stock, and are adding to the further capital.

There is thus a modicum of truth in each of the doctrines. The old doctrine, so far as it means that labourers must actually consume previously prepared wealth, is obviously true. Mr. George is also right in saying that it is not lent to them, and that labour employs capital; not that capital employs labour. He should have said, however, that the present consumable capital was being constantly exchanged by the labourers, and that the labourers who employed capital were the employers and not the servants.

In discussing the cause of interest, Mr. George offers new ideas. He refers to an illustration of Bastiat's which has been constantly used by other writers. James lends William a plane which has taken ten days to make and will last two hundred and ninety days. This is on condition of receiving back an equally good plane with a plank for interest. Mr. George shows that William must do all the work he would have had to do if he had not borrowed the plane. He must still spend ten days sooner or later in making the plane. And he will be a plank the poorer. Moreover, if he goes on borrowing on these terms, the income of the one will progressively decline and that of the other will progressively increase until James will obtain the whole result of William's labour. This is reducing an illustration to an absurdity.

Mr. George goes on to classify production into three modes, adapting (which would apparently include both mining, manufacturing and carrying), growing (which would include the raising of products obtained from animal or vegetable life) and exchanging. To the second and third only of these modes he attributes interest. The first he imagines is not a cause of interest. In the two later modes there is the principle of natural increase by reproduction of the capital used. But strictly, the second is the only instance of increase by reproduction. In the third case there is no increase of the quantity of the wealth, only an increase in value. And if, as Mr. George would have us believe, interest is the result of natural reproduction and consequent increase of the quantity of wealth, this case of his own must be omitted.

Mr. George seems to the present writer to have missed the point entirely. And although Bastiat's illustration may not be a happy one, it has not been disproved. First, observe what is clearly Mr. George's foundation idea. He sees that capital of the organic or living nature, whether animal or vegetable, is capable of natural increase by reproduction. He conceives that this is why interest is paid and the increase by exchange is analogous to it. The interest paid for various aids to adaptation in the way of machinery is in his view no cause of interest at all, but merely an equalising of interest.

But suppose in a country where manufacturing and exchanging were practically absent that this animal or vegetable capital were so plentiful that every one had as much as he cared to look after. Would any interest be paid? The increase by reproduction would go on as before. The capital might even double itself in a year, but so far from any one being willing to give one hundred per cent. for its use, he would decline to give anything. When each has enough already, it is useless to remind him that if he will use more it will increase in his hands by reproduction. He desires no more care and labour.

The same may be said with regard to capital used in exchange. If every one had a sufficient stock of all productions for his present needs, and was continuing to produce further wealth with which to obtain more of the productions of others, when he needed them, he would pay no interest to any one. It might occur that the process of exchange was long and tedious. The goods might be required to be carried long distances. But whilst each had a sufficient stock of what he required, and a further stock in course of transportation and exchange, interest could not arise. The carriers would require paying, but that would be wages, not interest. Neither party to an exchange would pay the other interest. Each gains by the transaction, and that is his reason for entering into it. In truth, this analogy of increase ought not to have been brought in even if natural reproduction had been the true cause of interest.

But increase by reproduction is not the great cause of interest. Nor is increase of value by means of exchange any reason for it above other forms of assistance to labour. The cause of interest is the desire to have wealth now rather than at a future time. It is true William must make another plane in addition to giving his plank. But if he borrows a plane which he could make in ten days, it is because he wishes to be using it in those ten days and not making it. He will get the advantage out of it or he will not borrow it, if he is prudent. And his reason, like the reason of every man for borrowing capital, is that by having it at once he can materially increase the results of his own labour. He cannot afford to wait until he has got his own stock ready; his life is going; and he had better pay some one a portion of the benefit for the use of their capital than wait until he has saved it.

The immediate possession of wealth may enable a man to produce treble what he could produce without it. Seed should produce a harvest. Ewes should bear lambs. But still more than this the possession of tools and machinery will assist his labour. The great need is to have them at once. Those who by their previous prudence, industry and thrift, have gotten these things, can either assist their own labour, or have something for the loan of them to those who wish to increase the products of their labour. But the capital needs using if it is to be of benefit. It cannot tend itself. And interest will vary according as those who are willing to use it are or are not sufficiently supplied.

The cause of interest, therefore, is the relative scarcity of useful capital. Interest is a value determined like every other value by utility and scarcity. This is another instance in which the expression value in use might conveniently be taken into the science. It does not mean mere utility, as it did with Adam Smith. It means value for the use of the capital for a time, as opposed to the value of the whole capital on sale or exchange. In the same way rent was value in use of the land temporarily, as opposed to the absolute value of the land itself.

In view of these considerations, it is evident that the rate of interest can be reduced by increasing the amount of available capital. The same might occur by more or less dispensing with its use. The value of the use of capital for a time is, in fact, subject to the same laws of supply and demand as the value of the capital itself.

Certain older confusions require to be noticed. As already mentioned, interest on capital was at first spoken of as profits. The whole of the profits of the farmer or manufacturer were treated as the profits of his stock. Nassau Senior then invented the expression wages of abstinence (already condemned) to express the idea that the employer was only paid according to his deserts. This was approvingly quoted by John Stuart Mill, who proceeded to separate profits into three constituents. These were interest at the rate current on the best security, compensation for risk, and remuneration for the devotion of time and labour. The division has been faithfully followed by Mill's school of writers. But it needs further examination. Of the three constituents the last is clearly wages of labour, and will be dealt with as such in its place. We have left, therefore, the interest at the rate current on the best security (which has retained the name wages of abstinence) and compensation for risk. Wages of abstinence is a phrase which should be abandoned as inexpressive of the truth. Compensation for risk should be remerged in interest for reasons which will appear.

It is perfectly true that a person lending money or capital to another, or determining to use it, will take into consideration the risk involved when he considers the interest obtainable or the profits likely to be had. But he will take other things also into consideration. He will probably consider the effect of the investment on his reputation. Possibly he will take into account the effect upon others of employing his capital in that way. He may desire an investment which will set him free to attend to other duties; or he may be prepared to use the capital himself. In the latter case he may desire a pleasant occupation even though his return be small. He will consequently take perhaps a farm instead of manufacturing or trading premises. Some modes of investment are regarded by various people as not only safer but more honourable than others. The ownership of land (with the capital upon it) appears to give importance. Hence a lower rate of interest will suffice to induce investment in such property. There are, therefore, it seems, several considerations to be taken into account as influencing the rate of interest. To separate compensation for risk would be inconvenient, and clearly an imperfect means of arriving at true interest.

Moreover, what place could be found for this compensation if it were separated? Wages of labour have been separated. It is not included in that. Interest on capital will of course be reduced by actual losses. But this will not be included at all. If the compensation for risk refers to the cost of making these losses good, it ought never to have been included in profits. The truth is, that interest will vary in different employments, just as will be seen hereafter wages must vary.

The interest on a particular quantity of capital will be more or less than the interest on another quantity. Other things being equal, there will be a constant tendency to equalise interest in all employments. But this equilisation will be more or less imperfect when different kinds of capital are considered, although it will be as nearly as possible perfect in the same employment.

The inequalities just referred to will not include those which arise from the more skilful and vigorous employment of the same species of capital. Such inequalities will be due to the exertion of labour and must be included in wages. But there are still other inequalities which remain even after deducting all the influences of extra skill or exertion.

The method of arriving at the proper rate of interest in any country by observing the rate paid for government loans is thoroughly bad. This mode grew up amongst the followers of Mill. It scarcely needs to be mentioned, however, that so far from this being a true test, the property referred to cannot even be called capital at all in the proper sense of the word. Interest on capital can only be ascertained by considering the various rates earned by the different species of capital. And this, it need hardly be said, can no more be accurately ascertained than the rates of money wages.

CHAPTER XI

WAGES OF LABOUR

THE shares of rent of land and interest on capital having been allowed for, the remainder is for wages. This appears from what has already been seen. But it will be further enforced in a succeeding chapter.

There is great possibility of a disturbing influence on this division in the case of land. For supposing that the soil of a country, while not fully occupied, is nevertheless fully held in ownership, wealth can only be obtained by the consent of the owners of the soil. If no tax is placed on the land except as the land is used, the owners can make practically their own terms with the landless. There is nothing to prevent their putting the burden of taxation on the shoulders of those who wish to occupy the land. It has sometimes been contended that rates of the nature of taxes levied on the occupation of land fell ultimately on the landlord. The argument is that if the rates were not levied, the landlord would be able to charge more for the land. This is true as referring to a single farm. If one landowner could be set free of these rates, he certainly would be able to increase his rent. But if all the others were also set free, then he would have to take the old rate. So that applied as the taxes are to the whole, they do not ultimately fall on the landlord. The farmer who would occupy land must pay these rates in addition to the rent, if he intends to stay in that country. He can only escape them by going to some place where they are not levied. In the case of local taxes, however, there are differences for him to consider between one place and another in the same country.

Another disturbing influence arising from the untaxed ownership of land, is that which arises from its occupiers having no security for the full enjoyment of the improvements they may make. The full discussion of this subject would require a more extended reference to the history of land tenures than is compatible with the object of this enquiry. Some little reference has been made in the chapter on Rent of Land to the nature of the economic difficulties connected with these systems. Speaking generally, they are survivals of conditions arising from conquest. The feudal system followed the older system (or rather systems) of the Roman Empire. In both of them the idea of personal superiority played a prominent part. So that these land systems in which the true economic ideal is impossible of being attained are merely relics of slavery which must pass away in the course of the progress of the race.

The difficulties arising from the monopolisation of the land do not apply in any degree to capital. It is capable of indefinite increase. Given land and labour, capital may be created to any extent desired. So far as capital is concerned, therefore, if there is any lack of it, or its owners require too much for its use, all that is requisite to be done is that other capital should be created. And, as already seen, the greater the amount of it, the smaller proportion of the value of the service rendered can its owners obtain for the service. The capital itself is something which, except to the loss of the owner, is not capable of consuming wealth unproductively. It does not usually increase in value by being retained; rather the contrary. A very small reward, therefore, beyond the maintenance of the capital itself would induce the owner of it to let it be used rather than it should remain unoccupied.

The wages of labour, on the other hand, can never be limited by any strict laws. For a long time it was half imagined that they were limited to bare subsistence. This might perhaps apply to slave labour. And many treatises on economics have compared for various purposes slave labour with free labour. But slavery as an institution has now been thoroughly discredited amongst all civilised nations, and it is useless to discuss it here. The subject of bare subsistence wages will be discussed in another chapter, as the theory has not yet ceased to exert a practical influence. It will be sufficient to remark here that the advocates of this theory never attributed the condition to the untaxed monopoly of land. Under certain circumstances that monopoly would in some sense justify the theory. Where tenants know that what they make above such a bare subsistence must go in rent, and their rent be still not fully paid, it is natural that they will produce only enough for their bare subsistence beyond the minimum rent, with payment of which they hope to escape. Their productions as productions will be limited in this way. But even then it must be confessed that there will be no law keeping the subsistence of one equal to that of another. Some will make a little more effort than others, and, perhaps, secretly live better or save money.

But the advocates of the theory of wages of subsistence suppose the balance after payment of those wages to be the profits of capital. Profits were perhaps loosely defined and more loosely grasped in the minds of the economists. But if there was anything at all in the theory, the contention was that the balance, after payment of subsistence wages, was interest on capital. That such is not the case has been amply proved. Interest is limited to a portion of the benefits conferred by capital; and the portion is determined by its relative scarcity. As between capital and labour, labour alone is capable of taking the balance, because labour alone is inseparably connected with the consumer of wealth.

Without doubt, the advocates of the subsistence theory made the error of confusing the interest of capital with the wages of the capitalist who superintended and used it. But that necessarily brings the balance, supposing the wages of subsistence theory were true, into the consideration of the present chapter. It would mean that the wages of the superintending labour of the capitalist who employed the labour of others included all the balance after he had paid wages of subsistence to his servants. That being the case, the considerations of this chapter will apply to such labour as well as to other labour. As was mentioned almost at the outset, there is no insuperable barrier between one grade and the other. It is purely a question of ability and energy. And these are matters to which attention must now be given.

This enquiry is not as to what wages ought to be paid, or what ought to be the principle on which they are fixed; it is rather what are the determining influences which naturally do fix them, just as the influences were noticed which determined the shares of rent and interest. So far as the total share devoted to wages is concerned, the enquiry is complete. But wages are not equal for all persons. The question still remains, What determines the inequalities? Some have contended that all wages should be equal. Such an arrangement is not likely to occur in the nature of things. It is difficult to realize that any means of securing such an equality could be possible. It certainly could not be just or beneficial. Very little consideration will show this.

Equal wages would surely presuppose equal labour. In the first place, the hours must be supposed to be equal. This would be very irksome and unfair to those who preferred short and intense application, but who found themselves compelled to drawl out their labours for a longer period to be equal to others. For, in the second place, equal intensity of exertion must be supposed. This would be disagreeable and unjust to those who preferred less exertion even at the expense of less wages.

In the third place, it would suppose equal efficiency of labour. Answer is made to this by some, that those who have greater powers should be willing to exert them for those who are less favoured. But such an answer neglects to take note of the fact that by nature large powers are coupled with large desires and smaller powers with smaller desires. There can be no pretence to justice in the idea that those to whom large desires have been given with corresponding powers are made amiss; that they should give up their powers and sink their desires to obey the will of others, especially of those whom nature has clearly endowed with more limited desires, and has accordingly fitted with more limited powers. Such notions are utterly false notions of equality. Human beings are not mere machines capable of being artificially rendered exactly alike in form, stature, weight, strength and appetite. There is a difference physically as all may see. It is still more the case mentally, as may be realized by those who possess minds of any importance.

Further, and in the fourth place, this equality supposes that all employments are equally agreeable. But as that is not the case, and as they are not capable of being rendered equally agreeable, some have so far retreated from absolute equality as to suppose that agreeableness of occupation, and longer or shorter employment per day, should be balanced against each other. If the territory of any nation could be sufficiently converted into a prison house, this would meet the first and fourth difficulties, that is to say the difficulties which relate to what is outside the individual.

Those who feel themselves compelled to retreat still further from this absurd equality, propose to meet the third difficulty and perhaps to some extent the second by conceding some inequality of wages. This is, of course, a very decided retreat. The contention of equality is practically given up. But the prison house idea of the artificial fixing of wages is not entirely abandoned. The natural rate fixed for the various abilities, exertions, employments, and grades of employment is supposed to be capable of being improved upon. The utility of the kind of labour is a matter of indifference or one to be determined by some person or body of persons on behalf of the community. This itself, which was not included in the enumeration just given, is enough to condemn the whole theory of enforced equality. For every one should be at liberty to express his own desires. These desires he expresses by means of his money, and this influences the price of labour as of other things.

Perhaps enough has been said to show the folly of the contention that other than the true value of labour should be paid for it. The true value is of course the natural value. It is determined, like any other value, by its utility and scarcity. There is no just method of determining the value of the service rendered by one to another except by regarding the benefit it confers. Of that benefit he who receives it must be the judge. If the benefit conferred is not to him of the value put upon the service by the person who has the labour to sell, then it is iniquitous to propose that the two should be compelled to exchange. That inequalities of wages should arise is inevitable from the fact that unequal benefits are conferred by different individuals. If the benefits desired require quali-

ties or exertions more scarce than other benefits, they will for that reason have greater value. Indeed, many of the inequalities are difficult to understand, except by reference to these considerations of scarcity.

One of the first of these considerations is that which relates to ability. All have not the same mental and physical ability. Even of those whose ability is perhaps equal, when taken as a whole some have abilities of a rarer type. If these abilities are such that their exercise is much sought after, a high rate of payment will result.

Another consideration is that of energy. Abilities may be dormant for want of energy to exercise them. The number of those who possess abilities is therefore reduced for the present purpose by the number of those who lack the energy to use them. This will further tend to raise the rate of payment of those who both have abilities and use them. Closely connected with this energy, and to be included under the same considerations, are persistency and perseverance of effort, together with a determination fixed on a definite object.

A third great consideration is that of character or reputation for trustworthiness. This has special reference to the moral character as opposed to merely mental and physical characteristics. It is evident that a man who has proved himself worthy of trust is for many purposes more sought after than one who has no such reputation. And in proportion to the scarcity of proved, trustworthy labourers the rate of payment rises. Perhaps moral qualities, other than mere questions of honesty with regard to property, should also be included in this category.

These are rough generalizations indicating some of the causes of inequality of payment. These three, and perhaps particularly the first two (although even the third cannot be excluded) indicate inequalities in the nature of things. But there are qualities of importance which have not been specially mentioned. Appearance and manner frequently afford means of increasing wages. This may seem at first sight unaccountable in a scientific sense. But people pay for the gratification of their desires. And appearance and manner give a pleasure for which payment is unconsciously made even when it is imagined only goods are being bought. Such qualities as these, however, must be supposed to be included in the first of the considerations named.

It must be borne in mind that the various qualities named give a cumulative value to labour. The lack of any one of them will materially reduce the wages a person can earn. They are all of them, however, capable of material improvement by training. The three qualities named are, so to speak, the foundation on which the sum total of wage-earning qualities is built. To the first particularly the expression rent of ability has been applied. But ability must be backed by energy, and usually both by character. Moreover, ability may be trained. Business habits giving a power to resist temptations to ease and pleasure may be acquired. Such habits would correspond to energy. Character may be strengthened and reputation can only be attained after trial. All these go to make up the person, apart from skill or knowledge of external objects.

Further, by means of ability technical skill is attained. By training it is possible, not only to develop natural ability but to acquire external knowledge or skill. This knowledge and skill, whether general or particularly relating to special industries, naturally commands more wages whilst it is scarce, and less as it becomes more common. This effect on the rate of wages is analagous to the similar effect on interest. The greater diffusion of education and skill corresponds to increase of capital.

All these are considerations affecting particular persons. There are other considerations which vary the rates of payment obtainable in different employments. This is analogous to the variation of interest in different employments of capital.

In the first place, some employments are cleaner, pleasanter, and more agreeable than others. For these there will be many applicants and a consequent tendency to lower wages. To this cause may be attributed the small wages of the lower grades of clerks and light employments not requiring special mental aptitude. Dirtier and more laborious work will command better wages for the same skill and training. This is even seen in occupations which are equally manual labour. The wages of coal-miners are higher than those of farm labourers and that for fewer hours.

In the second place, the necessity and difficulty of learning trades will deter applicants for places.

This makes the difference in wages between skilled and unskilled workmen.

In the third place, there are various degrees of security that the wages hoped for will in fact be earned. Some employments are more irregular. Workmen engaged in the building trade are frequently out of work for weeks at a time, on account of the season, whilst others are not affected by seasons. Trades are sometimes irregular in the employment they afford on account of artificial interference with the course of employment, but that is a subject for later discussion. Apart from that, however, there are other considerations affecting security of income. A foreman or manager at a fixed salary has to consider, before he gives up that fixed salary, whether it is wise to give up such a certainty for the possibility of a better reward for carrying on business on his own account. It certainly will not pay him to give up his certainty for the mere chance of an equal reward, and no better, if it is possible that the actual results will fall short of it.

In the fourth place, some employments and positions require much more ability, character and training than others. Without such ability and training the person attempting the employment is likely to fail altogether. Without approved character he will scarcely obtain even the chance of a trial. Thus in the case of the foreman or manager considering whether or not to commence business on his own account, it may be that, although well fitted for his present position, he lacks some essential quality, without which he will entirely fail when on his own account. Some employments require abilities of a peculiar type. Such are those of musical and other artists. And similarly, but more directly concerned in wealth production, are inventors. The learned professions also afford some scope for similar exercise of special abilities. In such employments it often occurs that a few can command very high rewards, whilst others entering the employment with similar hopes, find themselves receiving less than the average they could have obtained in other employments.

These considerations are somewhat different from the ideas expressed by Adam Smith. There is no pretence that they deal with the subject more accurately, and certainly not so fully nor with so much illustration. But this is the way in which the subject occurs to the present writer. It is a somewhat different aspect of the same truth.

One or two general considerations are apparent. There are some positions which at first sight appear easy to be filled. But they nevertheless command very high wages. The truth is, that in many cases it requires much more labour in the way of untiring mental effort and training than is generally imagined. And beyond this it has to be remembered that these positions require strength of mind and character, which are more or less scarce. Frequently the strength is of the nature of courage analogous to, but not actually, physical courage. The skilful commander of a ship is he who, in the most difficult, trying and dangerous circumstances, so far from losing his presence of mind, is more than ever cool and at ease. Similar qualities go to make a successful business man, who must steer through similar dangers.

That the best paid labour is, speaking generally, mental labour, can readily be understood. It is not always more difficult or irksome. But it is generally more useful, for it is capable of calling into its service the forces of nature. Steam, electricity, and the other natural forces have been harnessed only by the exercise of mental labour. In an advanced state of·civilisation, where so much physical work is done by machinery, it is evident that exceptional powers of mind will be more useful than exceptional powers of body. Hence, while the vast majority possess bodily powers, and whilst even those who have them exceptionally developed find no special call for them, those who have mental gifts above the average find them much in request. They are accordingly able to demand a higher price on account of the scarcity of their class of labour. This is so, perhaps, even for qualities which, in a ruder state of civilisation, would be comparatively more despised. Those who have only average powers of body and mind must naturally take their place amongst the employments and grades of employments requiring less ability and affording less wages.

Although it is true that these inequalities of wages must exist in the nature of things, it should be noted that the inequalities are not naturally so great as it is possible, through uncalled-for interference, to make them. The natural inequalities of wages will, under free and natural organization, be limited to the inequality of the service rendered. For the most part such inequalities would not be very great. At any rate, they would vary so insensibly that a sharp division into upper and lower classes could scarcely be possible.

Such are the obvious facts with regard to wages. Concluding with these facts, the division of wealth has been completely surveyed. There seems nothing particularly abstruse or difficult to understand in that division. It might have been expressed and even explained in very much fewer words. But it seemed advisable sometimes to enforce what was said. The same facts and theories have been stated in varying language so that, if possible, the danger of misunderstanding might be avoided. Even now, however, the matter cannot safely be left. Some long-standing fallacies with regard to wages must be examined and refuted in the following chapter. Succeeding that must come a demonstration of the futility and injury of external interference with wages.

The considerations already set forth should be sufficient to show the superiority of the natural modes of determining wages over any artificial contrivances. But artificial contrivances have obtained a strong hold on the popular mind in all the countries which can be said to have any political freedom. It is not sufficient, therefore, merely to give negative indications of the absence of necessity for interference. There must be positive demonstration of the futility of any artificial attempt to raise wages, and of the injury likely to arise from every such attempt, successful or unsuccessful.

CHAPTER XII

WAGES OF SUBSISTENCE

IN spite of the number and apparent variety of the fallacies which have obtained and still flourish on the subject of wages, a very little consideration will show that they are all closely connected with each other. Indeed, all the economic errors of the last fifty or a hundred years have features in common which are not difficult to recognise. The germs of all of them will be found in Adam Smith's great work—so completely has his personality dominated the whole science of wealth. The single tax on land had, as already mentioned, been advocated by the Physiocrats in France, though by untenable arguments. Smith did not adopt the tax. And no one ever boldly ventured to dispute Smith's maxim until Mr. George revived the single tax, once more on inaccurate grounds. Curiously enough those grounds were reached, as will shortly be seen, by adopting the errors connected with Smith's own writings.

The same domination of the science by Smith appears with regard to wages. The *Enquiry into the Nature and Causes of the Wealth of Nations* perhaps contained what, if rightly used, might have fully established the essential truths of the science.

It certainly did contain what were turned into the flagrant violations of truth which have hindered its progress. The law of rent was not reached until after Smith's time, but he had facts enough for it, and nearly reached it. With that exception, all the theories advocated for more than half a century might, in one form or another, have been found in his book.

To understand the various theories of wages which have arisen, it is only necessary to go back and see what Smith wrote. He clearly realized that employers of labour must themselves use their skill and industry. But he yielded to popular language, and treated as labourers only those who were commonly called by that name. He did not include the profits of the farmer or any portion of them in the wages of labour. He stated that in fact a portion of those profits was due to the farmer's labour, but he treated it all as the profits of the farmer's stock. For nearly a century he was almost implicitly followed in that respect. The modifications made were very slight indeed. The result was necessarily confusion, especially as those who followed put their errors much more concisely and definitely. It can hardly be said that this method of treating the labour of employers has even yet been abandoned. The fact is very evident, however, that it gives to interest a great deal which is really wages, and leaves a number of persons of the very small capitalist class almost entirely out of account. Under this method, no clear consideration can be given to the case of men who live, not as employers or employed, but as small farmers, traders, or artificers, performing their own labour, and dealing directly with their customers.

Having separated what are known as the wage-earning class from those who were not employed for stated wages, Smith proceeded to deal with their wages as if they were the only wages paid for labour. He was not very precise, but his followers took the same method, and in their hands it became a precise one. In Smith's discussion of wages, after referring to the disputes between employers and employed, we find this statement: "Though in disputes with their workmen masters must generally have the advantage, there is a certain rate below which it seems impossible to reduce for any considerable time the ordinary wages even of the lowest species of labour. A man must always live by his work, and his wages must at least be sufficient to maintain him." He went on to say that they must even upon most occasions be somewhat more. But he constantly referred in varying terms to the lowest rate at which labour could anywhere be paid—the bare subsistence of the labourer. This was 1775. Malthus about twenty years afterwards (1798), and more fully somewhat later still, brought forth his arithmetical and geometrical progression to show that population would inevitably increase up to the highest point at which subsistence was possible. The only merit about this work of Malthus was to persuade people that governments should not be over anxious to increase their population but rather to feed them. But between Smith and Malthus it got established that wages were wages of bare subsistence. Smith said they could not long be less; Malthus said they could not long be more. In about another twenty years (1817) Ricardo brought out his book, which established the law of rent previously suggested. In it he proceeded entirely on the assumption that wages were properly explained by referring them to bare subsistence. This has been called Ricardo's iron law of wages. Its subsequent history will shortly be noticed.

Smith, however, had gone to considerable trouble to show that these wages of bare subsistence were not the outside limit of wages. He showed by observed facts that wages did not necessarily vary with the price of provisions; that in truth lower wages were found with higher prices of food, and *vice versâ*. He showed this by reference to variations of season, place and periods of years. The facts could not be denied. Wages of bare subsistence were therefore supposed by later writers to be wages of subsistence according to the standard of comfort to which the labourer had grown accustomed. This was of course a convenient way of meeting the difficulty. But it was a very unsatisfactory way. For it amounted to saying that wages were the produce enjoyed by the labourers—a mere truism. The great master must not, however, be blamed for this aspect of the wages of subsistence theory. The idea that the better standard of comfort is the cause of higher wages is directly controverted by him. Speaking of the difference between the subsistence of the common people of Scotland, and that of a similar class in England, he says :—

"This difference, however, in the mode of their

subsistence is not the cause but the effect of the difference in their wages; though by a strange misapprehension I have frequently heard it represented as the cause. It is not because one man keeps a coach while his neighbour walks afoot that the one is rich and the other poor; but because the one is rich he keeps a coach, and because the other is poor he walks afoot."

This should sufficiently have answered the theory that the varying standard of comfort was the cause of differences of wages. Smith clearly saw that the difference of wages caused the varying standard of comfort. With him, wages were wages of subsistence always, and sometimes more than that. But even what to all appearance were only wages of subsistence varied, and this had to be explained by the standard of comfort theory. Adam Smith did not commit himself much with regard to wages of subsistence. But Malthus and Ricardo, to their own satisfaction, settled the whole matter to a nicety.

By Mill's time, and in his hands, the standard of comfort theory amounted to this: that if by any means wages were raised, the permanence of the rise depended on the labourers' growing accustomed to a better standard of comfort. Otherwise they would propagate and increase until the old rate was reached. On the other hand, a fall of wages might make them grow accustomed to a lower standard of comfort. This, it was supposed, would prevent their exercising that prudential restraint which was necessary to reduce their numbers as required to again reach the same rate of wages.

The whole theory, so far as it differed from

Smith's ideas, was the work of Malthus, or rather the result of the Malthusian theory of population. Mill could not disguise from himself the fact that population did not exactly adjust itself to subsistence, as the Malthusian doctrine would imply. His views are not without reason. But he nevertheless conceded too much to the standard of comfort theory, with which the doctrine was inseparably connected. For without staying to question the tendencies referred to by him, or altogether denying the influence of a standard of comfort on population, one obvious explanation of the tendencies is that poor people are more helpless on account of their poverty: and further, that even when better opportunities offer themselves, helpless people do not always take advantage of them.

There is, however, another fallacy to which Smith gave shape. It has already been mentioned that real wages must for the most part, be drawn from capital in exchange for the capital added to the total fund. The fund available for use as wages has been spoken of as the wages fund. There is some reason for speaking in this way of a wages fund; but it has been so much misunderstood that the most glaring error may be observed in the discussion of it. This wages fund theory is closely connected, as will be seen, with the wages of subsistence theory and, like the latter, it found place in Smith's book. The author of the *Wealth of Nations* stated that "the demand for those who live by wages, it is evident, cannot increase but by the increase of the funds which are destined for the payment of wages." These funds he conceived to be of two kinds: the surplus revenue of the landlord or moneyed man who, on the increase of his surplus, would naturally increase the number of his menial servants; and secondly, the surplus stock of the independent workman, such as the weaver or shoemaker, who had more than he needed to purchase the materials of his own work and to maintain himself until he could dispose of it. On an increase of this stock it was said he would naturally increase the number of his journeymen.

It would be difficult to find error more closely packed into half truths than in these passages. The author went on to enforce the position that "the demand for those who live by wages, therefore, necessarily increases with the revenue and stock of every country and cannot possibly increase without it." But he contended that it was not the actual greatness of national wealth, but its continual increase, which occasions a rise in the wages of labour. He had a wonderful command of facts, but his explanations were not always perfect.

Now in these statements we have the foundation of the wages fund theory. The connection with that of wages of subsistence is evident. The contention seems to be that an increase of funds will not benefit those now employed. Only on this ground could it be imagined that the increase would cause a demand for others. This could only be the case if the wages were practically fixed at wages of subsistence. And yet truth underlies the erroneous statement.

Suppose instead of demand for labour the phrase supply of wages had been used. It probably would not have seemed a great change. But it would have made the first of these two statements true instead of false. For the supply of wages can only increase with the increase of the fund from which the wages must be drawn; that is, by the increase of those desirable commodities and services which go to make up wages. Nor would the statement be a useless remark. For it would indicate the important fact that no good can come to labourers by attempting to limit the production of desirable commodities. This was the great argument used by Nassau Senior against the restrictive action of trade combinations. It is one still worth notice, although the expression wages fund has been so often misunderstood and perverted in its use.

As it was, however, the subject was brought into utter confusion. The demand for labour may increase before the funds for its payment have increased. The funds for its payment will be produced by the labour itself when a sufficient time has elapsed. The demand for labour is the first thing which arises. The increased funds for its payment will come afterwards. This is the explanation of what Adam Smith explained by referring it to the increasing state of the funds. In speaking of the rise of wages being due, not to the actual greatness of the national wealth, but to its continual increase, he proceeded to enforce his point by reference to new countries. He apparently imagined that the increase of wealth in those countries was the cause of the demand for labour and higher wages. But the increase of wealth was surely not the cause of more labour being required.

People labour and demand labour because they desire wealth, not because they have it.

The explanation is abundantly clear. The exertion of the labour is the cause of the increase of wealth. That must ever be so. The demand for labour in the new countries arises from the fact that the return for labour is so obvious, and that the institutions of the country have not yet begun to hinder the abundant production of wealth. Instances of new countries will hereafter be cited, in which the demand for labour has been hindered and the increase of wealth stopped by bad economic institutions. It is not merely the newness of the country which makes the difference. There may be poverty in such places in spite of the benefit of abundant natural resources. Economic evils have something to do with it. At any rate, it is certain that the demand for productive labour is owing to a desire that wealth should be produced, and not to the fact that wealth has been produced; whilst the supply of wages is owing to the fact that wealth has been produced.

Neither the landlord nor moneyed man on the one hand, nor the independent labourer, such as the weaver or shoemaker, on the other, would demand more labourers merely because he had the funds with which to remunerate them. The demand would arise because work was required to be done. It would not at all follow that any man would engage more servants merely because he could afford it, though it is true there could be no wages without the funds with which to pay them. These are very obvious corrections and seem almost unnecessary. But the errors were so changed in form as to become very real and tangible fallacies.

The fallacies just referred to have wandered about until they have produced a goodly array of error sprung from the original stock. The wages of subsistence theory has been traced to Ricardo. He used a method (Adam Smith's, like the others) of making labour the foundation of the value of commodities. He proceeded to treat of natural and market price. Market price was conceived to be merely an accidental and temporary deviation from the primary and natural price. The latter was determined by the comparative quantity of labour necessary to the production of the commodities. Natural price was alone to be dealt with. He went on to deal with wages in this way :—

"Labour, like all other things which are purchased and sold and which may be increased or diminished in quantity, has its natural and its market price. The natural price of labour is that price which is necessary to enable the labourers, one with the other, to subsist and to perpetuate their race without either increase or diminution."

This natural price which he thus described was really what he treated of as wages throughout his book. When this is remembered, and it is reflected that he paid no heed to the market price which labourers actually did receive, but set it aside in favour of this so-called natural price which was imagined necessary for subsistence, there can be no surprise at any amount of confusion. He continues :—

"The power of the labourer to support himself and the family, which may be necessary to keep up the number of labourers, does not depend on the quantity of money which he may receive for wages, but on the quantity of food, necessaries and conveniences become essential to him from habit which that money will purchase. The natural price of labour, therefore, depends on the price of food, necessaries, and conveniences required for the support of the labourer and his family. With a rise in the price of food and necessaries, the natural price of labour will rise; with the fall in their price the natural price of labour will fall."

This is quite enough confusion to quote at one time. In the previous passage he had satisfied himself that the natural price of labour was what would sustain the labourers and enable them to propagate their species. Now he states that this will be done, not by the money (which is of course true), but by what the money will buy. So that the natural price of labour becomes the amount of money which buys this wealth. This natural price will rise when food becomes dear, and fall as it becomes cheap.

Now the last statement, if it refers to real wages, that is, if it means anything at all, is untrue, as we saw in an earlier chapter. The natural price being assumed to be what will subsist the labourers, it is concluded that it should rise and fall with the price of maintenance. The whole thing is an assumption. Ricardo goes on to show that the market price may be above or below this natural price. He might as well have said that the natural price was purely ideal and had nothing to do with actual life and fact. He took the imaginary natural price as the foundation of all his arguments. There can be no wonder at the boundless confusion which consequently fills his pages. It was this celebrated iron law of wages on which Marx and his school built the whole of their arguments for socialism. Labour was supposed to be the cause of value. The wages of labour were bare subsistence, though even Ricardo showed that he knew the subsistence was sometimes better and sometimes worse. The capitalist exploited labour and took the excess value beyond bare subsistence for his profits.

It is all mere imagination. Money wages are not raised and lowered to suit the price of subsistence, as labourers have often found to their cost. It is contrary to experience and reason that a higher money wage should be given because the master finds the servant, on account of the higher price of provisions, is somewhat more at his mercy. He may even find that he cannot afford to engage servants at all because the higher prices compel him to reduce his own expenditure. This imaginary law is the economic foundation of Socialism, and without foundation the structure cannot hope to stand. Let it not be concluded, however, that socialism is thought to be entirely disposed of so easily.

The notion that wages tend to wages of subsistence, and need artificial remedies to prevent that result, has, however, obtained a very deep hold on men's minds. Mr. Henry George puts his inquiry into this compact form: "Why, in spite of increase in productive power, do wages tend to a minimum which will give but a bare living?" This is the problem he sets before himself for solution. Much depends on what is meant by the problem, but in one aspect of it the answer is very simple. The reason why wages tend to a bare living is that men only work for a living, and when they have that, there is no need for them to work more; they consequently cease. If anything more than this is meant, the problem is a statement which should have been well proved before it was taken as the foundation problem of an inquiry.

What is meant by a minimum which will give but a bare living? If it means that wages universally are, or tend to become, only sufficient to sustain life, the statement is absolutely untrue. In these times, for one reason or another, some fail to get even that. Some finish their days in starvation, or put an end to them by their own hands, rather than face starvation. But it is not because they are starving in spite of working, but because they cannot get the opportunity of working. If for a similar cause the wages of others are very low, it is not that wages tend to a minimum; it is that something hinders the full employment of labour.

For the same amount of labour actually exerted there can be no doubt that in most countries better real wages are now obtainable than has ever previously been the case. A few special instances to the contrary of perhaps newly-discovered fertile plains may have to be excepted from notice on the one hand, as also some cases of unnaturally abundant casual labour in civilised countries on the other hand. Speaking generally, however, no such natural tendency as that spoken of exists. Even if it can be shown that poverty has increased, it does not follow that real wages tend to be lowered. It may only show that by one means or another the production of wealth is hindered, that, in fact, labour is not exerted. In such a case it is incorrect to say that wages tend to a minimum. The work is not done. How, then, can wages be expected?

It is very true that, with the exception of those who save, wages only amount to a living. But there are those who save in all classes, and they must be excepted. As for the others, they only work for the living, and consequently get what they work for. But there is no law or tendency establishing that it shall fall to bare subsistence, or that it must of necessity be even that. Without the work there may not be even subsistence. So much for the wages of subsistence theory strictly expressed.

The standard of comfort theory, which is evidently a modification of the wages of subsistence idea, need not be further discussed. Adam Smith sufficiently answered it. And it needs little thought to realize that the demand for labour is the first in order of succession in the explanation of wealth supply, that supply of wages is next, and that standard of comfort comes after, and results from the supply. The raising of the standard of comfort will cause an increased demand for labour, it is true. But the standard of comfort can only rise by increased supply of real wages. The order is demand, supply, standard of comfort. Then trace them in the same order again, and again, and so on, while the system of industrial activity continues. Only let this be clear—the demand is never lacking. Man's desire for wealth is never satiated. But stop the supply, and the standard of comfort will be lowered. The effectiveness of the demand will by the same means be diminished. For supply is what gives effectiveness of demand. And this diminishing of the effectiveness of the demand will be worse than diminishing the demand itself.

The wages fund fallacy, as well as that of wages of subsistence, has had a history. Nassau Senior can hardly be said to have done much violence to the truth in his treatment of it. But that cannot be said of John Stuart Mill. His confusion between wealth and money has already been referred to. Add to this the theory that wages were determined by a wages fund; which, let it be remembered, was an absolutely limited fund, though its extent was not perhaps ascertainable. This was all that was necessary to establish with him that wages were fixed by what the capitalists had and intended to pay out as wages. These wages would be lent to labourers. This was the circulating capital the employer kept for his wages. It was always expressed as being advanced. That notion of advancement was probably another idea of Smith's, though its appearance in his work is not nearly so clear as in those of later writers.

With Mill wages were clearly stated to be limited by the capital devoted to their employment. This capital with Mill meant money. The wages fund, as it appeared in his hands, took some root. By means of it, and his confusion between wealth and money, he had succeeded in showing to his own satisfaction that a demand for commodities was not a demand for labour. The examination of his method of doing so is too complicated and not of sufficient interest to be set out here at length. But it may be stated that he practically relinquished the position by saying that, when a demand for commodities was a demand for labour, it was because of the vicarious employment of the labour by the farmer or manufacturer who produced the commodities. That would have been admitted at once. But he spent some pages in trying to show that a demand for commodities would not result in a demand for labour. What he really meant was that a demand for labour condensed into expensive luxuries for the personal consumption of the buyer, was not a supply of food and other necessaries to labourers. Stated in that way no one would deny it. And he would have arrived at the result immediately if he had kept wealth and money distinct in treating the subject. But it is obviously incorrect to imagine that a continuous demand for commodities can be supplied without the employment of labour required for their production. It is, moreover, useless to darken counsel by talking about a demand for commodities not being a demand for labour when, in fact, something else is meant.

There was, however, a decidedly evil tendency in the wages fund theory as it was developed. The notion was that the wages fund was controlled by certain persons, and it was only as they were willing to employ it productively that any benefit could accrue to the mass of the people from it. This notion perhaps reached its climax in the words of

Dr. Amassa Walker: "Wages are not high in proportion to the wealth of a community, but rather to the disposition that exists amongst those possessing wealth to pay it out for labour." Now, the only fragment of truth which can be conceded to any notion approaching this idea will not warrant such a statement as the words convey.

It may be, and without doubt is, true that abilities and qualities are required for organizing and employing labour which are not possessed by every one. And it is also true that those who possess the qualifications will not undertake the duties without sufficient reward. It is not to be expected that they should, when they can retain well-paid positions without the risks of independent business undertakings. But if the demand for the results of labour exists, and those who require those results are able and willing to pay for them, some will be ready to come forward and employ the necessary labour. If some will not, others will, provided the necessary conditions exist. It is not the confidence of employers or moneyed people, but the effective demand of consumers who are willing to supply wealth in return, that causes good trade and high wages.

These various fallacies are, it is true, capable of separation and distinct treatment. But they are all closely interwoven with each other. On them, or at least in accordance with them, have been based the various attempts to interfere with the natural rate of wages, and regulate by combination the relations between employers and employed. Dr. Smith referred to these combinations without any particular disapproval; although he clearly saw that if the conditions were favourable, their action was unnecessary to raise wages. Of subsequent economists, few have gone so far as Professor Jevons. Yet he only ventured to express his belief that their action had, on the whole, done no good; and that wages would have risen without their interference as much as they had with it. Dr. Smiles wrote against strikes, but he did not profess to be an economist, and he has had very few followers. No one seems to have come to the conclusion that the combination was bad from the beginning; or its interference an evil, whatever the immediate result with regard to apparent success or failure.

Nor did the theories which have just been discussed militate against the idea that the combinations were beneficial.

The idea that wages of labourers are those on which they can and will subsist, and consent to propagate their species, justifies as well as they can be justified strikes for higher wages. The labourers striking have a dim notion of the wages of subsistence explanation, modified, perhaps, by the standard of comfort theory, together with a sort of impression that by striking they are refusing to subsist unless they have higher wages. Their standard of comfort requires it. They must have a "living wage," which is the latest phrase used. The same theory supports the Trades Union and Socialistic idea of restricting the hours of adult labour and otherwise interfering with the labour of workmen besides those who ask for the restrictions. It is essential, they think, that others should be prevented from accepting less money wages in proportion to the work done. For it is obviously impossible that they should raise their own wages by refusing to subsist, unless the others will likewise refuse or can be hindered from subsisting by means of a legal enactment.

But of course labourers on strike do not actually refuse to subsist during the months in which they do not work. Mr. George has compared strikes to the Hindoo mode of compelling payment of a just debt called sitting dharna—the creditor sitting down at the door of the debtor and refusing to eat or drink until he is paid. Mr. George says that in their strikes Trades Unions sit dharna, but, unlike the Hindoos, they have not the power of superstition to back them. There is, however, another important difference: they never refuse to eat or drink. If their productions are essential, their success or failure depends on waiting until that is realized, that is, on their being able to obtain enough for themselves and their families to eat and drink to sustain them for a sufficiently long time. Meantime their work stands, and they, in common with the rest of the nation, are the poorer for it. A creditor sitting dharna, with a supply of provisions beside him, brought to maintain him while he waited, or one who asked others to bring him food and drink for that purpose, would have been an object of interest, not to say curiosity, to the Hindoos.

Mr. George is more correct in calling a strike a destructive contest. But even in that he might more nearly have approached the truth than by comparing it to the contest proposed by the money king when taunted with meanness. The contest proposed was that he and his taunter should go down to the wharf and alternately toss twenty-dollar pieces into the bay. But Mr. George should have imagined the masters representing the class of moneyed people, and particularly the wealthiest, committing to destruction paper money created by themselves. As far as regards the men representing their class and the poorer employers, the contest should be compared to destroying victuals, clothing, and the comforts of life. This will more clearly appear as we proceed.

The wages fund theory, moreover, has been so developed as to encourage, like that of wages of subsistence, the idea that capitalists can give better wages if they choose; that, in fact, the men have only to combine to get practically what they like. More than that, these theories help the notion that unless they do combine they will be crushed to starvation. Dr. Walker's words above quoted amply support the idea. But wages do not depend on the whims of a few wealthy people; it would be a sad calamity for mankind if that were the case. And next to such a calamity the most disastrous thing is that such fallacy should have been so prevalent. It would indeed be all the argument required to support strikes, trade combinations to raise prices, socialism, and all the economic ills from which any nation could suffer. Fortunately it is not true, and the mass of the people have a great deal more power to determine what wages shall be than such a notion gives them credit for. They must, however, for this purpose take to understanding and acting upon the laws of the science of wealth. The standard of living can be raised by the supply of which they are themselves capable. Such a supply raising the standard of living will itself be a demand for labour and a raising of wages, whatever those possessing wealth may choose to do or not to do. The demand will be supplied if the right course be taken. Nor for this purpose will any political measures be necessary; but it will be necessary that nothing be done to hinder any one from producing wealth to any extent he may choose.

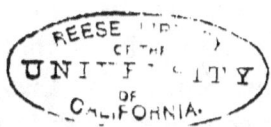

CHAPTER XIII

TRADE COMBINATIONS

IN dealing with Trade Combinations, it is as essential as in the case of other points already dealt with to define exactly the scope of the inquiry. A combination or society of any kind is not good or evil because it is a combination, but because of the action taken by the combination. The expression "Trades Union" has a sufficiently definite meaning to most minds; but it is better to at once confine the attention to the essential characteristic which requires examination.

The Societies known in common parlance as Trades Unions frequently call themselves Trade Protection Societies. In the United States of America the best known expression is that of Knights of Labour. But whether known by these names or others, the idea to be conveyed is the same; it is that of a Society, existing, by combination of the workmen of a particular trade, for the purpose of raising the wages of its members, and otherwise strengthening their position against their employers. Such a combination usually extends only to one trade. It may be one of several different trades engaged in the manufacture or preparation of a particular commodity. Occasionally, however, those of two or more trades will consider themselves to have interests sufficiently in common to induce joint combination.

These combinations frequently have as subsidiary objects those which are in all respects similar to the objects of Friendly and Insurance Societies. But whatever may have been true in the past, such objects have now become quite subsidiary to that of protection against the employer. These subsidiary objects include provision for sickness, loss of tools, and other misfortunes occurring to their members. On this point nothing is intended to be said. The principle of insurance against possible mishap, which may occur to any one, but which is not likely to occur to all at once, seems in all respects a good one. In such a case the many who are, for the time at least, free from misfortune, can, without appreciable difficulty, render assistance which to the one or the few is invaluable. To ask the one to sacrifice himself for the sake of the many is a very different thing, and will require further consideration. The difference will be commented upon in a later chapter.

Included in this principle of insurance is the making of allowances to members who are really out of work and unable to find remunerative employment. But it will not extend to making allowances to members who might have employment if they would accept lower wages than those fixed by the combination as the "Union rate of wages." This latter kind of allowance is a part of the system of controlling or attempting to control the wages of the members, and must be included in the main question.

One other point must also be noticed before passing to the consideration of that main question. These combinations have sometimes taken or received credit for their interference to raise the quality of the goods manufactured. Such credit is entirely gratuitous. So far as a workman can be induced to put his best and most conscientious labour into his handicraft, the quality of his work is improved. But it is clearly evident that this in no way depends upon combination; all the influence which is possible can be exerted without the combination. Nor do the Trades Unions make it one of their regulations or strong points, whatever the ancient guilds may have done. It is true that they frequently prescribe prices below which their members should not go; but that is a very different thing from inculcating conscientious work or prescribing qualities. This prescribing prices is, in fact, all that can be meant by their attempts to put on the market only the better classes of goods. The feature is not heard of in the case of those trades in which the workmen cannot control the quality of the article. None the less the duty of paying a good price for it is quite as strenuously maintained. In those instances in which a high quality is made a point of, there is no request for the privilege of making a good article for the money, but of making a good article and receiving a good price. The inference is that the price is the chief object, not the quality.

The privilege of making an article well worth the money will be readily conceded. But what class of goods, considered with reference to their prices, shall be made, it is not in the power of trade combinations to decide; that is purely a question for the consumer, and not for the producer. The producer can only be paid for what the consumer chooses to use. If he makes anything else, he will find that the market is closed to it, and he has wasted his time. So far as a person is a consumer, but no farther, and with regard only to the commodities he consumes, he can choose their quality; the producer produces for the consumer. If Trades Unions would influence qualities, they must persuade their members to give ungrudging work for their wages (which is not their present policy), and to choose only the better qualities when they buy. What they sell others will choose. Only by these means can Trade Combinations anywhere have influenced qualities.

On the subject of quality, however, it may conveniently be noticed here that nothing conduces so much to the general use of the better qualities of goods of all kinds as does "good trade." Few or none choose inferior qualities because they prefer them. It may be said, without much fear of contradiction, that the reason for their choice is that the price is all they feel they can afford. And in a period when all are at work, none wasting their strength seeking employment, and money flowing freely from hand to hand, there is much more likelihood that the additional money received will be expended in the better qualities of goods. Indeed, they are the more economical in the long run, but no man can expend money which he does not possess or control, even though it may be of advantage to him to do so. This contention with regard to better qualities being sold during brisker trade is confirmed by experience.

Apart, therefore, from the principle of insurance, which is not now an essential feature of Trade Protection Societies, and apart also from the possibility of Societies intimating to their members where remunerative employment can be had, which is scarcely a feature of these combinations, there remains only to be considered their chief and essential feature, which is their interference between employer and employed with regard to wages and other matters.

Strictly speaking, a combination being an abstract notion cannot interfere between master and servant, but the final result is as if such a thing were possible. For the combination of a number of men to fix their wages in unison inevitably results in their being represented by one or more individuals. These individuals are, so to speak, the embodiment of the combination. They may themselves be members of the combination and engaged in the same employment, or they may be specially set apart by the other members for the purpose of representing the Union. In any case the professed object is to act in the interest and on behalf of the employed. The idea is that by thus forming themselves into one mass and acting as though the individuals were not many but one, the members can obtain better wages than if they acted separately. In this way it has become customary for all the workmen of a trade extending over a whole district to have their wages fixed. The officials who embody the Union frequently deal directly with the masters, who in their turn occasionally choose a number of themselves to treat with the men's officials. In other cases the workmen individually treat with the masters, perhaps because the masters will not recognise the Union. But even in these cases the result is the same. The men do nothing without the sanction of their leaders, and thus become merely the mouthpiece of the Union.

Naturally the Union does as an individual would, in so far as it endeavours to raise the money wages as high as possible. Of course the workmen imagine that they will, by means of the combination, increase their wages. And there are many others besides the men and their leaders who favour these combinations as tending to better the lot of the workman. Not for a moment would any one doubt the sincerity of their belief. But it is intended to show that it is an entirely mistaken one. The truth is that these combinations cannot better the lot of their members, but can and do make it materially worse. This does not appear ever to have been definitely proved. Several economists have, however, shown their strong suspicion of the truth. Some of them were hindered by initial fallacies from reaching the truth. The mention of names, and the reasons apparently to be assigned for their failure in this respect, must be deferred until the subject itself has been to some extent dealt with.

Many methods of arriving at the truth are open, but some classification will conduce to clear apprehension. For this purpose a distinction between fixed and circulating capital, which has often been used by economists, will be useful. It has not been adopted as a primary distinction, because, in the first place, it is impossible to find a clear and at the same time satisfactory line of demarcation; and in the second place, as might be anticipated from the absence of such a line, nothing really important hangs on the distinction. It will, however, be convenient, and the reader may fix the line at his own choice.

The old distinction became almost worthless, for whilst fixed capital was truly described, circulating capital, in the language of Mill for instance, was an expression for money. Such a method inevitably led to confusion. Moreover, there was a difference between the methods of understanding the distinction. For while Smith referred to circulating capital as that passing from hand to hand and not consumed, Ricardo (whose method is here followed) meant by it capital more speedily consumed. There is a difference between wealth which is entirely consumed or altered in the using, and wealth which is not so consumed or altered. There are obvious difficulties in allowing much beyond arrangement to depend upon it. But there are certainly differences in degree, and to that extent a useful distinction. Food, for instance, can be consumed but once. Fuel also is consumed in the using. Clothing may be used more than once; but the raw material used in the making of it can be used but once for the purpose, and is truly circulating capital until it reaches the finished state. Moreover, it appears more convenient to speak of even the clothing as circulating capital until it actually reaches the consumer. A house, on the other hand, is fixed in every respect;

yet the material used in its construction is in respect of its use of the nature of circulating capital. Timber may be said to be consumed in the using. It probably only affords benefit after it has been used in the construction or manufacture of some commodity. Yet as timber it exists no longer after once used.

It thus appears difficult to find a satisfactory line of distinction. It is better to bear in mind that houses, mills, railways, and the like are fixed capital. Food and fuel are circulating capital in the sense in which the term is used by economists. Between the two are various degrees of fixity, and even the most fixed kinds of capital eventually wear out or are consumed.

Consider, then, in the first place the trades engaged in the production of circulating capital. As a type take coal-miners. Their pre-eminence in the matter of gigantic trade combination, in Great Britain at any rate, is notorious. Suppose that there is a great demand for coal, and the price is rising. Everything is favourable to the success of the combination. The leaders know that in such a market they can successfully demand a higher price for the men's work. As frequently has happened they demand and obtain the addition of a certain percentage to the money wages of all the miners. To many minds, and especially at first sight, it is doubtless difficult to imagine how this can be anything but a benefit to the miners. But the matter must be traced further. It is essential to see where the additional money comes from, and what the result is, before it can be concluded that the miners are benefitted.

No one would venture to say that in such a market

the masters would lose the additional sum paid to the men. It is contrary to business principles that they should willingly forfeit that sum. They cannot be expected to do so. The result must therefore be that the additional price paid is added to the commodity. It is true it is not calculated in that way. It is a question of the market. The price is fixed by supply and demand. But the only way the Union can raise the price is by stopping work or threatening to do so. Stopping work is in effect diminishing supply, which, as already pointed out, is a means of raising prices. Moreover, the threat to stop the supply has the same effect, by inducing purchasers to buy out of the regular course what they would have bought later, and by inducing the sellers to hold for the time of stoppage. As a matter of experience it is found that the addition to the miners' wages is at best only about one-third of the additional price paid for the coal. This proportion, however, is not essential for the argument. It is enough that from the nature of things the masters will have the additional price paid with some profit on it.

That is the first step in the argument: the additional price paid to the miners, together with a profit on it, will be added to the price of the commodity. The next and only other step is, that the miners themselves will pay that additional price, together with a number of further profits on it. It is true they do not require the coal for their own consumption, but the mischief is even greater on that account. They work for money because money will buy wealth. They desire, and, in fact, absolutely need that wealth.

The commercial world will only give it them in return for their labour. That labour is embodied in the coal they have produced. It is passed on with its additional price through a great variety of hands, a profit for the transaction being added every time, until it reaches them again. When it does reach them, they, having only received the percentage first added to their wages, are not able to pay the profits which, from the absolute necessity of the case, have been added. Their real wages, the wealth for which they worked, is accordingly diminished.

This result must follow from the nature of things. The master will get for the commodity the amount paid, together with his profit, or he had better give up his business. Every one who deals with the commodity will take care that the commodities he has to sell will recoup him, together with a profit, or he had better not be in the trade. And the original producer can have no wealth except by reason of his productions going the complete circle until they reach him again.

This point is important to make clear. If while he lives in England, the miner's bread is grown in the United States of America, and the raw material of his clothing produced in Australia, these things can only reach him because those who bought the coal from his employer used it to manufacture something which should be sent out to those distant regions. The people who live in those regions must pay the manufacturers for what they send. And included in the price must be the additional sum added by the threatened strike, otherwise the manufacturers will stop their works.

When the raw material leaves those distant regions, it must, as a matter of course, include the additional price paid for what has been essential to its production. That will include the wages of men who must have higher money wages to pay for the higher prices of manufactured goods coming to them, or must take care to go without them and stop the coal being of use at all. To that additional price must be added a profit, or the producers of the raw material will give up their business, and there will be no corn or wool. When these materials reach England, of course the higher price must be paid for them by the manufacturers of cloth and the grinders of corn. This again will be repaid, together with a profit, or no bread or clothes will reach the miner. The manufacturers and millers have also felt the rise in the price of coal, and have something to add to the price of the finished product on that account. In this way, therefore, the miner pays dearly for the addition he made to his money wages by means of the combination.

For reasons which are sufficiently obvious, coal-miners have been chosen as an instance by means of which to examine the subject. They have a powerful combination in Great Britain; they are the first producers of raw material; but other instances might have been adopted. There must be a complete circle, and any one in that circle may do the same thing, though it may appear less easy to trace.

There are other contentions possible. For instance, it might be contended that, even if manufacturers and other masters within the circle would either insist on being paid the additional outlay with a profit, or would cease to trade, yet they might possibly take that additional outlay from their own men. It would scarcely be an argument which would be offered on humanitarian grounds, and those are the grounds usually offered to support trade combinations. Nor would it tend to induce subscriptions from other trades in case of a strike. It might, however, be urged; and, as a matter of fact, that proceeding actually occurs. The result of it will be noticed in the next chapter. That result, it may be here stated, is not a favourable argument for trades unionism.

On the other hand, it must be remembered that many engaged in other trades (for their own protection as they imagine) form similar combinations. It is true their object is protection against the supposed rapacity of the masters. It is not ostensibly against a combination of other workmen which raises the price of the raw material with which they must work, or of the commodity they must themselves consume. They never notice that by these latter means their own wages must be reduced or the price of their productions raised. Still less would they realize that in the latter case they must eventually pay that advance with interest and profits. In endeavouring to protect themselves against some real or imaginary danger they are doing themselves injury. Yet that does not prevent their increasing the injury which the workmen of the trade first instanced did to themselves. These other trades also combine and raise their prices. The same results follow as were mentioned with regard to the miners. Thus, as the circle is traced, the evil is increased, not only by means of the profit which must be taken on the increased price of the first commodity, but also by the additional prices put on by other combinations.

This cannot, of course, go on indefinitely raising the price of the commodities. The limit must be reached somewhere. And the influence which counteracts that of the combination to raise the prices is found in diminished effective demand. Not that the demand in the sense that word has been used in this book is any less, but the means by which it is made effective are considerably reduced. Throughout the circle of exchange the workmen find themselves unable to purchase the higher priced wealth. By this means the prices are kept within reasonable limits. But it is a still further argument against the combination method. For it simply means that the commodities are kept cheap because the people have not enough to buy them with, and not because they are found in great abundance. And it explains why, as a mere contrivance to raise prices, trade combinations are ultimately powerless.

With regard to fixed wealth or capital, a slightly different method of argument may be adopted. The workmen engaged in building houses may be taken as a typical instance. The same method might be adopted with regard to those engaged in shipbuilding or erecting more or less permanent engineering works.

Suppose once more that the demand for houses is good. For it is desired to take the case most strongly against the writer. As in the other instance, the combination demands and obtains an advance of money wages. So far as the contracts then in hand are concerned, doubtless the masters must suffer the loss. But in making fresh contracts they will certainly make allowance for the current rates of wages and the cost of building other houses will be increased. Now, a person wishing to invest money in houses may either buy those already built or contract for the erection of others. No higher house rents can be obtained for the new ones built at the increased rate than for equally convenient houses built at the old rate. The result is, that all the houses already built have been increased in value by the advance in the workmen's wages. This benefit accrues to the owners of house property, not to journeymen builders.

Now no one will contend that the workmen should debar themselves from a possible benefit, lest the owners of capital should also be benefitted. But they can hardly suspect that the effort of the combination was really benefitting the capitalist to so much greater an extent than it was benefitting the labourer. The person against whom the combination is intended to be directed is the capitalist. And yet here is a very clear instance in which the capitalist has gained by the combination.

Moreover, the question requires discussion as to whether the workman is benefitted by the advance of wages so obtained. It is true the rents of houses are not raised by the advance itself, so that the workman does not necessarily pay more for his house. Nor would, for instance, freights be increased by a similar advance in the cost of shipbuilding. On the other hand, these advances do not increase the amount of money to be expended in house or shipbuilding. And as the cost of this building has been increased, it is evident that fewer houses or ships can be built. The workmen have a little more to spend if the same work continues to be demanded, but it would not be suggested that they would spend it all in house-building. Whether by their spending it they will indirectly produce that result is a question which shall be answered.

Now, of the money to be invested in house property, it is clear a portion will go to those owners of houses who, having built or bought at the old rate, are able to sell at the new rate. The money to be spent in actual building is thus decreased in the first place. Moreover, the remainder of the money will not now build as many houses as it would have built at the lower rates. The consequence is, that from both causes fewer houses are built. The result of this is, that the people must either live in worse houses or pay higher rents to induce money again to go to the building trade. By this means the owners of the older houses naturally increase their income. For the rents will of necessity be raised all round in a fair proportion.

Still the workmen have not yet felt the pinch, except so far as the demand has fallen off, and their services are not so much required at the new rate as they were at the old. This may or may not reduce their money wages to what they would have been without the advance; it may possibly bring them below that sum. But the only clear step yet is, that the chief gainers have been the owners of the houses built before the advance. We have seen, however, that rents must rise or the people be worse housed. In the latter case the members of the combination must share the misfortune which, so far as that point is concerned, is all we have to prove. It is true they will obtain more rest, unless they spend the exertion in seeking employment. But rest was not what they desired, or they might have had it without combination. They desired better wages, and, at any rate in respect of houses, their wages are worse.

If, however, increased rents result, they must be paid by the men themselves and by others. So far as the men themselves are concerned, the benefit of the combination is thereby lost. So far as others are concerned, the result is, that they must have either less of other comforts to compensate for the increased rent, or increased prices for the commodities they supply. Their receiving less of other comforts is not an argument likely to be used by Trades Unionists. But if the argument be used, an answer is ready. A tendency will be produced (which will be noticed in the next chapter) to come into the favoured trade and share the advantages that trade has obtained over members of other trades. If, on the other hand, the commodities are increased in price, the members of the combination take their injury in that way. The method becomes similar to that referred to with regard to circulating capital. The curse must come home to roost.

These two instances have been adopted as typical ones. Under one or other of the heads every trade must come. If the reader has any doubt as to which of the classes to put a trade in, he may combine the two. With regard to capital in existence, whether it be fixed capital or a considerable stock of circulating capital, the second method will apply. With that modification the first applies to all cases of circulating capital.

Incidentally it may be seen that each Trade Combination is an injury to those in other trades. But neglecting that aspect altogether, the combination is an injury to its own members. The gist of the whole matter is: first, that the additional money received will be put on the price of the commodity; secondly, the commodity must directly or indirectly be sold to those who will eventually supply wealth for the labourers combining, and who in the very nature of things, from causes both justifiable and beyond control, take care to put the additional price on the commodities supplied to those labourers. They must, moreover, have something as profit to induce them to continue the trade. The labourers combining therefore pay away all they get, together with a profit on it.

It has to be confessed that the operations here set forth are not always easily recognised. It is only possible to examine them by rigorously confining the attention to what in the nature of things must be, and closely reasoning the matter out. Economists have not always done this. For instance, some have stated that though it might be possible that competition would raise wages, yet that the combination could obtain the advance much more promptly than by waiting for competition to give it them. It does not seem to have occurred to those who argued in this way that the masters would not voluntarily submit to absolutely lose what the Union demanded, but would charge more for the commodity. If they had noticed this, they would have probably come to the conclusion that it was not the natural market which occasionally raised the prices to such an abnormal height, causing the Union to ask for a share of such prices. They would have realized that the combination itself had much to do with those abnormal prices.

For the time being, so far from the masters giving a portion of their gettings to the men, they were actually adding more to their own gettings by means of the combination's interference. No one could blame them for it. They were only adopting the same principles as the Union and following the universal law expressed in the third postulate. The combination had only itself to blame for the results which inevitably followed. Each man labours for the gratification of his desires, but in the complicated system of commerce under which we live the labour does not directly produce that gratification. The value of the labour is put into a commodity which is passed on to others. After various changes in form, the value of labour inhering in that commodity will come back. The capital by means of which the world sustains itself is, as it were, a huge cistern for storing up labour. If a number of men combine to interfere with the natural price of their labour, their interference will come back to them with increased disadvantage.

Nor will it avail them much at the very outset.

As is well known, commodities can be increased and kept high in price much more readily and easily than labour possibly can be. Those who have labour to sell must constantly have something for their consumption, and have not generally a large stock of consumable wealth on hand. It is easy to see, therefore, how the prices of the commodities they require can be immediately raised to meet the increased money wages by which it is imagined the Union has benefitted the lot of the workmen. The same spirit which actuates the workmen influences others.

One other point which was referred to earlier in the chapter must be dealt with here. It is the notion of some that by means of the additional money wages which the Union secures, some benefit may accrue to others, and by that very means exchange may be made more brisk. This is part of the very common error that money is wealth. The idea is that the men with their increased wages will go into the various markets: that the money they expend will cause others to spend more; in short, that the human species will be really better off because the men combining have obtained more money for producing the same amount of wealth. A little thought will convince any one that the reverse is the case.

It is not money we require, but what money will buy. The money, therefore, is useless except as an indication that its value has been started through the circle of exchanges and will eventually come round to these particular vendors. Now, if by means of the combination the wealth given for that money has deliberately been made less, it is clear that the combination cannot be looked upon as a real benefit to those who receive the money of its members. They bring money which represents less than it did before the combination went to work, and pass it off as of the proper value calculated in terms of wealth.

The arguments used and endeavoured to be classified in this chapter are capable of assuming very many forms, according to the form the error to be replied to may take. The reader may find those forms and many other arguments at his will. There is, so to speak, only one truth, but there are as many ways of reaching and proving it as there are errors and fallacies to be answered; as many paths by which to come back to it as may be used in wandering away from it. In fact, all this is part of the same truth; it is but a closer examination of a detail which has been undertaken. The next chapter must go somewhat more to the root of the error, and by examining the foundation on which the whole subject rests, prove still more conclusively the truth of what has already been put forward.

Throughout this chapter it has been assumed that the market was a rising one, and the attempt to raise wages therefore apparently successful. This, it is conceived, is the most favourable view to take for the combinations. If the attempt is unsuccessful, few would care to argue the advantage of the combination. If a reduction of money wages ensues in spite of the combination, still fewer would take its part. If wages are kept up in this way above their natural point, the result is the same as in the case of their being raised above that point. The additional price must be put on the commodity.

It has been seen already that the masters generally take care that they do not lose the higher price. But it must be conceded that they do lose under the combination method, on account of the irregularity it causes. The numerous strikes and other causes of loss are not more than compensated for by the increased prices. 'For there are certain expenses which must go on, and irregularity of employment is a very great source of loss. There still remains a possible alternative. By the keeping of wages above the competition rate the master may have his profits seriously diminished by a falling market before he can, or at least before he does, give notice to his men for a reduction. This, together with the cost of the necessary lock-out, probably does fall on the master. And that one point remains to be dealt with by another method. But it will be enough to say here that a master who loses in this way will not long go on employing labourers, and less demand will bring less wages.'

CHAPTER XIV

COMPETITION AND CO-OPERATION

A TRADE combination to raise wages is essentially a contrivance for restricting competition. To the minds of many persons competition is an evil to be as far as possible suppressed. This seems to be the case even with some economists. The reason for it appears to be a confusion between competition and the struggle for existence. This confusion is, without doubt, the reason why some economists have not before now reached the conclusions here put forward. It is imagined that competition and the struggle for existence are one and the same thing, and that restricting competition will diminish the struggle for existence. Mr. George very clearly falls into the error. Professor F. A. Walker has been under the same confusion. Only a mistaken notion as to the nature of competition prevented him from clearly perceiving that free competition was the true and only means of raising wages.

This was not the case with Professor Jevons. He quite understood that competition was the effort to supply. The reason why he did not realize more certainly what he evidently suspected is to be found elsewhere. On the whole he clearly thought Trade Combinations were an evil. Strikes he certainly considered an injury, whether successful or unsuccessful. But he stopped short of saying that the principle was entirely bad from the beginning. He apparently thought that possibly rich people paid some of the additional money obtained by combination, though the workmen must pay the greater portion of it. Whilst he saw that all workmen could not better their wages by combination, yet he seemed to admit that a few might do so. Probably the reason why he stopped short of the whole truth, was that he treated money too much as a commodity instead of a mere circulating measure. Although he quite realized that money was not wealth, he nevertheless probably allowed himself to think that metal money must be had and a benefit must result from getting more of it. This method would favour the trade combinations more than is due to them. For there is no denying that in the matter of money they do frequently, by means of strikes, increase their nominal wages. The result of that has already been seen, but to be fully realized it must be taken in connection with the fact that metal money or other legalised currency is more or less efficient in proportion to the rapidity of its transfer. And further, it must be realized that for many purposes the metal is quite unnecessary if something else in the nature of credit can be made to pass current to a larger or smaller extent. The only qualification is that it shall be current so as to get round without hinderance to the starting place, or wherever it may be wanted to keep industry in full operation. His thus attaching too much importance to money seems to account for Professor Jevons not reaching the full amplitude of the truth. Professor Nassau Senior, who was probably equally impressed with the evil of restrictive trade combinations, perhaps never thought of seeking to what extent he could carry his convictions.

In the previous chapter the evil of trade combinations has been sufficiently pointed out to answer most of the arguments urged on their behalf even by economists. In the present chapter it is proposed to show, not only that a combination of all the workmen in a nation would be an evil, and powerless for good, but that the principle is bad, even in the case of a combination of only two workmen. That will strike at the very root idea of the institution, showing that it is an evil in its inception and becomes worse in proportion to the extent it is followed.

Having thus stated the subject, it will be well once more to define the inquiry. The principle of which the evil is to be shown is the restriction of competition. The confusion between competition and the struggle for existence has already been referred to, and must be here explained. It is not true, as carelessly thought by many, that the two are the same thing. The truth is that they are the exact contraries, or rather complements of each other. The struggle for existence is the effort to consume—we have called it the demand. Competition is the effort to produce—the supply, as we have expressed it, and consequently the very opposite in its effect on prices to the struggle for existence. Competition is that by means of which the struggle for existence is successfully met.

Q

When once this has been admitted there seems little to argue about—and admitted clearly it must be. In itself the word competition means any striving between two or more, but as used with regard to human necessities it refers only to their supply. What is the result of increased competition but to reduce prices? In other words, competition is the effort to give more wealth for less money. It is true that this is done that more money may be had for the proportionately greater supply of wealth. That is to say, the competition is impelled by the struggle for existence. But the competition becomes an effort to render more wealth than another for the same money. It is thus the means by which human needs and desires are supplied, and clearly the more of it, the more effective it is, the greater the benefit to humanity. A little thought will satisfy any one that the charge against the strong competitor is not that he gets too much for what he gives, but that he gives too much for what he gets. He lowers prices. His offending is that he undersells his neighbour. He should be prevented from giving too much, and should be encouraged, and even coerced into asking for more, which seems quite superfluous interference.

The exact nature of competition may, however, with advantage be made even more clear than by saying it is the effort to supply, as distinguished from the effort to demand. Competition, when properly understood, is really co-operation, and full and free competition is the only perfect co-operation attainable.

Long ago it was shown by Say in France, in

dealing with gluts of the market, that what was called over-production was really under-production. Not too much had been produced, but too little had come to market to be exchanged for it. But this has not been clearly brought into the science, and has apparently not been well applied to the consideration of labour. In fact, it is a seriously entertained idea that there should be free supply of commodities but not free supply of labour.

Of the methods of co-operation which are generally understood there are two clearly distinguishable kinds. The first may be called co-operative distribution, in which the consumers join together, paying wages to their shopmen, and thus obtain their retail produce, taking the profits for themselves. The second, and it is submitted the better system of co-operation, may be spoken of as co-operative production. In it the producers get the profits. Speaking generally, this is the only true co-operation. The producers are really those who should get the profits, for encouragement should be to production rather than consumption. Only in a few special instances in which the consumers have some office to perform other than consuming wealth is the former a true co-operation. The desire to consume is in itself a sufficient motive. The co-operation of consumers for their own profit is not the distribution of wealth amongst its producers. In such co-operation the members can only be said to co-operate as capitalists and not as labourers.

Besides these systems of co-operation, however, economists have recognised that all division of labour is co-operation. According to Mill, the credit is due to Mr. Wakefield. Where several are engaged to lift the same weight co-operation is evident. This is simple co-operation. But as an instance of complex co-operation it must also be remembered that the different persons engaged in different processes of manufacturing the same article are co-operating to produce that article. The different persons engaged in producing clothing—from the sheep-farmer or the cotton-grower through all the processes, and including the manufacture of all the tools and machinery required for the different processes, up to the tailor or draper who sells the article—are all co-operating to produce clothing. So it is with food; so with houses; so with luxuries; so with everything required. And the different people engaged in producing food, clothing, houses, and what else, are in one great multitude co-operating to produce a living wage. The point now to make clear is that free competition is entirely co-operation, and the only means of attaining perfect co-operation. The following statement is submitted as explaining that expression, and in its turn to be explained and justified.

The most perfect co-operation of labour is that in which the service rendered will bring to each labourer the results of an equal expenditure (effectiveness being considered) of the labour of others.

That statement will explain and commend itself to most thinking people, but it shall be further made clear. First, it will be remembered that the causes which create the natural inequalities of wages were pointed out. The effect of the scarcity of the qualifications or inclinations required for certain occupations and grades of employment raised the wages in those cases above the level of other employments. This scarcity diminished the competition for such positions. Now it is clear that these qualifications and inclinations are regarded by those who are willing to pay for them as giving greater effectiveness in the matter of wealth production. We have here nothing to do with rent of land nor with interest on capital. These are determined by entirely different considerations. We have now to deal with the rewards of personal efforts exercised with or without land or capital; but if with them, then paid for after rent and interest have been allowed. The rendering of such services is open to the competition of every one capable of them. The amount paid for each one's efforts, therefore, is the value put upon them by the rest of the community having regard to their utility and their scarcity. Their effectiveness is in proportion to the felt want which they supply, which is only another way of expressing the utility and scarcity of the services they render.

Allowing for this greater effectiveness (in supplying a felt want), it is evident that free competition is the only system by which a perfect co-operation can be secured. To hinder free competition must be to raise the prices of some commodities without putting more labour into them. Some find themselves subject to less competition than before. The result is that others must give more of their labour than the results will produce an equivalent for. On the other hand it is very clear that, competition being free, the co-operation referred to will take place. It is evident that as soon as one labourer finds that he is not getting as much as he could get in another employment he will be inclined to change his occupation. The most unskilled, and consequently the lowest class, will most readily be able to change.

To further explain this co-operation imagine two men engaged in the simplest method of co-operation —lifting and carrying (one at each end) a flag-stone. That is evidently co-operation just as much as the two hands of one man co-operate. And quite as clearly is it competition—a real competition. Let one of them allow his end of the flag-stone to go down, even to a limited extent, and his toes (not his companion's) will be in considerable danger.

Now suppose two men getting their living by an occupation in which both their services are required, but in different processes, the resulting product being for the consumption of the two and not for exchange. That would be true co-operation as well as a competition. Each must compete with the other, so that he be not behind in his part of the operation. A very expressive vulgarism is that he must keep his end up. And yet it is co-operation, for they are working for the same object. This is the method in which the two find they can most advantageously work in order to effect the object they have in view. Let it be supposed that one of them has to perform a much more difficult part of the process than the other, and therefore contributes much more to the ultimate result. It is only fair that the rewards be properly apportioned between them. The proceeds are accordingly divided in proportion to the efforts put forth and the effective work contributed. It is still co-operation, and even the one receiving least receives more than he would have done working alone. It is competition only in the same sense as before.

Put any number of men into these processes, an equal number in each. They are still all co-operating; the people in the same process are co-operating with each other as well as with their companions in the other process. The co-operation is most perfect, and this even though each has results proportionate to his share in the effort to produce. Now let it be supposed that each set consists of three men. There may be any number of sets, and they are still all co-operating. Extend the three to four, or five, or a thousand, according to the extent to which it is found labour can be profitably divided. They still co-operate by competition.

The illustration may be varied. Suppose that instead of the first two individuals with the flag-stone being one at each end, the flag-stone had been a very large one, and they had only required one end of it raising. Suppose further that by some means a test of the effectiveness of their applied strength had been possible, and they were paid in proportion to the lifting power they each used. It would still have been competition each to lift the greater weight. And yet it would be the most perfect co-operation. The varying payment would be the only just payment. For not only must the result be considered, but probably the stronger man requires the more subsistence to make up for the additional physical waste. Carry this principle out to its utmost extent; spread it over the utmost variety of occupations, and it will hold good.

Let it also be clearly understood that this reasoning is direct and not by analogy. Reference was first made to two processes by way of assisting the mind to grasp the point more clearly. The number was gradually increased to show that it held good throughout. The illustration of the flagstone is used by way of assisting the mind to grasp the point by means of a visible and tangible model. The essential principle is the same, and must be kept so, as in the case of a working model. In this the argument differs from an argument by analogy.

Competition in actual life may be spoken of as direct and indirect. Each labourer competes directly with the labourers in his own trade and position, although clearly he is co-operating to produce the same stock of commodities. This would be direct competition and simple co-operation. Indirectly he competes with all other labourers. Some are able and willing to turn their hands to other occupations than those they are engaged in. Some will be likely to come into his trade if necessary. This indirect competition corresponds to complex co-operation. The same applies to capital. The freely changing capital (which is labourers' maintenance) is that which can be applied to the employment which most requires capital.

Now all indirect competition is evidently co-operation. No man can desire (if he thinks at all) to see stopped the production of what he requires. All the people producing that are helping to cause, not merely demand for his labour, but a supply of wages for him. Further it was seen that all those engaged in the same process were co-operating. And they were co-operating perfectly if the other processes were being kept up by a sufficient number to make complete sets.

So that there is a co-operation even amongst those who compete directly with each other. The only qualification required to make it perfect is that the wages shall be equal to those which are obtained by the same effectiveness of industry in another employment. At that point only is perfect co-operation. Amongst those competing directly with each other for wages in the same employment, if the wages fall below that point, it may be said there is a competition which is not a co-operation. There is in such a case a competition, not only to supply wealth, but for the opportunity of supplying it. There is a struggle for the privilege of working which ought not to exist. On the other hand, if the wages rise above the point referred to, then it is clear the persons engaged in that occupation are not fairly co-operating with those in other employments. They are getting more than their proper share of the proceeds, and perfect co-operation is interfered with.

Now if by any means the wages in one trade rise above those in another, after allowing for variations in effectiveness, it is evident that a tendency will set in for men to leave the worst paid trade, and go to the better paid one. If a change is impossible by the then present members, the same result will be effected by those who have to choose which of the two trades they will enter.

It thus appears that if each occupation is left to itself the exact number will constantly tend to be found in it which may be required for the purpose of carrying it on in unison with other occupations. The smallest variation below that number will tend to raise the price of labour in that occupation which will be at once corrected by an inflow from those who would have worked in other occupations. Any excess will tend to lower the wages and prevent others coming to them, if not to drive some out of the trade. This result, however, it is evident can only be attained by free competition.

It is clear that, setting aside special circumstances, every man will choose that employment in which he can obtain the best wages. These will be indicated to him by the price test. Money, though not real wages, will show the relative wages in the different employments. But if the price gauge be artificially altered, it will be no true test.

It should also be borne in mind that the cooperation of various occupations includes, not only that of the different trades, but also that of the different grades of persons in the same trade or process. To work effectively workmen require to be properly organized. To this end it is desirable that the proper number of persons be raised to positions of command and responsibility. Qualifications for various posts differ. According as the requisite qualities are commonly or rarely found, the wages will be comparatively low or high. But there is no absolute barrier between one position and another. As any position becomes undermanned or overmanned, the variation will make itself known by a rise or fall in the wages as compared with other positions. This rise or fall will have its effect on the persons already in or seeking to enter that employment. But every position as well as every trade is subject to the same law of competition. Whatever a man's position he will find that his wages must be limited by comparison with what other equally qualified men can earn in that employment.

Let the action of trade combinations be now examined in the light of what has already been seen. A number of persons carrying on one kind of work required in the production of a certain article combine to demand higher wages. They refuse to carry on their work unless they are given those higher wages. There are three possibilities with regard to the number of people already in that employment. They may be the number exactly required for perfect co-operation, or above or below that number. The supposition for convenience will be that at present they are the exact number required. If they are fewer than are required, it will be seen in the higher prices already. This will intensify the effect which it will be pointed out follows the interference. If they are more than are required (as may in fact result from interference) the interference will be delusive. The members of the combination will imagine they can secure in the trade what they can only obtain by getting out of it. They will all continue to struggle where they are not wanted, instead of allowing prices to send some where they are more required. This, however, is an anticipation, and will be more clear as we proceed.

The combination again may consist of two or more persons. If the combination is so small as not to materially affect the work accomplished, no result comes of it except to the men combining. To them the result is that the two or more have persuaded each other to forego the measure of satisfaction of their desires, which was possible. They have not suffered the work, but they might have accomplished that, acting singly had they so wished. That was not their object in combining. The object was that by one inducing another not to work others would be compelled to give them more for their labour. In the event, however, others have chosen to do without their labour, and they obtain rest when they desired work and wages.

If, on the other hand, the combination is large enough to hinder the work so materially as to influence prices, the result must be carefully sought. On a sufficiently firm interference by the combination there are but two chances: first, that the work shall stand, and secondly, that the men shall have more money given to them for it.

If their work stands it is evident that others needing their productions must do without them. If their efforts are only a step towards the complete production (that is in all cases except actual supply of the finished product to the very consumer), then the efforts of those who follow them will be stopped. And as the efforts of those who precede are only useful as leading up to the point at which the efforts of those now combining begin, their efforts also become useless. Thus the whole supply of that portion or kind of wages is stopped. In the case of those who actually supply the consumer, it is only necessary that their own efforts cease, and the same result will be accomplished.

Now if this method were to be applied to all kinds of commodities which go to make up the living wage, then the living is completely stopped, and life ends. That, in other words, has been pointed out often enough. But it has been thought the people stopping might possibly benefit themselves at the expense of others. While their work stands, however, they can of course have no wages; so that they cannot be considered to have benefited themselves so far. If the result of the stoppage is to give them more wages, it will come under the next point.

Suppose, therefore, on the other hand, that the work does not stand but the higher money wages are given. Every worker as an individual had previously found the best place he could for himself, that is, the place at which price told him he was most wanted. Now, however, a section of workers by threatening to stop altogether have obtained for themselves a better relative share of the total productions. What can happen but that some of the others will go to that section as quickly as they can, to get some of that share? The result of that proceeding is that, whereas they were co-operating, now they are merely competing for a place. They leave the work in which they were engaged, supplementing that of the men combining, and come for a place in the now improved trade. It would be very unjust to try to prevent their doing so, for it would compel them to accept less than their equal share. And yet there can be but one consequence, namely, that less shall be produced for the men who combined. The men who were producing it have come to their trade.

There is still an argument for the combination left to those who care to use it. The abstraction from other trades of some of those engaged in them will leave more work to be done by those left in them. Indeed, the work has been increased whilst the people to do it have been reduced. This is certainly true if the same standard of living for the combining trade is to be kept up. As the proportion taken by the combining trade is larger, both by the original action of the combination in altering the rate of payment and by the additional numbers in it, those remaining in other trades must materially increase their efforts, or they must accept a materially reduced wage. Possibly in such a case they may do both if the conditions are already much against them.

Now it may be argued that in this way the combination will avoid having to submit to a reduction of wages. Doubtless to some extent it is the case. But there must be a sufficient reason for this, and nothing but absolute necessity will induce it. Those who must submit to the most adverse conditions or starve will doubtless struggle on and get what little they can. But those who are stronger and in better circumstances will not submit to work harder and accept less wages. They will simply give up their business. If they must work at all, they will crowd into the now over full combining trade. Having by their skill and physical or mental strength sustained a higher and more difficult position, they probably find themselves easily able to displace others. In any case they add to the number who have left indirect competition and direct co-operation and have come to directly compete.

With the exception then of crushing more the starving wretches who cannot help themselves, there is as yet no way visible of keeping up the other processes. This would leave us at the point it is desired to pass, namely, that the trade combination can only raise wages at the expense of other trades. It is true it is now shown that so far as the supposed increase obtained by the combination is taken from other occupations or grades of employment, it is from the weakest. The point must be carried beyond this. Even these cannot increase their efforts to an unlimited extent. Besides which the tendency already noticed to enter the combining trade is all the more intensified. So that we are once more brought to the same point. The action of the combination brings some out of direct co-operation to direct competition. In other words, there is but one conclusion, which is that less wages will be produced for the combining trade and more people will have to share in it. The combination has brought others to struggle against its members in the same trade for the wages it will afford. And it has caused those now coming in to leave the work they were doing which was most required to make a uniform whole. That work is less efficiently done; there is consequently less demand for the work of those who combined, and more persons share what the demand brings with it of wages.

To enable the mind the better to grasp the point it may again be illustrated by means of the flag-stone. Imagine it, however, so large that a number of men are engaged at different portions of it. It may be taken to represent the standard of living. The flag-stone must be raised uniformly. In the case to be illustrated the production must be of those things which will find purchasers, and this no combination can control. Now the price test induces each man, whether master or workman, to go to the point where he can do the best for himself. That is where his strength is most needed. One section threatens to let the flag-stone go down unless the price test is modified for their benefit. The gauge is tampered with to satisfy them. Inevitably more lifters will come there to share the better conditions. Just as inevitably the flag-stone will be lowered all round whilst about that point a number of men cluster and struggle for a place to get hold in the hope of getting some wages for it. The more the process goes on the more will the flag-stone be lowered. In proportion to the strength of restrictive trade combinations (rings, trusts, and trades unions) will the standard of living be lowered. The members of the combination itself will suffer. Only a quantity of other commodities will be produced proportionate to the commodities produced by them.

It must clearly be borne in mind that a trade combination can only include those in the same department of production. If by any means other departments can be brought into combination, the more are included the more is the object defeated. The additional money obtained by combination must come out of one department or another of the production or from the consumer. The consumer protects himself by comparatively ceasing to demand —the truth is that his means are limited and he could not demand more if he would. Another department of production therefore must suffer. Trade combinations imagine the masters in their own trade must forfeit the price. Suppose they do. What occurs? Some of them would naturally be making only just a little more than some of the men. A man does not suddenly increase his earnings to an unlimited extent by becoming a master, or there would soon be more masters. On the increase of wages those who were earning least find they would be better off amongst those in the Union rather than amongst the masters against whom the combination was fighting. They therefore leave being masters and join the other class, struggling with them for the same wages, instead of competing with the masters for the labour of the other class. So that, even if it were true that the additional money wages must come out of the pockets of the masters, the conclusion is the same in the end. In an indirect way this driving of masters out of business does occur. It prevents men of small capital from undertaking business on their own account, and leaves the whole matter in the hands of great firms and Companies.

From these considerations it will be apparent how a man can better his class by getting out of it.

It will readily be perceived that the man who leaves one class of labourers and becomes a master labourer in producing the same commodity ceases to compete against the men he was amongst and begins to compete against the masters for men of the class he has just left.

From what has been said it will also be seen that there is no solidarity of interest amongst the weekly wage earners. There is only the interest which they have in common with all wage earners to the very highest—that wealth should be abundant.

It also appears that the evils attributed to competition are the result of stopping competition. This causes some to compete more than they should because others, under unwise influences, compete less than they ought. The natural remedy is more free competition—competition encouraged and not discouraged.

It will be seen that the gist of this method, like that of the last chapter, consists of two steps. In both cases the combination is taken at its strongest point. Every advantage is given to it in the argument. And so far as it is a combination to interfere with or hinder competition, in other words, to raise money wages, it is shown to be an unmitigated evil. In the previous chapter price was regarded. The two steps were that the additional price of the labour was added to the commodity, and that the added price with various profits must be paid by the members of the combination, who thus lost more than they gained. A counteracting influence to that was, however, noticed in the fact that not having the additional money to pay with, they did not, strictly speaking, pay more for the commodities, but were unable to buy them at all. Thus their real wages were diminished.

In the present chapter wealth production only is considered. It is noticed that the whole process under a system of division of labour and exchange is one of co-operation. What is required to be done is indicated by the rise and fall of the prices offered for the doing of it. These indicate the utility of any service to those who demand it. It is seen that this alone will produce a perfect co-operation in which every one finds the place at which his services are most required. The inequalities are natural and inevitable.

Now, supposing that by the combination of a certain number a better rate than free competition allows is obtained by that number, the evil is twofold. The production of wealth is hindered. In truth this is because of several tendencies. Probably the members of the combination do less. For even though they may not be inclined to work less at the increased prices, the demand is less on account of the higher price. But the tendency on which emphasis has been laid is that others will cease their own efforts and come to the work for which a better price is now paid. Herein also lies the other evil. For while their work is undone they are struggling with the others for the now smaller total of production.

If there was an unlimited supply of money, of which no one could hinder the circulation, the combination might possibly not injure their members; but in such a case the additional money could be of no additional benefit. All the money which circulates must measure wealth or services, otherwise it will not circulate. To hinder the natural exchange of labour and the production and exchange of wealth is to hinder the money circulating and to reduce real wages.

Again, if those who, by the combination, find themselves having to give a larger share to the members of the combination would consent to go on, regardless of the diminishing of their share of wealth, the combination might better the condition of its members at the expense of others. But would any one venture to suggest the probability of such a proceeding. It is against reason and all experience. For those who have possession of some secret it is indeed possible to raise their wages to a monopoly price. They may raise them to such a price that the market will decline to take their productions rather than pay a higher price. But such a result is because the secret operates as an addition to the ability and skill of the persons possessing it, and is not attainable by others. If the skill is attainable by others this influence cannot be felt.

Thus, a combination finds itself met by a tendency it cannot control. The employer will not willingly continue his work and submit to a forced increase of wages out of his pocket. Other workmen will not continue to accept a less share of the total productions because the combination have resolved to take a larger one. If this were possible, a few might, by combination, reduce the remainder to the condition of slavery under them. But the facts are otherwise.

The advantages of free trade in labour are thus amply demonstrated. And a restriction is an evil, whether imposed from without or voluntarily submitted to. Professor Fawcett imagined that strikes were an inevitable feature of the modern system of free sale of labour. He concluded that they were inseparable from free contracts. Strikes of individuals may be inevitable; but that was hardly his meaning. A strike by one at a time would do little harm. It is the principle of combination by which workmen injure themselves. And it has been all along insisted that they do injure themselves. Experience shows that to contend that they injure other workmen is not an argument which counts for much. It must be brought home to them that they injure themselves. One man may decline to work if he prefers the ease to the labour. He may persuade another to take a holiday with him, for the pleasure of his company. But if he imagines he will raise his real wages by inducing one or any number to join him in declining to work whilst the same trade is open to all; or if he imagines he will be in a stronger position to-morrow by declining to work to-day, he is mistaken.

These considerations will have an important bearing on those of the duties of government with regard to the production of wealth.

CHAPTER XV

POLITICS

THE science of economics has often been spoken of and for a long time exclusively so as political economy. The expression doubtless arose partly from the history of its study. For in its earliest days what has now grown into a Science of Economics was involved in the study of methods of government, and particularly in the mode of raising taxes. The expression is not altogether inapposite. What domestic economy is to the household, the art which corresponds to political economy is to the nation. The science in each case has reference to the feeding, clothing and housing of the family or nation. Yet it is very possible, and, indeed, convenient, to assign a special province to each of the two studies, politics and economics. It is with economics that the present inquiry is concerned. But as with other sciences, there is a point at which the two touch each other, and it is important to deal with that point. Briefly expressed, it is a question of what the science would indicate a government has to do with the providing of a supply of wealth to the nation over which it rules.

The more purely political questions will find no place here. These would include, for instance, questions of sovereignty, constitution and franchise;

of who may be spoken of as the supreme power in a state; who should manage the affairs of the nation; whether all should have equal rights in that management, or whether some should have more than others; if the latter principle should be adopted, who should have precedence; whether it should be decided by sex, merit, wealth or birth. The same remark applies to the form in which the visible authority should shape itself; whether the nation or sovereign power in the nation should decide each question by a separate expression of its will; or whether the authority should be delegated to one or more persons or chambers; and, in case the sovereign power recognised as possessing the franchise chooses to delegate the authority given by the franchise, how the persons to whom the authority is delegated shall be determined; whether by birth or by election.

These are questions of pure politics. The relations existing between the nation in question and other nations are also pure politics, except so far as the raising and expenditure of money may be concerned. Many questions with which governments have to do are rather questions of law than of either politics or economics.

Even some things in which the payment of money is involved are strictly questions of politics. For instance, the advisability or otherwise of paying members of a representative legislative assembly for their services is a question which does not come within the scope of what is here meant by economics. It may be stated, without discussion, that whatever might be the result of a full consideration of the subject, it is perfectly certain that no such payments should be made for the express purpose of enabling men to set up pretended class interests which true economics prove not to exist, and the setting up of which tends to national poverty.

The right of taxation has already been treated of as belonging to government, and the subject of the imposition of taxes has been dealt with at sufficient length. The expenditure of the taxes thus imposed will not be specially treated of in this investigation.

Two political subjects having special relation to the department of economics will be dealt with in the present chapter — government debts and government interference with the production and distribution of wealth. In a succeeding chapter the subject of coinage and money currency so far as it is or can be affected by governments, will be under consideration.

From time to time, governments have found and still find occasions on which they have deemed it necessary or advisable to expend money which has not been raised by means of immediate taxation, but obtained by way of loan. The contention has been that the expenditure was for the benefit of subsequent generations and not for the time then present. Now it may at once be conceded that it is advisable that taxation should, as far as possible, continue constant from year to year. It is not desirable that it should greatly vary up and down in succeeding years. For this purpose it might be contended with considerable show of reason that governments should occasionally have balances in hand and sometimes be temporarily in debt. Such a plan accords with the methods usually adopted by business men for their own purposes in their dealings with bankers.

The system of government loans now under discussion is, however, very different from that just indicated. The loans remain outstanding for many years, and come to be regarded as perpetual institutions. For the present purpose they may be regarded as divisible into two classes. In the one case the loan is expended for purposes which require that the wealth and services obtained by it should be immediately dissipated. It is not expected to produce revenue. Of this class are loans for expenditure in wars and military expeditions. In the other case the loan is used for the erecting of permanent works, which it is hoped will pay interest on the expenditure. Of this class are loans for the preparation and opening of railways. It will be convenient to deal with the two classes separately.

With regard to the first class, the money borrowed must of necessity be paid for one or more of three things—the stock already accumulated of war material and supplies for maintenance of those who are to carry on the war; the supply of further material and maintenance; and the wages of those who actually carry on the campaign. These three heads will include all the expenditure which can be incurred in this class of enterprise for which borrowing may take place: the stock previously prepared, the further quantity supplied before the conclusion of the enterprise (and not afterwards), and the wages paid for work before that conclusion. So far as this material and labour is supplied by the nation itself, for whom the borrowing takes place, it is obvious that there is no justification whatever for borrowing. The work is all done and the commodities are all supplied by the nation before the conclusion of the enterprise for which the borrowing takes place. To leave the nation with a debt to pay afterwards, is nothing less than iniquitous if the enterprise has been undertaken after a sufficiently long warning; or if it has continued for a sufficiently long time to enable the government to adjust its finances and impose the taxation. And this latter qualification must be understood to refer only to urgency of expense. If there has been time to impose the taxes, it is no excuse that it might have caused discontent. To imagine that the nation cannot bear the expense is obviously contrary to actual facts. The material has been supplied. The work has been done. The nation has done all this. To pretend that it must afterwards be paid for is merely a pretence. It may readily be seen that there was no excuse for the nation borrowing money from some of its number to pay for what in truth it actually prepared and did for itself.

What really takes place in such a case of borrowing is that at once all prices of property rise. The prices of war material rise out of proportion to other species of capital, but that is a matter which cannot be foreseen, and may be neglected here. The investment in that kind of capital might bring profit or might cause loss to the person investing. The unusual profit cannot therefore be discussed as a matter to be remedied. The general rise of prices is another matter. If, as the war or other enterprise proceeded, the taxes for carrying it on were annually collected, the whole matter would adjust itself.

Let the incidence of taxation be what it may, the work must be done: so far as the mass of the nation are concerned, it must be paid for: so far as all who actually supply the material and carry on the campaign are concerned, it is paid for. The additional prices caused by the unusual expenditure may raise money wages. For that very reason they will raise the cost of preparing the capital which must be prepared. That will raise the price of similar capital already prepared. But the same unusual expenditure and raising of prices must also raise the price of the land. It is necessary to the production of the wealth, not only that which is bought by the government, but also that which all those who are receiving these higher prices must have.

On whichever of the three elements taxation falls, it falls on something of which the price is already advanced, and on something, therefore, which is prepared to meet it without real loss. The method of taxation would be liable to the same examination as to the justice of its incidence as at other times. But the extraordinary taxation could only fall in the same way as the ordinary amount. As the ordinary taxation is more or less justly carried out, so that would be.

The borrowing, however, introduces another element. Instead of paying its way, the government goes into debt to some of its subjects. This can only be to those who already possess property, either in the way of money or of something on which they can obtain money. At once the money is paid away. Prices are raised just as much as if the money had been obtained by taxation. Those who need land or capital must pay for it as if the government were not preparing a legacy of debt. Those who labour must have wealth for consumption as at other times. Their wages are somewhat higher on account of the greater demand for labour, but the price of their subsistence is also increased. Since so many are withdrawn from ordinary wealth production for the special service of the time, more work devolves upon them to raise mere subsistence. They cannot obtain wages disproportionately high or even perhaps proportionately as high as usual. Their great need of wealth compels them to offer their labour at such prices as they can obtain. The additional price at least goes in higher prices of commodities. But meantime, those who could lend money get themselves installed as creditors of the government to be paid at some time when this special period is over, and out of the wealth to be then prepared.

It is pretended that these wars are undertaken for succeeding generations. It is open to argument whether the owners of property are not the people who have most interest in such wars and other special efforts. But let that be disregarded. A great undertaking has been accomplished by a nation. After allowing its people to undergo the privation of the effort, it compels them to undergo further privation to set themselves free from the claims of a class who happened to be possessed of property; clearly this ought not to be. It must not be forgotten that the property increased in price to the profit of its owners, whilst they managed also to get themselves credited with that profit for future redemption.

This applies to borrowing in the nation itself. Strictly the question is what amount of actual wealth produced and labour exerted was taken from the nation. But in the absence of any interference with the currency, the probability is that money borrowed outside the nation will again leave the nation for goods; so that the borrowing community will really have obtained its loan in such a case from another nation. In that case there would be a real loan from nation to nation of labour and effort. The preceding remarks would not, therefore, apply to the case. But it need hardly be said that a nation should not continue in debt in this way longer than was absolutely necessary after the conclusion of its special enterprise. After that there would be labour enough at liberty to repay the loan.

With regard to the other class somewhat different considerations apply. There is left, not merely a successful triumph and repelling of foes, or lesson of humiliation; a tangible, profit-bearing piece of capital now belongs to the nation. So far as the loan has been obtained outside the nation, it appears correct to conclude that the borrowing nation has really borrowed useful capital, by the aid of which it will be able to pay interest on the loan and the more successfully to produce wealth for repayment. Not that the obtaining of money from elsewhere is in itself the advantage. The prices are none the better for being raised all round. But the higher prices will tend to bring actual wealth from other countries, and will thereby save the borrowing nation from having to perform all the labour required for the special undertaking. Whilst that is on hand they will be provided with wealth from elsewhere, and will repay the loan after it is completed. A very amusing thing has, however, often occurred, in that nations or peoples have borrowed money from elsewhere, and then have set up, or at any rate maintained, a wall of protective tariffs to keep out the wealth, for the bringing in of which the borrowing was alone useful.

So far as the money borrowed within the nation for this second class is concerned, and to the extent to which the wealth which it represents is also produced within the realm, the same considerations apply as to borrowing for an unproductive undertaking. All the wealth has been prepared and the services rendered by the nation. There is nothing absolutely to require that it should not have been entirely paid for as the work proceeded. In fact, it is paid for. But from Peter the government borrows to pay Paul, who, in his turn, repays Peter for the use of the capital and commodities which he lends or sells to Paul. Of course Peter and Paul here are classes of persons.

There is probably not the same rise of prices in this case as in that of a war. But more is made of the need of borrowing than is necessary, even where something remains as the result of the expenditure.

The whole proceeding, that is, of governments

borrowing from those from whom they might obtain the amount by taxation, arises from the way in which those who are responsible for government allow their eyes to be blinded by money. They do not see that wealth is that by which alone the nation can be sustained and an enterprise carried on. They do not realize that money was there before they borrowed, and will be there afterwards : that they have merely altered the mode of its circulation. They fail to understand that the wealth by which the nation has been sustained and the enterprise carried out has all been produced at the close of the enterprise, and they might as well have had it by taxation as by the pretence of a loan.

But in the present case some allowance may be made. In the case of a war every right feeling would seem to indicate that all the nation should bear their share at once and carry it to a conclusion. Nothing will be left at the end of it by which it can be said the following generation is bettered. The country will probably be poorer, because the nation's energies have been diverted from the production of capital and devoted to fighting. In the case of a railway, however, for instance, the succeeding generation will be really the better. Its labours will be lightened by the use of that piece of capital. There is something real and useful as the result of such an undertaking as that. The men of the present generation may therefore without injustice make a claim. The succeeding generation will enjoy real benefit from their labours. There is no particular reason why the revenue to be obtained from the capital they have prepared should merely go to reduce the taxation of the next generation. To the extent of the capital actually left as the result of their labours, the government may, without injustice, resolve to borrow. Those who at this time are engaged in additional labour or possess capital may accordingly, if they so choose, save up the benefit of that labour by making themselves creditors of the government. Thus as old men they may enjoy the benefit or ease, whilst the next generation maintain them, in consideration of the work they did in preparing a useful piece of capital when they were younger. This is a mode of expressing the result. Some may of course be old even at this time, who nevertheless prefer to have a share in this undertaking. They do not need all their subsistence, and have a desire to leave something of a fortune to their own children or others.

By thus justifying governments in borrowing for works of permanent utility, it must not be concluded that there is any intention to commend the undertaking of all such enterprises on the part of governments. With regard to some works there seems no way but that governments should undertake them. This applies to sea walls and similar undertakings; including roads, bridges, and all permanently beneficial works, which produce no revenue directly. It is true that roads and bridges are not strictly works from which it is impossible to collect a revenue. It is none the less expedient that such things should be paid for by government out of taxation. They can be used by the people without any present personal service by government servants. This is a very different thing from a government undertaking to carry the subjects of the realm on railways free of charge. That implies the providing of carriage room, haulage power, and personal conduct of and attention to trains. It is one thing to give people a road to walk or even to drive along : it is another thing to carry them.

Even the very providing and working of such things as railways, though on the same method as in the case of private enterprise, requires careful consideration. In the case of works which are important to the nation, but which can produce no revenue by the ordinary methods, there is no inducement to individual enterprise. Yet the works may on all hands be conceded to be of great importance to the community. The great difficulty is in collecting the revenue from those who must benefit. In such cases the nation or community should, without doubt, undertake the work and obtain the cost from the taxes. A sea wall may preserve the land from which taxes must be drawn. And, of course, for that very reason, even if for no other, the land should bear the taxes—not, as generally occurs, some persons who have nothing to do with it and obtain no benefit from it. The same might be said of roads and bridges which also make land more valuable.

But the case of a railway which is capable of producing a revenue is altogether different. If that is needed individuals will be ready to provide it and reap the benefit of it. There is no special reason why a government should interfere in such a matter. In providing gas, electric light, water or tramways, for a place there is a special reason why the govern-

s

ment of that town or district should undertake the matter itself. It is essential that the undertakers of such a work should have a monopoly granted to them. And it may be laid down as a general rule that any government should itself undertake what can only otherwise be accomplished by the granting of a monopoly. A monopolist will naturally take care to have the best possible profit. Allowance must be made for the generally admitted fact that governments cannot carry on industrial undertakings as cheaply as private enterprise. There is still, however, a balance in favour of an undertaking reasonably carried on for the benefit of the community under the control of public representatives, over a similar undertaking carried on by a monopolist for his profit.

In the case of a railway, however, there is no need whatever for a monopoly beyond that conceded to all individuals of owning land subject to taxation. If after one body of persons have constructed a railway, another body should desire to construct another between the same two places, the government should offer no impediment whatever. Not only will the public be better served by the rivalry of the two companies, but a fresh district is sure to be traversed by the new railway to the benefit of that district. Even if the new railway should be proposed to be run parallel and near to the other, the government would have no objection if individuals think they see need for it and are willing to undertake it. That would seldom occur. For their own interests the new undertakers would endeavour to find as much new ground as possible.

Some have thought that governments would save waste by avoiding competition. But perhaps enough has been said in defence of competition in the preceding chapter. If two railway companies can both make profit by running in competition and practically parallel to each other it is evident there is need for them both. It must not be forgotten that more work is not necessarily accomplished by setting up one undertaking to take the position of two. And it is infinitely better that a man should be kept at his best by the remembrance that his neighbour is probably also doing his best. Each of them serves himself and the community better for this consciousness, even though they have so well shown their ability as to become high railway company officials.

It is sometimes argued that governments should construct railways for the purpose of opening up districts. Now it can hardly be denied that there are occasions when, for its own purposes, a government may expediently construct light railways. A newly-subdued district, the government of which is perhaps difficult, furnishes a possible instance. But if a district is ready to be opened up, if its productions are needed, and it is capable of profitable use, individuals will be alive to the opportunity. There is very great danger of governments being influenced by those who are more anxious to have money expended in a railway than to use the railway when it is constructed. Railways are or should be made for inhabitants. Inhabitants do not exist for railways. When the inhabitants have arrived or begin to arrive they will discover their own needs. Until they arrive the government can usually better employ itself about its own concerns, than by diverting people from the work of making their present district flourish to opening up districts which to all appearance are not yet wanted. It is useless for a nation to scatter itself all over its territory if it finds a portion of the district more profitable for its use. It is a matter for the people themselves to decide upon.

The next subject which it was proposed to deal with is that of government interference with wealth production. The assistance a government may expediently give to production has already been sufficiently noticed in dealing with roads and bridges and with the supply of water, etc., in towns. For it must be borne in mind that government generally is here spoken of without making any special distinction between imperial and local authorities.

There is, however, a very great difference between assistance and interference. It is one thing to supply what is on all hands agreed to be generally useful: it is quite another to hinder, or to prescribe minute regulations for individuals in the management of their business. There are two or three distinct grounds on which a government may claim to interfere in such management. The first of such grounds which will be here noticed is that of security to the life, health, and limbs of the persons employed. Now it need hardly be pointed out that a government must carry out its interference by means of officials. They not only require to be paid, but are not necessarily more perfect in their views as to the best means of securing safety than some of the remainder of the nation. They may, without doubt, make a special study of the subject. But so also may those who are actually engaged in the employments referred to.

With regard to the safety of life and limb there is a very obvious mode of saving much vexatious interference, and also a great portion of the expense of the inspection. If a person properly goes on the premises of another, and if by reason of the negligence of that other or his servants, injury is done to the visitor by any machinery or other contrivance, the person on whose premises the injury has been done is by a reasonable law liable to pay damages for the injury. Now if, in the same way, the occupier of the premises were liable to his servants for a similar negligence, it would afford abundant security that his best endeavours would be used to avoid any such accident. In England an exception has been made by the judges operating harshly in this respect upon servants, but it seems likely to be remedied by the legislature. When this has been accomplished there can be no need for any great amount of inspection. Such inspection as may be continued may take more the form of approving and certifying that certain arrangements are as good as can possibly be suggested than of absolute interference. This would throw upon the occupier of the premises the onus of continuing any arrangements he may prefer. It would thus prevent (what it is said has already been found to be a disadvantage) the ordering of arrangements which were probably no less dangerous than the arrangements the employers themselves preferred.

With regard to unhealthy employments, it is obvious that some occupations must remain unhealthy. Governments can, without doubt, render assistance by ascertaining the best means of minimizing the evil. They may, even without giving any good cause of complaint, rigorously enforce such regulations as are undoubtedly beneficial. Even in this case, however, there is a limit which wise governments will take care not to exceed in their interference. And the abolition of the poverty which arises from bad economic institutions would tend to avoid the ill health, for it often results as much from irregular and badly-timed work and inferior living as from the occupations themselves.

The second ground on which governments may claim to interfere with the production and distribution of wealth refers only to persons who may be said to be limited, with regard to their liberty, by age or sex. The principle of interference, not only with the conditions, but even with the hours of employment of women and young persons, has been fully admitted in England and elsewhere. This principle, of course, needs to be rightly applied, but with the principle itself no attempt will here be made to find fault. Nor is it at all likely that in its application it will be abused.

There is a very clear ground for admitting an interference with the labour of women and young persons still under the control of their parents—a ground which does not apply to adult males. That ground is the limitation of their liberty just referred to. Already, and from the necessity of the case, their liberty is incomplete. The interference of government becomes an interference to protect them, not against the freedom to contract with their employers, but against the influence which might be exerted upon them by those to whom their liberty is more or less subjugated. They cannot enter into an entirely free contract for their own benefit. Their earnings are not their own. This is clearly so in the case of young persons. And in the case of women the influence of the father or husband is a sufficient reason for the interference of the government. The government interferes, not to restrain their natural liberty, but to increase it. By their position it is limited. It may be spoken of as subject already to a minus sign, and the government further limits it by a minus sign which in the double minus becomes plus.

Finally, however, there is another ground on which governments have claimed to interfere with wealth production. At any rate, there is another case. The ground is not so clear. The case is that of limiting the hours during which adult males may carry on their employments. To describe this as mere wanton interference with individual liberty would doubtless cause resentment. And yet no other valid ground can be suggested. The truth is that the interference is undertaken at the instance of combinations, who imagine that they can better their conditions by hindering the production of wealth. A person starting from the idea that he can benefit himself by persuading another not to labour or produce wealth, will naturally desire to persuade as many as possible to the same effect. Having done his utmost in persuading them that they also will be benefited by the combination to work less, the transition is very natural from persuasion to coercion. Those who will not be induced by persuasion to labour less must be restrained by legal restriction.

Now if there were any truth in the idea that one man could benefit himself by hindering another from working, then there might be some ground for a legally imposed time limit. As the truth happens to be, however, that he cannot thus benefit himself, the whole ground for the restriction is abolished. No man will perform labour except for what he regards as a sufficient reason. It is equally certain that he will not unduly prolong his labours, except to gratify a desire which influences him more than the desire for ease or pleasure. It would therefore be a hardship upon him to interfere with that lawful gratification of desire. And seeing that the hardship is not called for by any benefit it can possibly confer upon others, the restriction must perforce be described as mere wanton and vexatious interference with liberty. It is admitted that this follows from the demonstrations given in the previous chapter and apparently now for the first time given, but it is none the less true for that.

CHAPTER XVI

COST OF PRODUCTION

THE laws which influence prices in the market were considered in a previous chapter. We are now in a position to observe to some extent the ulterior influences on the prices of wealth. The market is the central feature of the science. In it the demand and supply with which the science has to deal are balanced. In this sense the market extends to all the places and transactions which come within the sphere of buying and selling; whatever may be the subject of the transaction, whether land, labour, or commodities. Howsoever the place may be usually known where the buying and selling takes place, whether as market, exchange, shop, auction room, warehouse, or office, the same general laws apply to the prices of the transactions which take place. But outside the market there are other influences affecting and being affected by it.

Some little mention was made of the method adopted by Adam Smith, and elaborated by Ricardo, of referring values to the labour included in their production. These values were spoken of by them as the natural values to which the market values constantly tended to approximate. Now this method has all the subtlety which is necessary to sustain almost unlimited error. There is some truth underlying it. Commodities which require much more labour in their production than others are likely to realize more when they reach the market, or very soon cease (absolutely or comparatively) to be produced. But it is not for that reason true that differences of value are owing to the different amounts of labour which have been required to produce commodities. A brilliant artist full of a grand inspiration will sometimes create more value in a few days than even he himself could at other times create in as many weeks or months of much more tedious effort; while most people could not create that value in years of more toilsome labour.

It would be monstrous to pretend that if no more labour has been necessary for the production of one commodity than another, it is no more valuable. Even the most abandoned Socialist, who contended that all the labour of every individual should be confiscated to the State, would not pretend that a better painted and more artistic picture, for instance, was not more valuable because it had not taken more painting. Even though the nation laid violent hands on every picture painted, it would even then know that some of its pictures were more valuable than others. And no one would think of fixing on the most valuable by asking which had required the most labour. If it be answered that there is a difference in qualities of labour, and that also must be considered, then the method is at once abandoned in favour of some other method of ascertaining values. For it is not merely the intensity of labour which causes a difference in the value of its product. There is beyond that a difference which can only be valued as other differences are—in the market. It may not be a perfect method of valuation. It may be that the tastes of those who determine the value are not at all what some would desire. But it is the only method available to us. Value can only be fixed by reference to the desires of those who must enjoy it.

If ulterior causes were admitted in this matter of value, it might not be altogether absurd to speak of the value of any commodity as the maintenance of the labourers necessary to produce it. This is really what Ricardo's natural value means. But a natural value conceived of in that way is not only impossible to be ascertained, but absolutely untrue. It is beyond dispute that labourers' maintenance operates as an ulterior cause in the creation of values. For commodities which are desired and cannot be had without labour must of necessity have value. Labourers require maintenance. They will not undergo fatigue to satisfy the desires of another without something which will give them maintenance. But their maintenance is not the measure of value of their labour. Ricardo admitted that when he spoke of a market price differing from the natural price. If it were so, there could be no measuring the value at all. For maintenance is so very varied that there could be no perfect settlement as to what maintenance really consisted of. That is the first uncertainty about taking ulterior causes as bases of argument. The labourer requires subsistence, but that is a varying quantity, and is not then the value of his labour. That also varies in quantity, intensity, and quality.

Again, even supposing that labour were all equally

efficient, there are other things to be considered in ascertaining the value of a commodity besides the labour contained in it. Ricardo endeavoured to reduce values to differences of labour by bringing into the value of commodities, not only all the labour directly applied to them, but also labour required for the production of the capital necessary for its assistance. Thus the value of commodities carried by sea included the labour required for the building of the ship. That is interesting as a reflection, but it is not the proper means of ascertaining the value of the commodity, even if it were a possible means. A number of contingencies may enter into the question even of cost of ship hire. The main object of the ship's journey may be something else, and the owner can afford to accept a lower freight for that reason. Or the ship may have been built under other conditions from those now obtaining; so that its owner is in a better or worse position to require payment to recoup him for his outlay. If improvements have been effected in ship-building, the fact that his ship was built under the inferior system will not give him a higher freight for his commodities; or make it or them more valuable. If by any means ships have become more scarce, he will not accept less because he obtained his for less money, nor will the ship be itself less valuable. A still better illustration may be found in the case of the produce of the earth. The value of corn does not vary exactly with the labour required to bring it to market. The season has much to do with it. A bad harvest will make corn dear without any additional labour, just as a good harvest will make it cheap.

So that, even though cost of production were entirely the determining cause of value, it would be inaccurate to refer it all to differences of labour. The natural value of Smith and Ricardo was not the true natural value. The method was entirely bad. The natural value is the market value. By no other means can value be ascertained than by bringing the object to market, or comparing it with what is in the market. That this is the natural value a very little consideration will show. There may be ulterior causes, but all the ulterior causes would have to be considered; and what Smith and Ricardo have taken as the determining causes are only some of them. There is no warrant for any one to take his own ideas of ulterior causes, and then to say that although facts indicate one value, yet that another value is the natural one. Once again let it be observed what determines value, so that it may be seen what is in truth the natural value.

The first question to ask in determining the value of any commodity is this, Is it wanted? If not, it has no value. If nobody cares to have it, it is worth nothing, no matter how much labour has been expended in its production. That is the demand. Now, the method which speaks of natural value as determined by differences of labour, entirely ignores the fact that the demand must be considered. This was indeed the great fault of the method. There could be no wonder at economists imagining they found a natural value distinct from the market value when they neglected such an important factor.

The next thing to consider in determining the

value of a commodity is not what it cost to produce, but how much is available to supply the demand. It may be very valuable, although originally obtained at little cost, if it possesses rarity and beauty or other desirability. And it may have cost a great deal to obtain, and be worth very little after all, for another abundant supply may be available. This is the natural value—the real value, and not some ideal set up as a natural value.

Now these are the very considerations which were noticed as determining the market value, namely, demand and supply. Not only is market value the only ascertainable value, it is the true and only real and natural value. It is where the demand and supply meet that the value is determined. The subject and its complement must be brought together in the market for the most part. To only a small extent do people in a high state of civilization supply their own wants without buying or selling. It is in supplying these wants that the value is fixed. That behind and away from the immediate point of connection which determines the value there are causes to be considered in their proper relation does not admit of dispute. But they must be kept in their place. And the causes behind each must have due weight.

In speaking of ulterior causes of value, it is necessary not only to consider what influences supply, but also what influences demand. Now, more than one influence may affect the demand. Demand will naturally rise with increase of population. The same result will, however, be brought about by the opening of connection with new markets; that is, with markets in populations which have previously existed as peoples, but not as purchasers of the commodities in question. Further than that, the same population may be induced to consume much more of a commodity if it become more accessible to them by reason of its reduced price. For human beings can greatly increase their consumption of wealth if sufficient variety be offered. As mentioned at the outset, they do not stop at the supply of mere food and water. It is true that their demand, to be effective in influencing the market, must be accompanied by a supply of other commodities in exchange. This is true with regard to both increased population, new markets, and increase of demand in the same population. But this simply points to another influence at work affecting the demand. Anything which enables the same population to produce more wealth will tend to increase their demand for the commodities of others, provided that their own wealth is not the same in kind. If they have abundance, they will consume more wealth. As they will prefer variety, they are likely to be all the better customers for the commodities of others. All these are influences outside the market operating to increase the demand, and consequently to raise prices in the market. Whatever tends in a contrary direction will have a contrary effect—a diminished population, the loss of markets, the making of the commodities in question more difficult of purchase, and the smaller productions of possible customers. These influences operating outside the market will tend to reduce demand and lower prices.

But, on the other hand, there are influences affecting the supply. It was remarked that the price in the market of commodities would ultimately tend towards the cost of bringing them to market. This may be spoken of as the cost of production. But the price in the market is not immediately referable to the cost of production. It may be higher or lower according to the circumstances of the case. It is fixed by the state of supply and demand. Other influences at work may affect the prices, but only by affecting supply or demand. Competition to supply may lower prices by increasing supply. Trade combinations and protective tariffs may raise prices by diminishing supply. Artificial contrivances must act on supply. A strike diminishes supply. So also do the steadier influences which form so large a feature in the operation of trade combinations. Such is the fixing of rates of wages below which members of such combinations are expected not to accept work at all. Such also are the various contrivances for keeping up prices by adhering to old methods of work, and even of preventing the importation of work done in other towns. The insisting on apprenticeships is probably no great cause of diminishing supply, especially seeing that, in proportion as a trade is difficult to get into, there will be competition for places in it. It is not the contrivances for keeping new applicants out, but the real difficulty of learning a trade which influences the supply of men to it.

So far as trade combinations operate at all, they do it by influencing supply. And the same applies to all other artificial contrivances. The demand, which depends on the consumption of wealth by others and the supply of wealth in exchange for it, can only be increased by the supply of more wealth. And that can only be done by encouraging natural competition to supply.

But although no influence can affect values except by acting upon supply and demand, it is nevertheless true that cost of production of commodities has a great effect upon prices in the market. It is perhaps not sufficiently accurate and expressive to say that the market price constantly tends to cost of production. Cost of production, strictly speaking, can only be said to be the actual cost to the master labourer who sells the commodity. On that he must put his profit. For by the profit he is paid for his labour in carrying on the business. In the case of undertakings, the profits of which are paid to the capitalists who originally supplied the capital (or those who now hold their shares), any additional profits go to them and not to those who have managed the undertaking. But for the present purpose no difference is made by this fact. The excess over cost of production goes to pay the proprietor of the undertaking whatever form that proprietor may assume. And if on the other hand the commodities fail to realize the cost, that proprietor must bear the loss. The supply in the market is influenced by the existence and amount of that profit. If the profit be abnormally high, it will have the effect of bringing others into the business to compete against those already in it. Thus by the increased supply the prices will be lowered.

T

If there is no profit, but a loss, or even an exceptionally low profit, the tendency will be that others will avoid the trade; and some will even leave it at the earliest opportunity. By that means supply will be diminished and prices raised.

Only in this way can cost of production influence the market. The price is not determined by the cost of production. In a sense the cost of production is determined by the price. For the cost to the consumer may without impropriety be called the cost of production, although it includes the producers' own profits. And those profits are capable of modification to meet the market whether the modification means increase or decrease. But on the other hand, the cost of production to the seller does influence the price by affecting the supply. In a word, cost of production is one of the influences outside the market which affect price; as was noticed with regard to the influences operatting upon demand. Cost of production operates upon supply.

Now all the influences which act upon prices through supply, may be said to do so by affecting cost of production. This at any rate applies to the ordinary industries, in which the relations of employer and employed obtain, and in which raw material or rent of land is an element to be considered. So that these influences affect the market through an ulterior cause which is itself outside the market. Cost of production is outside the market: these influences are outside that cost. To speak of value as though it were merely the cost of the labour required to produce an article is to neglect some steps in the reasoning. At each of these steps other factors must be taken into account. To make this clear, let it be considered what are the elements which go to make up or affect cost of production.

We may begin with the cost of labour, as well as at any other point. Let the cost be taken in money, and the efficiency of the money as a purchaser of wealth be disregarded. Even then, the person who employs the labour has to consider not only the money cost but the efficiency. A high-priced labourer may be cheap when the cost of his actually exerted labour is calculated. This is because of his greater effectiveness as a labourer. A low-priced labourer may be dear, when the benefit he has conferred is considered.

So that here at once is an element which itself varies in something besides the mere cost of labour per unit of time. But even more than that is true with regard to labour. There may be those who are paid by results. Their labour is paid for at a uniform rate per unit of work done. And still a difference may occur. For if their work be done irregularly and not steadily as required, their labour will become more costly. In most cases other men must be paid to attend to other matters in connection with their work. The wages of these others probably must go on as fixed charges. In almost all cases there are many fixed charges, which must go on, whether the men work or not. Now if by strikes and stoppages of one kind or another the work is irregularly done; and if occasionally a period of loss is suffered through the men not being at work at all; their labour becomes more costly than if they maintained a steady unfluctuating supply at the same prices. Even when there is no actual stoppage, if by a combination the market prices are affected through diminished supply or threatened strikes, the trade will become irregular. Additional cost will for that reason have to be borne in the way of fixed charges. The labour accordingly becomes more costly.

But labour is not the only element which enters into cost of production. In most instances tools, machinery, or fixed plant will be necessary. The cost of that so far, at any rate, as depreciation and interest on original expenditure are concerned, must be taken into account. Ricardo would have referred all this to the labour of preparing the capital. But that is another step backwards and must not be taken in here. There would be other factors to take into account again. That labour has been merged in the capital and must no longer be spoken of as labour. Capital enters as a distinct element in the production now under examination. The payment for its use as such is the element of cost now to be regarded. It is not the original cost of production of the capital but the price actually now paid for it. That again must be considered capable of modification, with regard to interest on the total, in proportion to the greater or less quantity of capital seeking employment.

Here then is another quite different element of the cost of production, varying by laws of its own; and capable of material reduction or otherwise, by influences which might have a very different effect upon other elements of cost. It is true as already mentioned, that sometimes interest on capital is paid out of profits which are ascertained by differences between actual cost of production and selling price. But in those cases, the managers who carry on the undertaking, instead of taking its additional profits, are paid fixed salaries which must be treated as part of cost of production. In the ordinary instances the interest is regarded as fixed charges, and the employers find the payment for their services in the profits.

Another element of this cost of production must be taken into account. Land is an essential in practically all wealth production. Raw material is drawn from the earth. But manufactures and trade cannot go on without land on which to place mills, factories, workshops, warehouses, shops, etc. And this latter land if smaller in area is not less costly. This is because of the value given to it by situation.

There has been much confusion as to the influence of rent on prices. Even Adam Smith said that rent entered into the composition of the price of commodities in a different way from wages and profit. "High or low wages and profit," said he, "are the causes of high or low price, high or low rent is the effect of it." This will readily be seen to be erroneous in view of what has already been pointed out. It was a survival of the teaching of the Physiocrats. It neglects to note that price depends on demand as well as supply. High or low profit and wages depend on price as much as rent does. Rent therefore enters into the cost of production just in the same way as the other elements of cost. But rent may also vary, according to the institutions of a country and other causes. When a person may hold land untaxed, there is great danger that he will retain it unused until he receives a higher price or better terms than he would be willing to accept under taxation ; that is, if on monopolising it he had to pay taxes upon it, whether he used it or not. This is even beyond the natural increase of rent, arising from the greater necessity for the use of land ; which is the main cause, and affects the price of land through demand. There are other causes influencing rent of land, such as the comparative prohibition against importing commodities from elsewhere ; which is the practical effect of protective tariffs.

One more item must be mentioned as entering into cost of production, namely taxation. This might, and ought to be, merged in the previous item —rent, and thus an item of cost saved. But as it is not, it must be regarded as an additional influence affecting prices by way of supply through cost of production. This also is subject to variation. Taxes may be high or low. The government may be economical or otherwise. The cost of unnecessary interference with its subjects must be paid in the taxes. A National debt is also a costly burden to maintain. And this is an item of cost of production which might easily be saved. The spurious might easily be made real by the imposition of taxes and the payment of the debt. For in all probability it would not be spent on present pleasures, but rather invested in real capital for which the nation would be the better.

These appear to be the items which affect cost of production, with some considerations concerning them. Cost of production is what influences prices, by affecting the supply side of the balance. Some few things are brought to market by producers who have little cost besides their own maintenance to consider. In those cases, supply and demand are not influenced so much by ulterior causes. The commodities in question, are, so to speak, always in the market, if indeed it ought not to be expressed that the labour comes to the commodity market directly.

The question is sometimes discussed whether high or low prices are desirable. All sound economists hold that commodities should be cheap. But there is danger in so expressing it. Everything depends on the cause of the cheapness. For as will shortly be noticed, there is a cheapness which is undesirable. This occurs when the cheapness is through insufficient effective demand brought about by an artificial dearness. And yet it is safer to say that all commodities should be cheap, than that all commodities should be dear. Many hold that goods should be dear. Some of them perhaps notice that in times of good trade, prices have been high, and they have a confused notion that it is the high prices which cause the good trade. Whereas the truth is, that the good trade causes the high prices. Low prices are the inducement to good trade, and high prices tend to slacken the pace of exchange. Others desire dear goods because they imagine that if high prices are paid for goods, high prices must have been paid for their production. They apparently imagine that if the goods can be made dear in any way, the wages must of necessity be raised—which is the most hopeless confusion of cause and effect. Some other confusions are also made to do duty as arguments in this direction.

Others again naturally desiring that their own productions should be high priced, and that the productions they must buy should be low in price, do not realize exactly how it is desirable to them this should be caused. They therefore think, that if by combination affecting supply, they can cause high prices of their goods they will benefit themselves. Whereas it is only when the high prices are caused by an increased demand for those productions that they are benefited. On the other hand, they find cause for rejoicing in the fact that goods imported from elsewhere are cheap; even when that cheapness is the result of their own poverty, and inability to effectively demand the commodities. They should rejoice only when the cheapness is the result of low cost of production.

Perhaps it is better not even to say that commodities should be cheap, though certainly not to contend that they should be dear. In either case it is necessary to observe the cause of the high or low price. The one thing which is certain is that wealth should be abundant. For this purpose, all that can be said to be desirable is that cost of production should be kept low. There is no objection to prices being high if they are the result of a large effective demand from customers who have abundant wealth to offer in return. And there is an objection to prices being low if it is because some economic evil has been hindering trade and production. For this means that, while the persons affected by it have been making their own goods dearer, they have been unable to find employment, and are consequently too poor to buy the productions of others. But still more, and for that very reason there are great objections to goods being purposely made dear by their producers. That is hindering trade in them and causing poverty. High prices from scarcity of wealth are not beneficial.

Of those who have given arguments against cheapness Mr. Henry George stands out prominently. His ideas though, as will be seen, not correct are nevertheless sufficiently clear to merit examination. Amongst the remedies currently advocated which he considers inefficient to remove poverty are : greater economy in government, diffusion of education and improved habits of industry and thrift, and co-operation. These have the one feature in common that they add to the productive power of labour. And the cheapening of commodities, he imagines, but adds to rent. On the other hand, whilst he includes combinations of workmen as one of his inefficient remedies, he nevertheless says that " they can advance wages, and this not at the expense of workmen, as is sometimes said, nor yet at the expense of capital as is generally believed, but ultimately at the expense of rent." The same fallacy is apparent throughout. It is the notion that to cheapen productions will simply result in the payment of the balance in the way of more rent; to make them dearer will prevent the payment of rent.

The error may easily be answered by regarding the holders of land at a rent either individually or collectively. Suppose an individual taking a farm or other land. The adjoining land is unoccupied. But this farmer pays a rent for his somewhat better land. By some improvement in machinery he materially reduces his hours of labour. The landlord can get no more rent for that if the adjoining land remains unoccupied. Or by other means he discovers that he can materially increase his production; he will not on that account pay more for rent, if the other land continues without a tenant. Even though he may find a family growing up around him, if he can find employment and support for them on his own farm, he need pay no more rent while the other land awaits occupation. All this is supposing that he might, if necessity arose, use that land to similar effect. What would compel him to pay more rent would be that the productions of his present land were so scanty that he must take more land for his sons to labour upon. Or the same effect might be produced by some other person coming to take the adjoining land. If the other land would produce a rent, and if his own was still as much better than the other as it had ever been, he must now pay more. Rent is the excess produce over that of the worst land that must be cultivated. Now this is directly contrary to Mr. George's argument; it indicates that rent as a proportionate share is reduced by cheapness and plenty, and is increased by scarcity. The greater the scarcity, the worse land must be cultivated; the greater the plenty, the better land it is that is alone required.

The same result follows if the community be considered. As was seen in the chapter on rent, the greater the abundance the smaller the relative share of rent. Mr. George's idea is that since men's desires increase as they are satisfied, rent must continually encroach on the rewards of capital and labour. But surely it must not be said that rent has swallowed up a man's wages when, having reached a certain standard of comfort, he desires and is willing to pay for more land on which to enjoy a better living? That itself is indication enough that he is receiving better wages. Rent may increase a little, as was seen, but it cannot be said to have increased at the expense of wages when wages have increased still more. It is a question of proportionate shares. And in the matter of relative or proportionate shares rent is reduced by cheapness and plenty. Combinations of workmen do not benefit themselves at the expense of rent by making wealth more scarce.

Mr. George, like others, has neglected to take note of the fact that men produce in order that they may consume. He imagines that better machinery, and all the contrivances for increasing and cheapening the supply of wealth will but increase rent; that habits of sobriety and thrift will not make a man better off, but increase his rent; that to save a man from paying taxes will increase his rent. And all this, forsooth, is because men desire more as their desires are fulfilled. Not only does he neglect the fact that, if they spend it they enjoy it, and not the landlord, but also that if they save it, it is for themselves and not for the owner of the soil. He thinks that to say that men will be better for increased industry and thrift is like asserting that every one of a number of competitors might win a race—which is nonsense. It is not a question of one arriving first, but of all having abundance of wealth. Confusing wealth with money might give his results. So far as money is concerned, it is quite true that it is useless to imagine all can have more of it, for it cannot be much increased. People would be no better if it could. But this simply disproves Mr. George's own argument for dearness. So far, however, as wealth is concerned that can be increased. All may have more by increased industry and thrift making the wealth cheaper. It is not true, as Mr. George says, that "if one individual worked more hours than the average he will increase his wages, but the wages of all cannot be increased in this way." The wages of all can be increased by more work, if they prefer to have more wages and not to be content with what they have. This, of course, refers to real wages; money wages are a matter of indifference.

To put the matter briefly: cheapness which is not the result of artificial dearness is good for the nation in affording satisfaction to desires and avoiding poverty. It is also good (when it is the result of low cost of production) in inducing plentiful exchange for the productions of other districts and communities. To the poor it is especially beneficial. It permits them to consume their own productions, or the productions of others taken in exchange for them, and by that means to raise the price of their own labour. With regard to those who have been producing wasteful luxuries, and rendering frivolous services to the few rich, the cheapness enables their labour to be employed in the supply of necessaries, and even luxuries, to the many.

This cheapness, and the consideration of consumers rather than of producers has frequently been advocated on the ground that all are consumers, but not all are producers. This, however, is scarcely a sufficient argument; the true argument is, that consumers in the nature of things are considered first. Production is only required for consumption. Every man who produces does so because he is a consumer. Moreover, those who fondly imagine that they alone are producers, and that to raise prices benefits producers rather than consumers, forget that no one enjoys any produce except on account of his real or supposed services in production. The landlord and the capitalist receive their rent and interest for their share in production, and not otherwise. To make commodities dear is to raise the latter shares also; indeed, these shares particularly; for they are just the shares which increase relatively by scarcity and decrease by abundance. The reward of labour is constantly increased by greater abundance. For the labourer himself consumes the greater abundance, while land and capital do not themselves consume at all.

Now it is quite true that men cannot cause good seasons and plentiful harvests, nor can a government or anything of that nature cause improvements in machinery and other means of abundant and cheap production; but they can avoid waste. A good business man will take care, as he daily inspects his premises, to remedy any cause of waste. Amongst the causes of waste in any country are taxes improperly imposed or wastefully expended. A National Debt is a constant cause and indication of waste. Institutions of all kinds which hinder men competing to supply wealth are causes of waste. Trade depressions and men spending their efforts in seeking employment are fruitful sources of waste. Efforts spent in anxiously seeking work are quite as irksome as actually performing useful labour if more than that is not true. Whatever, therefore, tends to cause irregularity and difficulty of finding remunerative employment causes waste of national effort.

It has been generally thought that trade depressions, with all their waste of effort, which are a marked feature of modern commerce, were irremediable evils. Professor Jevons endeavoured to find a connection between them and sun spots. Good and bad harvests affect trade, and sun spots may affect harvests. It has been noticed that trade rises and falls in periods of ten years. But none of these things, even if admitted, prove that trade depressions must exist in the nature of things. It is very easy to see how trade depressions may be either caused or avoided. If after a period of depression, and consequently low prices, it should happen that the low prices induce greater demand, and exchange becomes more frequent, prices are likely to rise. Now if when prices begin to show signs of advancement, some combination or other demands something more than the market rate for labour or wealth, then prices will rise more suddenly. At once the higher prices will tend to stagnate the trade. After a period of feverish speculation induced by the higher prices, a crisis is reached, a collapse ensues, and prices again fall rapidly. Then follows another period of depression. If, on the other hand, when prices began to rise they had been left alone, competition would soon have brought them to their normal level without any falling off of demand. For as the demand afforded higher or lower prices, the supply would have accommodated itself to those prices. But a combination of any sort attempting to set at defiance and disregard the condition of supply and demand must hinder exchange; exchange is forbidden except at prices which the market will not afford. This does not apply merely to labour combinations. It applies to attempts by governments to regulate prices by tariffs or other means. It also applies to the holding of land above its present market price, which taxation properly applied would tend to avoid. But the action of trade combinations has the same effect. The settlement of wages by whole districts at once, instead of by each individual for himself, must cause irregularity. It can only at best be described as similar to the use of octagonal wheels instead of circular ones for railway engines and trains.

Besides the even supply which free and unhindered competition would give in these respects, it is important for the attainment of perfectly smooth working of trade that the money standard should be invariable. That point must, however, be dealt with in the following chapter.

CHAPTER XVII

COINAGE AND CURRENCY

The nature of money was discussed in a former chapter. The question to what extent the present monetary arrangements were perfect, was, however, left for further notice. The measure of value furnished by money in connection with the production and distribution of wealth is capable of being affected by artificial arrangements. But for that fact money would scarcely require any notice beyond that already given to it.

Reference was made at the close of the preceding chapter to the causes of variations in value and irregularities of employment. Not only for the purpose of avoiding these evils, but also for other reasons, it is desirable that values should continue constant; and that the standard by which values are measured should not vary. A buyer of property of any kind ought not to be in danger of suffering loss by a general fall of prices. Nor should there be any inducement for persons to buy land or wealth, which they neither require for their own purposes nor intend to distribute in the way of their trade. It is undesirable that speculation should be brought about by the existence of any cause, to hope for a general rise of prices. This speculation is one of the causes of trade depression. It is moreover, incompatible with perfect justice that values should rise so as to become a source of gain to some with outeffort. That, by consequence, is a source of loss to others. The latter suffer on account of the change of the standard by which they made their contracts.

Money as a medium of exchange need not be discussed at great length in this chapter. Its use as a measure of value is what will occupy the more attention. So far as the monetary substances are concerned, a very few words will suffice, especially, at any rate, when money is regarded as a medium of exchange. The monetary substances of savage nations need not be discussed at all. Amongst civilized peoples, by general consent, the precious metals, gold and silver, have established themselves as desirable monetary substances. They have the qualities necessary for adoption as such. They are generally esteemed for their inherent qualities. And they are scarce, so that they possess high intrinsic value. They are, moreover, easily divisible for the purpose of measuring large or small values. For they may be melted without injury, and may be separated into smaller quantities and reunited if desired without loss of value. This is not the case with precious stones, for instance. The metals are capable of being perfectly tested as to their purity. As they are indestructible, and only a small quantity is obtained yearly compared with the previous stock of them, the quantity available does not greatly vary from year to year. Indeed, it is probable that no more is got than the increased demand requires. This tends to give stability of value.

As a medium of exchange, money should be portable, divisible, and easy to recognise. These qualities are possessed by the precious metals in a high degree; the portability and divisibility depending on the value and homogenity previously referred to. Nor are they more costly, as has been imagined, than paper bearing authenticating marks. It is true they are more costly to obtain in the first instance. But once obtained, there is no more waste in their use than there would be in using paper for the same number of transactions. There is some waste by constant wear; yet when the number of times a coin is handled is considered, it will readily be seen that a paper bearing that denomination and handled as frequently would soon be worn away. More waste would occur than in the case of the metal. In the case of larger sums, it need hardly be said that paper is the more convenient medium.

As a measure of value the chief quality desired is stability, and this also seems capable of attainment by the use of the precious metals (with paper for larger sums) more perfectly than by other means. But it cannot be too clearly understood that the stability of value is required in the standard itself, and not in the metal which is used as the medium of exchange. To make this clear, it is important to fully understand what is meant by a standard of value.

As a first step, it may be well to make clear what is the standard which obtains in transactions between persons of different nations. It was pointed out that (with the exception of countries producing the metals) nations traded with the metals as money, and not as commodities. Traders accept them to be used as money, and not for consumption in the arts. In fact, for the most part they trade by means only of paper referring to them (or rather to the standard of one nation), which is obviously money, and not a commodity.

In discussing the standard of value in international transactions, it will be well to suppose two nations each having the value of a given weight of gold fixed in its standard. At a certain price per unit of weight there is in each of those nations free coinage into the currency of the country. This arrangement is not an essential one, but it will help the present explanation. The coins will vary in name and weight, and the units of weight will vary. But in every case a proportion can be found between the units of weight. From that result a proportion can also be found between the weight of metal in the coin of the one nation and that of the coin of the other. Now the value of the weight of metal thus ascertained by the relation to the standards of the two countries is the international standard.

But it is essential to observe that the standard is not the gold itself. The mind must abstract the idea of a measure, that measure being the value of a weight of gold. The gold itself is not wanted. But it denotes money to each of the traders. They would not think of accepting the gold for its own sake in return for their wealth. But money visibly represented is something which they can pass on in return for whatever else they desire. And this money they find in gold of a certain fineness and weight. The standard with them, although they have doubtless never taken the trouble to consider the fact, is the value of a unit of weight of that metal. It is not the metal, but the abstract notion of the value of a weight of that metal. In their own minds it assumes the form of pounds sterling, francs, marks, dollars, etc., according to their nationality. But as they deal with another nation, they reduce pounds to francs, or marks, or dollars, or as the case may be. The bankers and brokers then settle their accounts for them in their own currency.

It is quite true that persons occupying representative positions in these various nations imagine gold is the standard, and it is the gold they want. They even think that the benefit of the foreign trade is to amass a stock of gold. But that is merely because of their own imperfect powers of mental abstraction. What the traders require is money which they can pass on, and not the gold itself. Reliable paper would be equally useful as money for most purposes. Even the money, whether it assume the form of metal or paper, they only require for what it will buy. Though that again it is unnecessary for them to realize until they take some position which requires a knowledge of economics.

It will now perhaps be more possible to grasp the nature of a national monetary standard. The case of England may be taken as furnishing a very good instance. It is said to have a gold standard, and is held up as the most perfect instance of a gold standard country. Its money is usually expressed in pounds, shillings, and pence. The pound sterling, as the monetary pound is called, is the chief unit of the standard. The other monetary units used are fractions of it. Now the question arises, and must be answered, what is a pound? Economists have been accustomed to regard a pound as simply a certain weight of gold coined at the mint. They have spoken of price as value in gold. Money was simply gold and silver, varying in value with the cost of mining, and all prices were values in metal; as though the metal itself, and for its own sake, was of the value it represented as money. A little mental effort will serve to dissipate this notion.

The notion has its origin very much like that of natural value as mentioned in the previous chapter. It is an imperfect attempt to arrive at the nature of an object existing only in mental contemplation. Just as they failed to realize the nature of the abstract notion called value, so they failed to realize the nature of the abstract standard of value which money furnishes. They saw the medium. In its commonest form it was a weight of metal. They concluded that price was value in that metal. They only imperfectly realized the nature of money as something to be passed on. Still less did they realize that the metal was only money reduced to a tangible form, or that value was only a measure of mental desire. The abstract idea expressed in the phrase "measure of value" or "standard of value" was not separated by them from the notion of the visible medium.

A pound has been conceived to be a piece of coined gold weighing not less than $122\frac{1}{2}$ grains. Now, it so happens that there is another name for that piece of coined metal. It is called a sovereign.

It is the metal coin which is referred to when that word is used. But it is not the coin which is referred to when the word pound is used. When that word is used, the measure of value is referred to. In the case of a shilling or penny there is no separate expression. The same word does duty for both the metal coin and the measure of value. But in the case of a pound, what is meant is not the coin known as a sovereign, but the abstract notion of a quantity of money. The money itself is an abstract notion when it is referred to as a measure of value. It is a mental measure. It may be represented by a sovereign or by twenty shillings, or by anything which is regarded as equally valuable, such as a cheque. This, then, is the standard of value divided for ordinary purposes into shillings and pence.

A little further attention to the matter will show that it is erroneous to speak of the English standard as a gold standard. The international standard before referred to might, perhaps, without impropriety, be referred to as a gold standard. It is not the weight of gold which forms the standard in either mind, but the pound, dollar, etc., as a measure of value. Yet the weight of gold is the means of comparing the two measures, and its value thus becomes, in a not unreasonable sense, at any rate, the standard of value; though a strictly gold standard would be one which definitely referred to a known weight of gold. But the English standard is not a gold standard in either of these senses. The Englishman who has to make a bargain simply thinks of the price in pounds, shillings, and pence. The price may be paid to him in one of several ways. He is compelled to accept, in payment of debts, silver up to £2 and Bank of England notes up to any amount, as well as gold. The medium may, in fact, assume the form of cheque, bill of exchange, bank notes, or metal. The standard is a mental measure which he knows as a pound, and the money will probably soon assume the form of an entry of credit in some book or other.

Even the total quantity of money in the country can be increased or decreased, and prices accordingly affected, without any change in the quantity of gold. When a panic occurs, and there is great demand for money, it is not for gold, but for Bank of England notes. And yet the standard of English money has been called a gold standard. The truth is that England has, like other countries, an abstract standard of value represented by a medium composite in its nature, and comprising paper, gold, silver and bronze. Of paper, Bank of England notes are legal tender to any amount at any place except the Bank itself. Theoretically, they are always convertible. If there were any real attempt to get them all converted, they would be found to be inconvertible paper. But the Bank's credit is such that its notes are freely accepted even in other countries. Gold is legal tender when coined, but not otherwise —in spite of the phrase "gold standard." Silver and bronze coins are legal tender to limited amounts. This is the composite nature of the currency on which the standard is based. But the currency is one thing, the standard is another. The standard has for its chief unit the pound. The medium may assume a variety of forms.

At the outset, therefore, if the subject is to be understood, it must be realized that money is in the first place an object desired, because of its usefulness in the purchase of other desirable objects. It is essential to get hold of that idea, and to keep it distinct in the mind from the notion of the forms which money may take. Then it must be realized that money furnishes a standard by which the value of other objects is measured. That standard must be kept clear in the mind from the medium which represents the money. It is not the gold, or silver, or paper which is desired, or which forms the standard, but the money which they represent. The money is counted by Englishmen as pounds, by Americans as dollars, by other nationalities under other names. It furnishes, rather than is, the standard. And, finally, it must be fully grasped that the money which is desired for its purchasing power, and which also furnishes the standard, may assume various forms as the medium of exchange. No one or more of those forms is the standard. The money which affords the standard is an object which may assume those visible forms as a medium, but which has an abstract and invisible existence as a standard, and which, even as a medium, may assume the abstract and invisible form of credit.

This is what the money of an advanced community becomes, although it originally grew from the use of some object as a common medium of exchange. It is not altogether improper to say that the money is the standard reckoned, for instance, in pounds, shillings, and pence. But it is quite incorrect to say that the gold or medium is the standard. That is but the visible representative of the money which furnishes the standard, and which itself exists in calculation only. It is well enough in ordinary language to speak of the form it assumes as money. To properly understand the subject, however, the notions must be abstracted. Money must be regarded as the foundation notion (being itself a purchasing object), forming by its value a standard of value, and in its various visible or invisible forms being also a medium of exchange. Those forms are not the standard. All that is meant by England having a gold standard is that the price of gold is fixed at the mint, and there is unlimited free coinage of gold into sovereigns of a certain weight, each of which sovereigns, when coined, represents a pound sterling. But it is by no means the only form of money used in the country.

Now that an effort has been made to make clear what is meant by the standard of value, it may be well again to remark that what is desirable is that the standard should not vary; not that the price of the medium should be invariable. It should be no concern of the nation whether gold or silver fluctuates in price or not, but only that the pound should bear a constant value. This is important, so as to avoid a general rise and fall of prices. The price of a particular commodity may, without injury, rise or fall with its scarcity or abundance. Indeed, it is desirable that it should do so, even if it be gold or silver. But the standard of value should not fluctuate.

Now if the precious metals were used as money simply by weight, it is not likely that the standard would vary as much as it constantly does under the systems of coinage now obtaining. Large gettings of gold would increase the supply and diminish the value, whilst a demand greater than supply would have a contrary effect. The same would apply with regard to silver. But there would at any rate be the advantage of the law of substitution if both were subject to the full operation of the laws of supply and demand. And that is not the case at present. Moreover, if no coinage were undertaken and the metals were weighed, any fall in their value would be likely to increase their use as commodities. The additional demand would tend to raise the value again, and thus, by balancing the effect of the supply, keep the standard constant.

Very different, however, are the present results. Gold is in many countries fixed in price,—that is, in money value,—and is subject to unlimited free coinage. The result is, that if a large influx of gold occurs, instead of the value of gold falling, the standard of value falls. The money value of the gold is fixed by an artificial arrangement, so that it cannot fall as it ought by the increased supply. The most convenient means of selling it is to have it coined. The consequence is that a great quantity of gold coin is brought into the currency for which there is no real demand, but of which there is plentiful supply. This increases the stock of money in proportion to the demand, and that in one of its important forms. The value of money consequently falls. This is the case not only in the sense in which the expression "value of money" is understood amongst money brokers, a value in use for a time, but also with regard to the national standard of value. Prices rise not because of the ordinary influence of supply and demand, but because the standard is lowered. It is as though men began to call six inches a foot, with the consequence that men of six feet became giants of twelve feet. In the case of the money standard this is a great evil. And there is a further evil when the standard goes back to its old condition.

How this evil is to be avoided is a question demanding consideration and settlement. It is obviously desirable that the metal used as the medium of exchange should be coined. By that means its purity and weight is authenticated. Its genuineness and value as money is thus guaranteed; just as paper money is authenticated by the marks it bears. There is no better arrangement than that the government of any country should undertake the coinage. By its coinage it can at any rate indicate what it will accept in payment of taxes without any undue interference. That in itself would be enough to establish a currency. Nor is it a hardship that all others should be forbidden to coin money. For to permit such coinage would probably open the door to abuses. But why a government should coin money in unlimited quantities without payment of the cost there seems no valid reason whatever. Yet it is done the civilized world over. And this appears to furnish the cause of the evil previously mentioned.

Suppose that instead of the free coinage now obtaining, the government were to make a charge which would cover all the cost of the mint operations and the loss by wear of the metal used. Coins somewhat worn, but genuine and only worn, it would accept at their full nominal value in payment of taxes. The attention may still be confined to gold coins. At first sight it may appear that the only change from the present system of fixing the value of gold would be that the mint price would be fixed somewhat lower. Gold would apparently bear that constant value, and would not be subject to the influences of supply and demand. Something beyond this will have to be mentioned. But even with such a fixed price important results would follow from the adoption of the more natural system. In the first place, it would not be so profitable in case of exporting gold to export the coins as to export uncoined bar gold. Coined gold would now be more expensive than uncoined. The metal coined might be relied upon to stay in the country. Those who understand Gresham's law will readily see how it would be met by this arrangement.

In the second place, however, more important results would follow on the other hand: that is, with regard to the amount of metal coined and put into the currency. Whilst it is undesirable that the cost of coinage should be wasted by the coined metal being sent out of the country, it is equally undesirable that metal should be put into the currency for which there is no demand. That is what depreciates the currency and lowers the standard of value. Some means must be found for securing that the metal coined shall be the amount required, and not more.

The great use of metal money is for payment of weekly wages of workmen. But naturally this money is paid to tradesmen and others. It thus finds its way back to banks, and is again used for a similar circulation. Besides which there are purposes for which metal money is needed, even by those who are accustomed to make the greater part of their payments with paper. So far as money is required for these purposes, those who require it will be willing to pay for the use of it. Their payment for its use will reasonably include something for the gold having been coined, as well as for its having been mined.

The point to be made clear is that such a charge for coining would not only ensure that the coined money should not easily leave the currency, but also that it would furnish means of keeping out of the currency the gold not required in it. It must not be left to any one person or body of persons to decide whether the coin is required or not. Yet some means should be found for preventing more being coined than is required. Before that question is proceeded with, however, it is advisable to show that no difficulty would arise in finding the ratio of the English standard to the standards of other countries.

It must be borne in mind that whilst an ounce of coined gold would still be worth £3 17s. 10½d., the mint would pay only say £3 15s. for the ounce, and that in coin. The remainder would be retained for cost of the country's coinage and currency. This would, of course, not be a depreciation of the currency. The sovereign would contain the same amount of gold as before. The pound would, on the contrary, have to be considered as worth more francs, dollars, etc., than under the present arrangement. Whilst under that arrangement an ounce of gold will produce (roughly) £3⅞ at the mint, it would then produce only £3¾. So that the pound would become somewhat more valuable as compared with the standards of other countries. As metal, so far as the mint was concerned, gold would be worth only £3 15s. an ounce for import or export. But as English money, when so coined, it would be worth £3 17s. 10½d. Other nations, however, would compare their coins with English sovereigns at the rate for uncoined gold. It would be only as gold that they could take it for their own currency, even though coined. The cost of coinage must be wasted if they took it away and melted it. On the other hand, nothing could make their coins worth more at the English mint than £3 15s. an ounce, the price at which it could be turned into English money, except what would have a similar influence on any gold.

That there would be a loss on taking the money representing £3 17s. 10½d. and melting it to £3 15s. is the very object desired in order to prevent that proceeding. It should be paid to government or to persons in the realm, and its full value as coin thus secured. Even if it were taken abroad, as might occur in small quantities, it should, and generally would, be kept as English coin. The charge for coining would thus cause no difficulty in fixing the ratio of the standard with that of other countries. It would be simply determined by the price at which gold entered the mint—not at which it emerged. If coined metal had, through special circumstances, to leave the nation in considerable quantities, the loss of the cost of coining would be sustained by the nation as now; but through the rate of exchange, and not through the government. It need hardly be said that 2s. 10½d. an ounce is an altogether hypothetical amount, assumed for argument's sake, as the cost of coining and loss by wear, and is probably somewhat too high a rate.

The discussion of the export of coined gold in quantities will serve as an introduction to the other question which must be discussed. An important result of charging for coinage would be that gold would begin to have a market value. Indeed, that is in one aspect the object to be secured by the charge and by the other arrangements to be mentioned. At present it has no such value in the so-called gold-using countries, although silver has a market value. The value of gold is artificially fixed at a certain price. The erroneous idea obtains that gold is the standard, and fixing the price of gold is fixing the standard. All movements of gold have to be influenced by discount rates acting on rates of exchange, and not by market value. The marvellously complex movements are beautifully balanced by the natural laws of supply and demand. But there is still wanting the freedom of movement which a more natural system would offer. And once again be it said, the standard is consequently liable to unnecessary variations.

It may readily be seen that if a charge were made for coining, the market price of gold would vary. The mint would only give £3 15s. for an ounce of gold, although it would require £3 17s. 10½d. of the gold when coined to make up an ounce. The remaining grains of gold would be retained for coinage. But if gold were in demand, a little more than £3 15s. would be given, although it must be parted with to the mint at that price. Banks, for instance, would do this when their customers required metal money, and the customers would pay for it in their commission and interest. It is no new thing that the market price of gold should exceed the mint price. Though it must be confessed that the causes which have sometimes operated in that way have not been desirable ones. The mischief has been in the causes, however, and not in the fact.

Now suppose that by continued good trade internally there had been great demand for gold money, and almost the whole of the stock of metal had been coined and spread over the country; and suppose that by some means a great demand for gold were to arise for export purposes. It is not impossible that the price of gold would actually reach a little over £3 17s. 10½d. an ounce. It might then be worth while to export coin. If such interest were offered for money elsewhere, that it was profitable to invest money there instead of at home, those who had money would send it. The rate of exchange might get very high against this country, and yet no attempt would be made to lower it by sending bills of exchange back. The money could be so much better used in the other country. When the rate of exchange was so high that it was profitable to send bar gold, it would be sent. But if the bar gold was nearly exhausted, and there was still money to be sent, the exchange would get still higher, and coined gold would be bought if the process continued. This would happen even though it was at such a price that coin worth for internal circulation £3 17s. 10½d. had actually to be bought and sent away to be melted at £3 15s. The difference would be found in the better investment of the money.

Between the two rates mentioned there might be great variation. The market price might, as already mentioned, even go above the higher rate. It would depend on the inducement. In that direction, however, the amount indicated is a large advance on £3 15s., the normal rate. But some advance on £3 15s. might easily be caused by the exigencies of internal circulation. Even if there were no internal demand beyond that supplied by the metal already coined, the same results might follow. There might still be such a demand for gold, either for export or for the arts, that £3 15s. would be exceeded to a greater or less extent.

We next turn to the still more difficult question of the possibility of a fall below £3 15s., and of keeping out of the currency of the country any superabundant supply of gold. It has already been fully shown that gold might rise above £3 15s. if the supposed charge were made for coining. While above that price there can be no doubt whatever that the gold would not be coined if it were not required as money. That would imply positive and immediate loss. But, apart from its being re-

x

quired for coinage, it could only rise above that price by a demand for export or the arts. Could it, without inconvenience or injury, be made to fall below that price, so as to still further induce a demand for export or the arts? If not required as money, could it be prevented from going into the currency? That is the ultimate object to be reached.

It is but reasonable to suppose that if other nations retained free coinage the surplus gold would find its way into their currencies. Their prices would consequently get so high that exports to them would greatly increase. These exports would be paid for in gold when the rate of exchange was so much against them that it would afford the cost of conveying the metal. If money remained more plentiful in proportion to demand here than with them, the exchange would not get so high. But while the increased exports continued there would be likely to be causes operating to raise the exchange against them. The volume of trade and increased production of wealth would, in the first place, find employment for more coin for internal circulation. Besides which it would be likely to cause more demand for metal for use as a commodity in the way of ornaments, and for other purposes. But, on the other hand, such a condition of affairs would be likely to enable the nation thus more rapidly producing wealth either to lend money to the other nation on more or less permanent loans, or otherwise to invest with them. This money being sent in paper would tend to turn the exchange more in favour of the free coinage nation.

The effect of this lowering of the exchange would be to proportionately reduce the amount of gold transmitted. But the gold would only be retained by the nation getting into debt. The ultimate consequence of that would be a continual export of gold or commodities in succeeding years by way of interest on that debt. We have, however, to find arrangements under which any considerable import of gold to the nation not having free coinage would of necessity be because the gold was required. This is the point to keep ever in view.

But suppose that the other nations protect themselves in like manner against the superabundant supply of gold. An outlet must now be found for it if it is not to find its way into the currency. The importer of bullion may make different uses of it according to his business. For it must be supposed that he may turn to any business so as to make profitable use of his bullion. In other words, any person or body of persons must be supposed capable of importing the metal. In applying the argument to countries where gold mines exist, importation must be regarded as including mining operations. Moreover, to obtain conclusive arguments, a time must be taken at which all the gold at present in the country is required in the coinage, and is actually coined. It will not be sufficiently conclusive to take a period when the gold has already stagnated in the bank vaults, and might, for all useful purposes, as well have been left in the mine. The nation must be supposed to be busily at work, and using as money all the gold which has not been taken into the arts. But a further flood comes, which cannot be taken into the currency without affecting and lowering the standard. If that can be avoided in such conditions, it can be avoided under all circumstances and at all times.

The most difficult man to deal with for the present purpose is the man who imports gold and exports other commodities, paying in metal the wages of workmen employed in manufacturing those other commodities. He does not at present exist. The two trades are carried on separately. But, as already stated, he must be supposed capable of coming into existence if it is profitable to combine the trades of two distinct classes of persons. He finds gold so abundant and easy to be obtained that he can now pay for his export commodities very easily. He therefore rapidly imports gold and exports commodities in return. A similar result would follow from the opening of a mine within the country and the payment of wages to workmen for mining. The standard is in great danger of being lowered by this great supply of gold. What is to prevent it? The abundance of money actually being paid, and the very satisfactory condition of trade, will create an increased demand for the gold as a commodity. But that cannot yet be relied upon to avert the danger of the lowering of the standard, which would raise all prices, and cause trade depression and poverty.

Now this flood of gold must reach the banks, and particularly the Bank of England. England must be still considered the instance taken for argument's sake. Even supposing that the importer takes his gold to the mint, and pays it away as gold coin, it must pass through the hands of the tradesmen into the banks. If it does not, it will do no great harm. If every man keeps a few extra sovereigns in his pocket, the result will be just as if he had hung them on his watchguard as ornaments. It is the money which circulates which must alone be regarded as money, and as capable of affecting the standard. Probably, however, the importer would take his uncoined gold to the Bank of England, and thus save himself trouble. The additional gold, therefore, must now be sought in the banks. It may have affected the standard slightly before it reaches that point. But the influence can only have been slight so far, even though the importer had the gold coined. Now, however, arises the difficulty.

With the Bank vaults full of gold, and the discount rate consequently low, there is every inducement to merchants to buy goods with their bills of exchange. This is where the mischief begins. It goes steadily at first, and gradually increases its rate until the time of the panic and collapse. Even the bar gold, which will generally be found in the Bank of England, has its influence, as well as the coined metal. The bars may at any time be coined if wanted. It is true that the low discount rate tends to the export of the gold. But we are supposing the other nations protecting themselves like this nation, and already well supplied. Unless that bar gold can be got below £3 15s. an ounce, and thus turned into another channel, the danger cannot be avoided. The bar gold will probably be either with the Bank of England or with the mint, except so far as it has not yet left the hands of the importer. The importer may have some in hand, but those who have bought gold as a commodity will require it as such. The remainder is coined.

The Bank of England must not be supposed to be bound to take the gold at £3 15s. an ounce, and give coined gold or its own notes for the bars. As soon, therefore, as the Bank found they had so much gold on hand that it was not being employed profitably, they would naturally decline to give money for the gold. They might take it on deposit at some rate, but they would pay no interest for it. And the importer might as well accept a little less if he could get the gold into some form which would pay him interest.

At the mint, however, the gold is still taken at £3 15s. an ounce. Money is given for it. Very true it is metal money, but it will buy commodities which the bullion dealer wishes to export. The importer is, therefore, still putting gold into the currency and affecting the standard. For the trade still continues, and he can use the money for his purchases.

Meantime, however, the mint is accumulating gold. It gains a little on every ounce of gold it coins. When the light coins come in after a period of wear, they are melted again into bars. All this gold is ready to be re-issued. But since gold continues to come in so fast, and since the banks have already more than they have use for, no one will take the gold at its full price. It is useless for the mint to offer it at less than £3 15s. an ounce for other purposes if the purchasers might at once have it coined and obtain the full £3 15s. That would be nothing more nor less than issuing £3 17s. 10½d. in money for a less sum than that. There could be no clearer case of depreciating the currency. But the mint has the gold, and if it goes on coining, it will accumulate a great stock of gold for which it has no use. There is nothing arbitrary in declining to coin more until it is rid of its present stock. Here, then, is the means of reducing the price of gold below the mint price, which was seen to be necessary to keep the standard invariable. And it is secured automatically. It follows from an arrangement which is self-working.

There can be no hardship or injustice in this proceeding, nor can the nation complain that it is robbed of its money. The ratio of the national standard was fixed by a reference to £3 15s. an ounce for gold. That price the Government would give as long as ever there was need for the money. As soon, however, as its own stock of gold indicated that there was no further need or use for the money, it would cease coining until there was again demand. Meantime, the additional gold imported or otherwise obtained must be sold in the open market. It thus becomes subject to the ordinary laws of supply and demand, and is carried off into the arts. It is used as a commodity, and the benefits of its desirable qualities obtained by those who will buy it. The price is regulated in such a way as to secure purchasers. If more is wanted in the currency, it can at any time be had. As soon as any one will take an ounce of coined gold at the price which as money it will produce for them, they may have it. The mint only refuses to part with it at less than it actually represents as money. When an equal sum of any other form of money is offered the coined gold may be had. This would, in practice, be done through the Bank of England. But while there was gold money lying idle in the banks, there would be no demand for such money, and no further stock would be coined.

The same method might be applied to silver without any danger of depreciating the currency. A ratio to gold would be fixed, and that ratio would be maintained in all the silver coins issued. But the silver coins would only be issued when there was need for them as currency. That would be established in the same way as already mentioned with regard to gold. Both silver and gold would then have their market prices. In the currency they would bear fixed ratios, and the demand for them would settle exactly the amount put into the currency. But in the market each would have its own value as a commodity.

The mention of silver leads to another subject which must now be grappled with. The difficulty which arises from a rate of exchange varying greatly and continuing to move in one direction was briefly mentioned. It will be seen that the rate of exchange is influenced by two great causes. One of these is the temporary cause which determines to which of the two countries in question metal must be sent. The exchange is against the place which must send it. Strictly, this cause includes several causes. The apparent indebtedness may arise in several ways as previously stated. Paper may have been sent by way of loan, interest on loan, gift or payment for commodities; but the supply of paper indicates that metal money must be sent. This is the merchants' side of the matter, though their influence may be and is greatly modified by that of the money brokers who have most to do with the exchange.

The other great cause is the depreciation of the standard of one of the countries. If for any reason it becomes possible to obtain the money of one of the countries much more easily than before, it may be expressed as a depreciation of the standard of that country. If, at the same time, the standard of the other country is not depreciated or only to a less extent, the money of the first country becomes worth less proportionately than that of the other. The latter country will therefore decline to send its money except for more of that of the other country. Thus by the issue of inconvertible paper (that is, of paper which cannot be exchanged for metal) it may happen that more of the currency of any country will be given for gold than the gold when coined will represent. Those, therefore, who have gold in other countries, will decline to part with it except for more of the inconvertible paper currency than bears its nominal value. Between the country which can have gold for its currency at any moment and the country which must give more of its currency to obtain that gold, it will naturally happen that exchange will be affected. The rate of exchange will be raised against the place which, if it must send gold, must pay more for it. The exchange is calculated by the respective standards. Even if it is to receive gold, that gold will buy more of its currency than it would of that of the other country. In fact, although by the weights of gold one ratio is fixed, yet by the actual values of the two standards another ratio is fixed. And this is found in the rate of exchange.

The same result as from the issue of inconvertible paper will follow from the unlimited free coinage of a metal which becomes superabundant. As was seen in the case of a flood of gold, it is possible to depreciate the value of a currency by coining a flood of silver. And if silver finds a market price in one country below its mint price, while in the other country it is freely coined, the exchange will be turned against the latter country. That country has, in fact, lowered its standard by taking unlimited quantities of silver into its currency. In the other country the silver has not been taken in. It can be had at much less than the price it would have to maintain in order to keep the same ratio when sent to the silver-using country. Thus India has permitted every man to bring silver for free coinage into rupees. When the silver could be obtained cheaper elsewhere, it has simply occurred that the rupees have become less valuable in proportion to the other currencies. This ratio entering into the rate of exchange has raised that rate against India. This second great cause of variation is not a merely temporary one which can and will be removed by the importation of metal. The only remedy for it is to cease admitting as currency that which has depreciated the standard.

The theory known as Bimetallism suggests that when one nation has depreciated its standard by admitting unlimited quantities of metal, the method to adopt is for other nations to depreciate the value of their currency also. This is proposed to be done by allowing the free and unlimited coinage of silver as well as of gold. But as already seen, even the admission of unlimited quantities of gold is an evil in itself. It may sometimes cause great mischief. To admit also unlimited quantities of silver would be to increase the mischief. The fault is with the country which allows its standard to be depreciated by taking in all the metal presented. But that country must also suffer the misfortune in its increased prices. And the evil should be removed by it. Each nation may defend itself against the evil. And no nation can be worse for finding that it can buy more cheaply the currency of another nation. It is the nation which finds its own money less valuable as compared with other nations which is the sufferer. There is a hindrance to trade, but the nation with the depreciated standard suffers most as a nation.

The question may not unreasonably be asked what the result of the system here advocated would be if the cause of gold stagnating in the banks were some interference with trade and not an influx of gold. For instance, a very large combination of the workmen employed in one of the great staple industries of a country might, by a strike of a few months, very greatly hinder trade. Comparatively speaking, such a thing would stop the national industry. A great amount of money previously in circulation would get laid aside in the vaults of banks. For other trades also must stop, and the circulating medium would drain itself into great pools of metal. It need hardly be said that the event could not happen without hardship and loss, whatever might be the currency arrangements. It is impossible to prepare for such contingencies. It can never be foretold how long a strike will continue, or that there will be any stoppage at all. This uncertainty and fluctuation applies to all interferences with the natural course of supply and demand. In a slightly different way a similar result would follow from the imposition of a protective tariff. Indeed, all improper taxation has a similar effect to a greater or less extent.

It is impossible that perfect monetary arrangements can prevent all economic evils. But the better the system of currency, the better the results, even in face of other evils. No injury could result from keeping metal out of the currency when a large stock has already accumulated in the banks. For that stock might as well, for present practical purposes, have been lost in a shipwreck. It could not directly influence prices or answer any useful purpose whilst lying there. It might lower the discount rate to some extent. But it is not desirable that the discount rate should be lowered merely in order that prices should be raised. That is but to make wealth more difficult of access. And it is one of the ways of causing collapse of trade. If the discount rate is low with regard to money while interest on capital is high, it is evident that some economic evil is at work. A low rate of interest on real capital arising from the abundance of wealth is good. A low rate of interest on mere money whilst interest on real wealth continues high is bad. There cannot be too much wealth. But there can be too much money. For when balanced against wealth, money represents the scarcity and famine side of the scale.

The money already in the currency must of course stay for a time. The evils of strikes cannot be destroyed in a day. But there is no reason for taking more into the currency. The result of keeping it out is that it goes to the other countries. Their prices are raised by it. And trade tends to revive for the strike district by those raised prices. So far as the strike district is concerned, prices may tend to be lowered. The strikers may not like this, but it is better for even them to be brought as quickly as possible to a reasonable frame of mind. Moreover, it will make wealth more accessible to them, which is the great object of the study of economics. Indeed, so far as the whole district or country is concerned, the lowering of prices will have the effect of enabling them to obtain wealth and get to work again as quickly as possible. For it must be remembered that the strike or other interference has for its effect the lowering of the standard. By artificially raising prices the standard is lowered, and the lowering of the prices by a good monetary system is only bringing the standard back to its true position.

With free competition the government would not for long have to keep metal out of the currency. The arts would soon take what metal was not required for money. But whilst they stopped coining, how would the rates of exchange be fixed? The case of other nations allowing free and unlimited coinage has been sufficiently noticed. But suppose that other nations adopted the same system, and there were various hindrances to competition. The market price of gold might get below the mint price in all those places. It might, and probably would, however, vary in the different countries. And that would have its influence on exportation. The rate of exchange based on the nominal ratio between the standards would accordingly be fixed practically as now : that is, by the demand for bills created by the ordinary international transactions modified by the movements of metal. This already occurs, but the metal can only be moved between the gold-using countries by the rate of exchange, and not by the true market value.

In concluding this subject, a passing reference may be made to the Bank Charter Act, passed in England in 1844. Its object was to limit the issue of bank notes, though it need hardly be said that it was impossible, by an Act of Parliament, to hinder the substitution of other forms of paper money. It may be stated briefly that the Act was passed under a misapprehension of the cause of the evils it was intended to remedy. So far as the Bank of England is concerned it has practically no effect except in panics. At those times, after it has done as much injury as it is thought advisable to permit, it is suspended. Failing the entire repeal of the Act, it seems very desirable to avoid the evil generally wrought, before its suspension is asked for, by permanently suspending it on the same terms as it is on those occasions temporarily suspended.

The mischief lies in the superabundant supply of the money which must be accepted as such, not of that which all are at liberty to accept or refuse. Moreover, the latter being paper and for larger sums, reaches generally only those capable of judging of its merits or otherwise. The former passes into the hands of the mass of the people in payment of wages, and in that way also becomes the basis of the currency.

The portion of the subject attempted to be dealt with in this chapter requires, it need hardly be pointed out, much more elaboration than can be afforded in this book. Either the charge for coining or the refusal to coin except when there was a demand for the metal money might be adopted separately. There are other aspects in which the arguments might be put, and other ways of treating the subject with the same result. But it is sufficient to have indicated a system of coinage at once natural, self-working, and capable of operating with smoothness and elasticity. By this means a perfect balance is constantly kept, and the standard of value is maintained invariable. On such a basis the creation of paper money might safely be left quite free, and all danger of shocks or financial panics would be averted.

CHAPTER XVIII

COLLECTION OF RESULTS

It is of importance that the results of any scientific inquiry be as far as possible gathered together. Only by this means can it be seen whether or not any system runs through the inquiry, and its results. This method will show whether the results harmonize with each other. The focussing of the light will exhibit more clearly the practical outcome of the study of the subject, besides showing the connection of the several parts. For nature is one and the same. If we would study any specific subject, we must examine each portion separately; but we must never forget that the whole is one subject. And that one subject is part of a larger subject. And the larger subject is again a portion of the one truth of nature.

An endeavour has been made to keep the science as clear and distinct as possible from other sciences, and at the same time to show its bearing on other portions of truth. This method differs from that which neglects the surrounding truth as much as it does from that which confuses other subjects with the subject under consideration.

Passing the chronological introduction, it will be remembered that the first point to be noticed was man's need for wealth. This is the whole subject.

Value and exchange, land, labour and capital, rent, wages, and interest, money and discount are all portions of it. It is seldom they are treated in such a way as to show the connection, but it is well that they should be so treated. It is, however, well also to avoid dragging into the inquiry a discussion of the proper foods, drinks, clothing, and pleasures required for healthy living. Nor can the economist determine by his study whether it is good or evil that certain persons should choose to enjoy their wealth in this way or the other. He will take care to suggest such conditions as, when applied to actual life, will prevent any person or persons injuring others by hindering their obtaining the wealth they require. But that is all he will have to concern himself with. The one object constantly kept in view throughout this inquiry is that every man, woman, and child should be supplied as required with an abundance of wealth. Some have low ideals of life. But no good can come of keeping them in poverty and starvation as a means of raising their standard of comfort or their notions of enjoyment. The present business is to show how the needs as they exhibit themselves can be met until perhaps a better ideal of life can be taught. There can be no doubt that want is a poor uplifter of the human race in general.

Man's power to labour is taken for granted. And this power to labour is clearly sufficient to supply his needs if his employment can be regular. Moreover, if all take their fair share of the labour, it will not be irksome or over-difficult. It must be borne in mind, however, that labour includes all human effort directed to useful occupations. Mere physical labour, differing in relative degree only from that called mental, is not alone labour. It is in truth the most common, and in advanced civilization the least important, although it is useful in its place. The tendency of advancing civilization is ever to transform physical labour into skilled and mental labour, leaving the mechanical work to machines. Care is to be taken also to keep wealth clearly distinguished from that which is not wealth in the sense of this science. Particularly must it be kept distinct from human skill, labour, land, and money. Capital, it will be remembered, is wealth regarded as an element of production.

So much may be considered to have consisted of mere preliminary analysis of the subject. What men should consume, and how they should attain the skill necessary for producing it, are no part of the subject. It is enough to know what the essentials for production are, and that, in fact, they exist. As noticed, they consist of land, labour, and previously prepared wealth known as capital. But as soon as wealth is brought to market, however wide the market may be considered to be, the science of economics finds place. Indeed, it was seen in due course that the science must also concern itself with the influences which interfere with or encourage the production and distribution of wealth. The laws regulating value and price are proper portions of the inquiry, and take a prominent place in it. On this point it will be remembered that greater utility or increased scarcity, producing greater values and higher prices, consequently tends to induce supply.

Whilst less utility or decrease in scarcity reduces values, lowers prices, and tends to reduce the supply. There could be no more perfect arrangement than this, no matter how great the wisdom devoted to its invention. Utility, it will be borne in mind, is ascertained by the expression of desire.

These are the natural laws of the market. They govern the value and price of wealth, land, and labour. But wealth may be produced as required. It will, at the same time, be constantly in course of consumption. So that supply and demand rule its price entirely. Speaking generally, the laws of the market govern its price altogether. Land, however, cannot be increased, and its price depends ultimately on the demand for its use as wealth producer and otherwise. But on that subject more must be said. Labour, ultimately, depends in price, to a great extent, on the supply of wealth. Opposite in this respect from land, it increases in value as the supply of wealth increases. This will be seen to harmonize with the fact that increased labour produces increased wealth for the labourer.

It was stated that under the influence of these natural laws the process of exchange and distribution of products would go on until each had his desires so far satisfied that he preferred to be content with that measure of satisfaction rather than to work more. It was noted, however, that the natural process was interfered with to the injury of mankind. Governments have endeavoured to prevent the people over which they ruled from trading with other nations. Sometimes they have tried to stop the exporting of wealth, and sometimes to prohibit the importing of it. Both methods appear to be in disregard of the fact that the people would not wish to carry on the trade with foreigners but for their own benefit. The foreigners are as useful to them as they to the foreigners. In every exchange each party gains and neither loses. Each gains what is more useful to him than what he parts with. In this interference with free trade we find the first hindrance to the supply of the human needs and desires which are the subject of the inquiry.

Not much attention has been given directly to setting forth the advantages of free trade in commodities. Those advantages have been conclusively demonstrated over and over again. Mr. Henry George's able treatment of the subject may be referred to as a recent instance. But the same conclusions also followed indirectly from the arguments here offered on the subject generally. The most subtle form of the protectionist error is that of List, which advocates tariffs as a means of establishing new industries. The more obvious objections to this idea are two. First, it gives to the persons who may be in power as rulers the right to choose the employments of the nation instead of leaving it to the people themselves to choose their own employments under the inducement of the rewards offered. Secondly, it accomplishes this by keeping from others the objects of their desire, so as to compel them to offer more to keep persons employed at an otherwise unprofitable employment. The error thus started, however, works itself out like other errors to its fullest possible extent, producing high tariffs all round, and causing great injury.

Following the subject of exchange and distribution of wealth, we notice the division of wealth amongst its producers. The share of the owners of land is noticed first. A law is observable with regard to this share amongst persons free to contract for their own benefit. In view of the inequalities of the value in use of land, the rent will amount to the excess value of the land over the worst which is worth using. In the absence of improved powers of production, the proportionate share known as rent rises as worse land must be used. There is in such a case more land above the margin of cultivation, and there is nothing to compensate for the additional cost of producing on worse land. The share of capital and labour taken together is found at the margin of cultivation, and as that falls their relative share falls in proportion to that of rent. Every fresh supply of worse land which the needs of the people require adds to the amount which rent takes of the whole. Though care must be taken to remember that these are relative shares. Improvements in the efficiency of capital and labour may at the same time add still more to the shares of interest and wages. It is only when worse land must be taken because of the unsupplied needs of the people, and when no means of improving production are found to balance that necessity for using worse land, that rent encroaches. If the increased demand arises from an already better-supplied condition of the people, and from their capacity to produce and consume more, the rent rises at the same time as interest and wages. That is to say, the actual shares all increase. This also harmonises with the fact that increased production is on all hands desirable, though the relative or proportionate share of rent will decrease under such circumstances. In other words, whilst increasing, it will not increase so much as the other shares.

The consideration of the share devoted to payment for use of capital bears out the same conclusions. That share consists of the portion of the benefit it confers, which from its greater or less scarcity labourers will be willing to pay for its use. It is evident that the greater the amount of useful capital there may be in existence, the greater the benefit it will confer. But beyond this it is also true that this greater supply of useful capital, whilst it may from its increased quantity produce a larger actual share for its owners, will nevertheless produce a smaller relative share for them. This also may be expressed in other words. The share of capital may increase with its increased quantity and the greater benefit it confers, but the increase of benefit to labourers will be still greater on account of the abundant supply of the capital. In proportion to its abundance capital will take a smaller share of the benefits it confers. It must also be noticed that, whilst land tends to be more fully occupied, and to become scarce in the progress and increase of population of a people, capital in the natural course of events becomes more plentiful. This increase of capital appears capable of more than counterbalancing for productive purposes the decrease in supply of land relatively to demand. The increase of benefit from the greater abundance of capital is in addition to the constantly improving knowledge of mankind. That improving knowledge continually points out better means of increasing the products of the earth by the application of capital and labour.

Another hindrance has, however, to be noticed to the full enjoyment of the benefits of increasing capital. This is found in the monopoly by some persons of land which they hold without using. The permission granted and secured thus to hold land without taxation, and the imposition of taxes only when the land is used, stands much in the way of the land being made as productive as is possible. The holder of this untaxed land can in many cases impose his own terms on persons desirous of cultivating or otherwise making use of the land. He frequently requires as part of his terms the handing over to him of capital and improvements put upon the land. This has the effect of preventing the improvements being made, or the capital being created.

The imposition of taxes by governments has, however, to be noticed. The discussion of this subject leads to the conclusion that a just and natural system of taxation must be based on the value of the land monopolised by each person. That the land must be monopolised for the production of the wealth is beyond dispute. But governments are territorial. And the obviously proper method of taxation is that in which the taxation is calculated on the value of the monopoly held by each individual of the territory ruled over. This would accomplish two objects at the same time. In the first place, it would equalise the inequalities arising from differences of quality of the land held. In the second place, it would prevent men holding land they did not use.

Another result may, however, be noticed. It was mentioned that land ultimately depended only on demand for its price. As the supply could not be increased by human effort, human need alone was the creator of its value. In the market supply and demand ruled its price, but outside the market (unlike the case of wealth) there could be no additional supply of it. The taxation of land would meet this difficulty. The government's need for taxes, by compelling every one who held land to pay taxes on it, would induce a supply to the market of land which otherwise would not have been forthcoming. Not only by the rise of price in the market through increased demand would supply be induced, and the price again brought to its normal condition—that, indeed, would not always induce a supply; but by the demand for taxes the supply would be enforced just as man's inevitable demand for wealth ensured a supply of labour, or of other wealth to exchange for it. This again is fully consistent with, and helpful to, the great object of providing a constant supply of wealth to all the nation and the race. Professor Sidgwick has expressed fear lest the adoption of the policy known as *laissez-faire* or non-interference by government should have evil effects. A particular possibility referred to by him is that a man might choose to keep his land unused. But the imposition of taxes is nowhere regarded as contrary to the doctrine of non-interference. And if a proper method of taxation is adopted, no man is likely to do much harm in the direction indicated. Nor can this be called with any truth confiscation in the sense in which that word is used. Confiscation would imply that if a man did not choose to pay taxes on a sufficiently high value, he must give up the land on payment for the capital he had put upon it. That is not advocated, though it might possibly be a matter for discussion if the land were being occupied for the first time. Even then it is open to doubt, in view of every one's possible loss by the capital he puts upon land. But, as here suggested, he would, on disturbance, be paid his value of the land as well as a good price for his capital upon it.

The further discussion of interest on capital need not be noticed again here. The results have just been referred to, and their harmony with the other results commented upon. The causes of the inequalities of wages may also be dismissed without much further observation. It will be recollected that those inequalities which must arise by the influence of supply and demand are the natural result of the greater satisfaction of desire which some offer than others. In other words, they are inequalities of reward obtained for like inequalities in the supply of wealth or other object of human desire.

Another evil interference with the supply of wealth has, however, to be noticed. Mr. Henry George, whilst fully realizing the advantage of free trade in commodities, and whilst also pointing out the proper method of taxation, becomes after that inconsistent. It is quite true that protective tariffs are an evil, and a cause of poverty. It is also true that to permit a man to monopolise land, free from taxation so long as he takes care not to use it, is another evil and a further cause of poverty. But why is it an evil? How does it cause poverty? Clearly by hindering the production of wealth. Any other cause which has the same effect will be a similar evil, and in like manner be a source of poverty and want. Even though it be added that the untaxed monopoly of land enables the landowner to take also a large share of what is produced, it must furthermore be said that the same poverty may be produced by hindering production in the first instance. Now this effect is brought about by the action of combinations of workmen to raise prices by in one way or another limiting supply. Strikes are one of the methods adopted. The workmen simultaneously decline to supply labour and create wealth except for higher prices. Frequently they attain their object so far as higher money wages are concerned. It was shown, however, in the discussion which occupied two chapters, that they did not benefit themselves as to real wages by this method. The result was rather the contrary, while others also suffered.

To meet this method and to reverse its effects, masters adopt the policy of insisting on a simultaneous reduction of the money wages of their workmen. The resistance to this becomes a further hindrance to the supply of wealth. In the same way also the fixing of a standard price below which the workmen are expected by the combination not to work has the same effect. Other methods also are adopted for the same purpose, and with the same results. The evil of this interference is found in its hindering the supply of wealth both directly and by its indirect effects. It is one of the causes of the disorganization of trade—that is, of exchange and distribution. It should be mentioned that before discussing the action of these combinations it was shown that wages were not, as had been thought, merely the amount required for subsistence, nor were they limited by any fixed wages fund, but increased with the increased application of labour. This again is a further confirmation of the previous results.

The relations of governments to wealth supply were discussed. It was seen that their creating debts by means of which the taxes of succeeding generations were expended in payment of interest for which no benefit was conferred on those generations was an unwarranted and unnecessary evil. When nothing remained of a useful character as the result of the expenditure, there could be no reason for borrowing. Even in cases of the creation of capital which remained for the use of further generations, it was pointed out that frequently the supply should be left to private enterprise. That would be sufficient to induce it, if the demand really existed. If it did not exist, the expenditure was wasted. It was further observed that all unnecessary interference with wealth supply should be avoided by governments. Only the minimum of interference is consistent with the most abundant supply of wealth.

The influences affecting prices and the supply of

wealth were discussed with special reference to the cost of production. It was pointed out that high or low prices could not be commended or condemned without reference to their causes. High prices arising from abundant supply and demand, and a consequently fuller and ampler national life, could not be regarded as an evil. That would be altogether inconsistent with the object in view. If an abundance of wealth is supplied and consumed, and if for that reason labour requires high rewards to induce its application, the economist has no occasion to be dissatisfied. But high prices arising from scarcity and need were referred to as an evil. It was shown that the cost of production should be kept as low as possible. All irregularity of employment, for instance, was spoken of as waste of the national resources. Amongst the causes of this waste may be mentioned all interference by governments to determine what kinds of wealth shall be produced by a nation. All improper taxation may be included, the most economical being that previously mentioned. In truth, everything which hinders wealth production adds to cost, and is an evil. Only when further cost arises from the already abundant supply of wealth, increased effectiveness of demand, and diminished compulsion to labour, can it be considered that increased cost is not an evil.

A further cause of irregularity and loss as well as of injustice was found in the imperfect systems of coinage and currency obtaining in civilized communities. Briefly expressed, the error consists in artificially fixing the price of a monetary substance under the impression that it is the standard. The standard was, however, shown to be a mental measure known as value, and not a visible substance, or a weight of such substance. The means suggested for remedying the evil were such as would keep the standard constant, by ensuring that only as much money as was needed should be coined. At the same time, and to help in that purpose, it was shown to be desirable that the monetary substance should be made to find a true market value.

So far as paper money is concerned perfect freedom should be left. That does not affect the currency so long as it continues freely convertible. What affects the currency is the metal money which must be had for various purposes, and of which a superabundant supply is occasionally found. It gets into the currency, and cannot be so readily annihilated as paper money and credit. This induces the creation of paper money which would not otherwise exist. The result of the lowering of the standard which generally follows from these imperfect arrangements is to raise prices, and make wealth more difficult of access. Besides which it produces the collapses of credit, which cause trade depressions. These also have the same influence in hindering the production of wealth.

The whole subject is thus rapidly, but completely surveyed. It will have been noticed how persistently the supply of wealth has been kept in view in collecting these results. That is the object to be aimed at. Man's need for wealth was the subject, and the supply must be constantly brought to balance it. But while that is the one object, it will be seen that there is also one law running throughout the whole of the results. From beginning to end the importance of permitting the free play of supply and demand perpetually discovers itself. In the market and out of it, supply exists for the purpose of balancing demand. Whatever hinders its doing so freely and to the fullest extent is seen to be an evil. This is the case when the particular point is examined as well as in view of the larger aspect of the inquiry. Unrestricted competition is the one means—the only perfect means—of supplying the needs of the race. And the hindrance to competition may arise from the action not only of the government, but of some other organization. It is not enough for governments to abstain from interference if other institutions have the same effect. There must be free trade in all the objects with which the science has to deal. The arrangements must be such as to encourage and secure free trade in wealth, the object desired, free trade in land from which it must be drawn, free trade in labour by which it must be produced, and free trade in money by means of which it must be measured and exchanged.

This latter expression does not mean that there must be free coinage of all the monetary substances which any one may bring. It means that if any artificial means be taken to afford a supply of monetary substance the arrangements must be such as to secure the full influence of supply and demand. This influence should operate not only on the price of that monetary substance, but also on that of money in all its forms. The notion that every one may issue money at his will is quite correct, as far as that money bears only the power to circulate which his own credit can give. It is a very different thing when he is permitted to create money which others must perforce accept as money. But the object to be secured in this matter, as in others, is that money shall be subject to the influences of both supply and demand. The theories hitherto accepted have placed it only under the influence of supply, with the result that a demand was created which did not naturally exist. By this means the money has been circulated, the standard depreciated, and collapse and depression have followed.

The one law is that the influences of supply and demand should be permitted to have free play in all respects. Whilst the object to be secured is kept always in view,—that is to say, the supply of abundance of wealth to all,—this law runs through the whole, and constantly crops out as the inquiry proceeds. In the market, and out of it, the same considerations apply. Prices are affected only through the influence of supply or demand. Artificial arrangements must act through these natural influences, or they fail to have any effect. Unfortunately for the advocacy of artificial arrangements, they can only act on supply. If the object in view be once realized, it becomes obviously impossible that artificial contrivances can effect it as well as allowing the natural supply to meet the expressed demand. The very statement that any government or combination can decide what prices shall be better than those who need the object to be purchased is absurd on the face of it. Surely every man knows his own requirements better than any one can settle them for him. And if he can better satisfy them in one way than another, he should be permitted to do so. If one can supply his demands better than another, that one should not be hindered. If high prices indicate a need for more men in any grade of employment, the price should be allowed to induce the requisite supply. Possible aspirants to the position should be encouraged and not prevented from entering it. What is the use of money, the measure of desire, if some government, combination, board of conciliation, or other unnatural contrivance is to fix the prices for a whole country or district?

The perfect application of the law just noticed as appearing in every department of the inquiry is the natural, the only natural system. Where art was necessary to be noticed, endeavour was made to approximate as nearly as possible to nature. Nature is always more perfect than art. Art is perfect in proportion as it follows and imitates nature. This is not the first time that a natural system has been advocated. The first economists were called Physiocrats, because they advocated a natural system. Bastiat, again, has done so since their day. And the answer has been, forsooth, that matters were not perfect, and therefore a natural system was not the best system possible. We repudiate with scorn the insinuation that a natural system has prevailed these many centuries. Only in the newly opened countries has such a system obtained. The results all have noticed, but they usually gave wrong explanations of the observed facts. With the inventions of civilization, and an equally natural system of using them, mankind might ere this have enjoyed the beginning of a millennium. We are told that free competition has failed to produce the benefits claimed for it in the present century. The reason is but too obvious. It has never been tried. On all hands are contrivances for restricting competition. And unrestricted competition is then judged and condemned for the results of its absence. One by one the departments of the subject have been examined. In each separate instance the benefits of a natural system were clearly noticeable side by side with, or by inference from, the evils of artificial interference.

Another point to be borne in mind is that throughout the examination of the subject perfect justice has always been placed in the foreground. It cannot be too clearly insisted, that justice is reached by the exact balancing of rights. To give more than justice is to do injustice by giving less to the other side of the balance. In answer to this the cry is raised by the tamperers that they see injustice and wish to stop it. But they take the very means to increase it. They see the effects. They cannot understand, or never look for, the cause. And they proceed to do exactly that which magnifies the effects. An effect must be altered by modifying the cause. Frequently it occurs that to regard only the effects is to entirely fail to influence them for want of reaching the moving cause. The way to steer a coach is to look to the reins, not to

z

handle the wheels. The evil to be remedied in the matter of wealth supply is that the poor have too little, not that the rich have too much. Yet to remedy this evil the plan is on all hands adopted of reducing the supply or hindering it until a certain preconceived notion of utter unimportance has been realized.

Others say that justice must be subservient to expediency. The disgraceful argument is put forth as if true expediency could be founded on injustice. But the fact is, the expediency referred to is the notion with regard to the fitness of things of those who hold the doctrine. Some contend that all should be equal not in rights, privileges, and opportunities merely, but in all respects. Unfortunately for them, facts are against them. By the providential plan, inscrutable or clear, men and women are unequal in capacities and powers for both enjoyment and labour, as they are in stature and strength. To many, including the present writer, there seems infinite beauty and usefulness in this design. For the capacities and powers vary not only in quantity and degree, but in quality and kind. And in this fact of variety, pervaded as it is by harmony, is found the inconceivable grandeur and beauty of the infinite universe. Whatever views may be held on this point, however, it is certain that men are and ever will be unequal and various in themselves. It would be as easy to ensure that all should be of the same height as that they should be equal in other respects. The value of their efforts must vary. Why one or many should pay to another more than that other's efforts are worth to him or them is past comprehension. It certainly is not justice. Nor is it expediency, in view of the different positions which must be filled in a perfectly organized community. The truest equality is the natural equality.

But it is hard for human beings to realize that matters can be well managed without their interference. The system here suggested will be declined by many because too simple. The philanthropist often declines natural remedies because they leave so little scope for his efforts. Men love power. Ambitious mortals aspire to rule, and manage all things according to their notions. If the human race could have influenced the earth's course in its orbit, they would before this have presumed to steer in another direction. The experiment might have been interesting, but in all probability the results would have been disastrous.

And yet the earth pursues her course in perfect safety under the influence of two natural forces. All that is required for a similar perfection in the matter of wealth supply is that the two natural forces with which the science of economics has to do be allowed a similar freedom of action. Where artificial arrangements must be made, let them follow the justice of nature. The demand exists, and ever must exist. Men struggle for wealth because it is essential to existence. Let them also compete to supply it, and take care that nothing hinders competition or exempts any from it. In this way the supply and demand would be perfectly balanced.

Natural justice will secure this competition. All

must have wealth. Those who are without it must compete with their labour to supply the needs of others for services. Their need for wealth prevents their shirking their share of labour. Those to whom they sell their services must also compete with their compeers to supply the wealth that all must have. This is the competition of labourers, both masters and servants. The owners of capital, too, must compete if they would have their capital used. Without its being used, it will not only produce no income, but it will generally deteriorate in usefulness and value. If it is to be of service to its owners, they must use it or lend it to others. In either case they must compete. For the borrowers of wealth, like the purchasers of it, naturally satisfy their desires as easily as they can. And the greater the competition by owners of capital, the more will be the service rendered for the same reward.

The owners of land, too, must use it or have it used if it is to produce wealth. At first it seems unfortunate that land is capable of being monopolised and held idle without loss to the owner. In view of its necessity to wealth production, it appears inevitable that poverty must result because some can avoid competition by laying hold of the land. But a further fact must be considered in the necessity for taxation. The consideration indicates independently that taxes should be based on the value of the land. A fund created by demand alone is available to the community as justly its own. The equitable and natural method of taxation ensures that the land produces wealth because wealth must be paid for the requirements of the community.

This very need causes a supply of land, a competition to have it used.

And now the whole circle is complete. Let but the demand at any point rise, and the supply will increase to meet it. If the landowner finds himself master of the situation because the demand has increased, that very demand will prevent his holding the land idle by creating a greater need for taxation. If the capitalist finds he can raise his interest, the labourer will create more capital to compete with him. As the labourer finds himself better supplied he will demand the more: if he demands without supplying, he will soon discover that prices rise against him, and then he must bring his supply to the proper ratio. Even if the community unduly increase its taxes, it will find the source of its taxation so decreased in value that it is likely to get poorer by asking for more. There is absolutely no need whatever for trade depressions or poverty, as that term is understood. Sickness and old age must come, but even for those who must bear these burdens it is possible to be well provided. Some trades cannot be carried on in severe weather. But even in those trades provision might easily be made, or other employment readily found, were it not for artificial hindrances to competition. The unemployed need not exist. Want of employment, in the ordinary sense, is an unnecessary evil, and its creation a foolish and iniquitous proceeding.

It is true that all times would not be equally busy. The earth does not move with such regularity as that. Its orbit is not a perfect circle. The velocity of its revolution is not perfectly constant. But no disaster occurs. When one of the controlling forces is slightly increased, the other also increases, and the perfect balance is restored. The nearer approach to the sun, and consequent greater attraction, is balanced by accelerated motion. The same might occur with regard to supply and demand. There is but one further qualification required. Supply and demand are balanced by means of money. Money must remain constant in value for perfectly smooth and regular operations. But that condition is secured in exactly the same way. The arrangements must put the substance used under the influence of both supply and demand. The recurrence of periods of bad trade at intervals of ten years, and their identification with sun spots, should drop out of discussion. Trade should be good, and perhaps better, but never bad.

It is a common thing for those who advocate encouragements to trade and disapprove of interference with it to be denounced as friends of the capitalist. The cry against them is that good trade with them means capitalists' profits. Now if the mass of the people are to be kept in poverty and semi-starvation, and some to die outright from want, lest a few of the more energetic should make fortunes, then the science had better be left alone. All the books previously written on it should be burnt by the common hangman, and future study of the subject forbidden. But it would be well also to forbid talking and writing on the subject without study. The human beast should be written down once for all as an ill-disposed brute who deserved all his misfortunes and more. Good trade does not benefit capitalists only. Nor does it benefit only master labourers, who are the people really meant by those who thus talk of capitalists. Its benefits are perfectly general. And whilst it affords opportunity for a greater number to provide themselves competencies, it does not tend to the great inequalities of fortune which obtain under restricted competition. It is the hindering of wealth production which results in overgrown fortunes and wasteful luxury side by side with want and starvation.

Nor is it correct, as some have imagined, that hindrances to competition in one respect or by one class can be balanced by restricting competition in another. There can be no balancing of errors in this matter. All the errors are on the same side. Demand remains untouched by all the contrivances yet invented, except so far as it is influenced by supply. And all the artificial influences on supply are to restrict it. Professor F. A. Walker found good in trade combinations because in his view they increased competition. But the fact is, they diminish it. He imagined that without these combinations the workmen would not be sufficiently alive to their own interests. But the combinations, when they attempt to raise wages, do it by requiring or encouraging their members to abstain from working except at a higher price than that offered. The price offered may be one which, for their satisfaction, they would be willing to accept in preference to stopping altogether. But they are persuaded that to stop their competition will enable all to get better wages. All the contrivances of which Socialism is the extreme form of expression require the individual to obey the will and seek the benefit of the community. They are not recommended to him as a means of benefiting the community, but of benefiting himself by declining to compete with others. Whatever competition means, such a hindrance is absurd.

The demand for wealth is the one side of the balance. Its supply is the other side, and all the errors consist in hindering that supply. The hindrances cannot balance each other. The abolition of any one of them is a step towards the desired end. Nothing has here been said, or will be said, against trade combinations so far as they act as friendly societies or encourage their members to get the best wages they can. Wherever they can get the best wages, that is the place where they are most needed. By all means they should be informed of it, and be encouraged to go to it. The mischief is that they are gathered into a combination not to work except at certain specified prices. And a sentiment has grown up that it is an injury to their fellows if they do not refrain from working, and thus leave more work for others.

One would think that the great thing to be desired by every man was not wealth, but work; not satisfaction, but want. The secret, however, is that they have confused wealth and money together, and are hankering after money when they require wealth. This has been the cause of all the errors. It is seen in the desire expressed for the imposition of taxes to keep wealth out of the country, so that higher prices may be had. And the higher prices which would, in fact, keep a nation out of the markets are desired as a means of increasing trade. So far as it is not the result of interested influence, the same error is seen in the arguments against the proper principle of taxation. The fear is that it will reduce the value of land. Now the wealth of a country is not greater because of its greater value in exchange. Value is the combination of utility and limitation of supply. Scarcity is one of its elements, and it is obviously absurd to increase scarcity by way of making a country richer. A nation becomes more wealthy by increasing the sum of its utilities—by satisfying the demand, not diminishing the supply. The same error is seen in combinations of workmen not to produce wealth by adding to utilities, but to raise values by increasing scarcity. And the error is very clearly seen in the cry for more money, which is the chief request generally made on the currency question. Indeed, it is very remarkable how the craving seems always for something which is simply the reverse of what would render benefit. Socialism certainly finds the strength of its influence in the economic disease of the community. But it is the cry of pain and the expression of desire for what will increase the disease, and not the description of a remedy.

One other fact may be mentioned as proved by the examination of the subject, and for the present it may be regarded in its purely selfish aspect. For the mass of the nation or of the human race there can be no class interests and no national interests antagonistic to the interests of the race. The welfare of each is the most perfect welfare of all. And the welfare of each is best secured by conditions which leave him and all others to satisfy their desires in the way they deem best. One nation cannot be made rich by seeking the poverty of another. It is better for both nations to allow the individuals of both to grow as rich as free exchange can make them. On the other hand, no nation need be poor because another nation has bad economic institutions. It might be that trade with the other nation would be beneficial did they not prevent it by tariffs. But high tariffs, by raising prices, usually allow free trade nations to undersell the people protected even in their own country and in spite of the tariff. And certainly free trade gives an advantage in the open markets. Besides which, every country up to the present might, if necessary, find enough subsistence for the nation inhabiting it. The hindrance is that some are kept by restriction of competition from the employment where they would be most useful.

Nor can the mass of the nation benefit themselves by separating themselves into a class of poor people. They had better leave every individual amongst them who is able to do so to grow rich, and thus to enter the classes where he can render service to themselves by competing against the members of those classes. Even the few who form the classes cannot benefit themselves in the aggregate quantity of wealth by hindering its production. They can only keep the mass of the nation more nearly in a condition of subjection and slavery. And if they desire that, there can be no better plan of obtaining it than by means of Socialism. For that of necessity must rest on the personal subjection of the individual to the community as represented by the government. The government in its turn must in actual exercise consist of visible persons.

For the well-being of the nation, however, a truth expressed in some words of Adam Smith's may well be applied in this connection. But the words of the great Scotchman who is so prominent a figure in the science must be extended in their application. They must be regarded as including not only statesmen, but all leaders of men. They must apply not only to a man's capital, but to all his means of wealth production, to his method of conducting his business, the hours of his labour, and the amount he shall accept as recompense for it. He says :—

"The statesman who should attempt to direct private people in what manner they should employ their capitals would not only load himself with a most unnecessary attention, but assume an authority which would safely be trusted, not only to no single person, but to no council or senate whatever, and which would nowhere be so dangerous as in the hands of a man who had folly and presumption enough to fancy himself fit to exercise it."

CHAPTER XIX.

APPLICATION.

THE examination of the subject is complete, and the results have been collected. They remain to be applied. The science has little to suggest in the way of an art of government. The most perfect conditions for satisfying human needs are indicated to be the full and free play of supply and demand. In so far as a government must actively interfere in the matter of the production and distribution of wealth it will be as regards taxation and currency. In those two departments the science indicates that art must imitate nature. The same influence of supply and demand must, as far as possible, be secured in those departments as in others. Unrestricted competition is that to which the science points as the most perfect condition. As much as possible of nature and as little as possible of art is the truest art of government for ensuring a wealthy nation. Any active interference beyond that just indicated must be justified by some other considerations. For it cannot be justified by the truths of economics or the necessity for a supply of wealth. Free and unrestricted competition is the only means of increasing wages, raising the standard of comfort, avoiding trade depressions, and diminishing national poverty. Whatever restricts or hinders that competition will be injurious to the extent of the restriction or hindrance. Any political conditions which cause poverty will have that effect simply because they prevent free competition. What those who wish to benefit their fellows may do for them, and even what help the state may render, is matter for a different inquiry. But there is one thing they cannot do without causing injury, and from which the state must by all means refrain. They must not interfere with competition, or hinder the cheapest and most abundant supply of wealth.

The application of the science to the art of government is soon accomplished. Even with regard to borrowing and finance generally, all that is necessary is to apply the same rules to a nation as would be applied to an individual. Borrowing for the purchase or preparation of capital which will be an aid to wealth production and a source of revenue is justifiable. But borrowing for immediate consumption is only justifiable in those cases in which it might be warranted in the case of an individual. That could only be a case of a temporary loan. And a nation, like an individual, becomes richer by paying off its debts.

But besides the application of the science to the art of government another application must be made. If the conclusions are true, they should explain all the facts with which the science has to do. Trade depressions are entirely matters for explanation by this means. Poverty, so far as it is the result of the conditions of society, and not of the idleness, extravagance or vice of the individual, must also be explained, or the science is still not understood. That the conclusions are true the writer has not the slightest doubt. If some detail has not been properly filled in, he will still hold to the main conclusions. Those who dispute them must find the errors and flaws in the reasoning as he has done with regard to the doctrines he has attempted to refute. He is prepared to maintain those conclusions, and undertakes to find and point out errors in the reasoning on which any opposing conclusions can be based. And the theories here set out are put forth as sufficient to explain all the problems of trade depression and poverty if but the facts of the case be known.

It is unnecessary to do more than take instances to which the conclusions may be applied. Other instances may be taken at will, and the science can only be expected to explain economic problems. Drunkenness, vice, crime, and idleness open out other inquiries, though good economic conditions are capable of a general uplifting.

Probably no better instance could be found for examination than the economic history of England during the nineteenth century. The eighteenth century saw great improvements in the machinery by which natural forces were made to assist mankind in wealth production. Their adoption resulted in the rise and growth of the factory system. In connection with that system there can be no denying that much cruelty was practised in the early part of the present century. Children and young persons particularly were the victims of this cruelty. It was no necessary concomitant of the better means of production that women and children should be driven to greater toil. Still less was it essential that they should, by means of the lash and otherwise, be treated as slaves. But, with the confusion of cause and effect which has distinguished the notions of so many well-meaning reformers, the factory system has been blamed for the evils by which it was accompanied. The invention of labour-saving appliances has been made responsible for the toilsome bondage of the weaker labourers. Freedom of competition has been spoken of as accountable for the white slavery which social reformers with no great love for political economy themselves strenuously maintain to have been actual slavery.

It is needless to say that slavery is not an institution approved of by the economist. It is the very opposite to unrestricted competition, and is more in accordance with the policy of restriction. With regard to the boys and girls who were the victims of the oppression now under discussion, it has already been shown that state interference would have been justifiable without clashing with true economics. But the ironical fact is that the cruelty was first made possible by the community, and was not the work of individuals as opposed to the community. The children were at first taken from the workhouses. On them the greatest cruelty seems to have been practised. But even after that was forbidden, and other poor children were taken in their places, free competition was not the bane. Competition by persons who are not free cannot be called free competition. There was no injurious over-production arising from free contract when the producers had to be driven to and from their labours, and kept hard at work by chains and beating. Even if it be argued that the poverty of the parents drove them to permit their children to be thus ill-treated, it still remains untrue that competition caused that poverty. What did cause the poverty must be pointed out.

The beginning of the century now drawing to its close found England at war with France. The fighting was done entirely abroad. Napoleon's threatened invasion never took place. But the wealth had to be produced at home. A great number of men were withdrawn from wealth production for fighting purposes. Large sums of money were being sent abroad to carry on the campaign. The importation of provisions was hindered by the war. Corn had to be grown on worse and worse land. Prices were high, and it was the high prices which caused the manufacturers to ask for the children whom they received from the workhouses. None of this could be laid at the door of free competition. The high prices, not the low prices which competition causes, were the evil. The truth was that the wretched children were carrying on a great Continental war. They were at least producing the wealth for it, and it was England's wealth which enabled her to hold out in that struggle. The hollow mockery of the pretended borrowing has been noticed. The wealth was being produced in the factories, and by means of it the war proceeded. The choice was between this wealth production and starvation. Even surrender would have meant despotism after the war became one of mere conquest.

Meantime, however, economic conditions were not perfect. It was enough that such a war had to be carried on. And only by means of competition could it have been accomplished so well. But economic science was badly understood, and still more badly acted upon. To avoid starvation worse land must be cultivated and the share of rent consequently increased. The landowners flourished at the expense of the country. The famine prices gave also large profits to those who had capital. The nation was too heavily laden to create fresh capital to compete with it. The government borrowed from moneyed people, sent the money out to raise prices still more, and left the nation in debt for having defended the country—for the benefit chiefly of landed and propertied people. If it could be thought that they realized what they did, no words could be too strong, even in such a book as this, to express horror and disgust at the proceeding.

In the first place, therefore, the misfortunes of the nation arose, not from competition to supply, but from exceptionally great need and imperfect competition. But the war came to an end. Even before it actually concluded the landlords were in fear for their rents. The political power was in their hands. The importation of corn must reduce the poverty of the masses, and lower the rents of the landed aristocracy and gentry. Corn must therefore be kept out of the country. The first of the economic evils which has clearly emerged above others during the century is found in this interference with free trade in commodities. At the very beginning of the century several evils applied. In addition to the war and the expenditure of borrowed money there was the absence of a proper system of taxation. The system adopted permitted the landowners to escape their share of the extraordinary effort, and even to gain by it. Inconvertible paper money was issued, which was another evil. And trade combinations were only less injurious because other evils were greater.

The corn laws, which form the most important part of the protection of the time, then became distinguishable as the chief evil. They were not the only evil, but they stood out prominently. Perhaps England could have produced all the corn necessary for the maintenance of the nation. But the mischief of interfering with competition is not that it absolutely stops production. The wealth might be produced if the persons capable of producing it could be persuaded that they should go on with it, regardless of the profits or absence of profits. But the strong men decline this, and naturally take the best places they can get. It is useless to preach that they ought to be more enterprising. Men are enterprising for reward. And the way to make them enterprising is to allow such free play as will secure them such a reward as is likely to induce their efforts. Failing that, they will fall back on an easier if less ambitious mode of obtaining a livelihood. If by that means others are driven out of employment and suffer poverty, it is not the fault of those who might have employed them had an adequate reward been possible. It is the fault of the restriction which hindered them choosing what would naturally have been a more profitable employment. In such a case the weaker ones who are incompetent to take the position the strong have declined to take can but stare at each other in blank despair. Their cry should be addressed not to the strong to give them work, but to the organisation establishing the restriction to set competition free.

This evil continued until the middle of the century. Other evils also remained. An unjust poor law still survived. Trade combinations were not powerless for mischief. But the greatest curse of the period was the hindrance to free trade in commodities.

After this another evil came to the front. The system of taxation still left much to be desired. But free trade in commodities alone was a great boon gained. The greater supply of wealth should have induced a further demand amongst the mass of the nation. The poverty resulting from the restriction of competition should have been followed by a great demand for those kinds of capital which were beneficial to the commonest class of labourers. Better houses and clothing should have been in great demand. The interest on such capital of the kinds necessary for this purpose as had already been prepared should have been very high. Its price should have so increased as to induce a supply of further capital, with a great demand for labour and an increase of wages. The increased amount of money required for wages should have caused the discount rate to rise comparatively very high, corresponding in this respect with the increased interest on capital. This would have caused the manufacturers and other employers of labour to have increased their stock of ready money, and would also have given a stimulus to the saving of wage-earners in the narrower sense.

Instead of this, however, it so happened that there were such discoveries of gold in Australia and California that the quantity available was greatly increased. As this was all admitted into the currency, the discount rate generally remained comparatively low. The manufacturers and others, therefore, to whom greater profits had now become possible, found that they could so easily obtain money for their wages that they invested their surplus profits in other ways. So far as there was a demand for capital as opposed to land the price would accordingly be affected. But, with the discount rate low, incomes from other kinds of property than money tended to become low in proportion to value. Or rather the value tended to become high in proportion to income, on account of the greater quantity of money available for the purpose of purchasing. The result was that prices of property rose. Land particularly greatly advanced in price from the middle of the century to a little after 1870. Prices rose all round, and much of what should have gone in increased wealth went in increased prices. By these effects owners of property, and particularly of land, were the chief gainers. What the wage-payers should have devoted to the fund out of which they individually must pay their wages went to buy property. Instead of wealth being kept low in price by a continual supply to meet the demand, property greatly advanced in price by the depreciation of the standard. This is an instance of the effects of the bad system of currency which was noticed.

It has been contended that there was no considerable depreciation of gold during this period. By this is meant that the standard was not greatly lowered, for this accords with the ideas as to what the standard is, of those who put forth the contention. But there can be no denying that land greatly increased in value during the period. Yet most land should rather have fallen in value during that time. Wealth also, instead of bearing about the same ratio to money as in say 1850, should have become much more abundant and cheap. If, in view of all this, however, prices of wealth were somewhat higher, and the value of land greatly increased, it could only be that the standard had depreciated. Professor Jevons showed that it did so.

There was, however, an end to the operation of that cause of poverty. And then another evil came to the front. It was not by any means new to experience. It had existed for hundreds of years, even in the form assumed in recent times. And the ancient guilds were, in some aspects, nearly related to it. But it now for the first time came quite to the front. The laws forbidding trade combinations to raise prices by causing scarcity had been repealed. No argument will be offered against the wisdom of that repeal. The very existence of those laws appeared to the minds of workmen to prove that the combinations were a help to them as against their political superiors who made the laws. The reason why the combinations should not exist was not that they hindered the masses labouring for the satisfaction of the classes. The evil was that they injured the masses themselves. This is still the argument, and the proper policy is not to make laws against the combinations, but to show the members their futility. While, however, the laws against combination had been repealed, the injury to the combiners had not been realized.

Political power had passed into the hands of the masses to a much greater extent than previously. They had to some extent emerged from poverty. But ignorance still remained. For a long time they had been oppressed by the classes above them. After that they had been oppressed by events for which no one was responsible. For though the system of coinage was not good, it had not been wilfully made bad. And no human oppressor could be blamed for the discovery of great quantities of gold.

But now the masses began to oppress themselves. In their ignorance of economic causes and effects, and thinking to benefit themselves, they combined as never before to raise their money wages. Shortly after 1870, when prices had reached their highest point, the coal-miners especially made themselves prominent in this respect. The demand for coal for manufacturing and other purposes enabled them to obtain these higher prices. The addition was simultaneously made to the money wages of the miners of all districts. The price of coal advanced to an unprecedented extent. The strikes and high prices produced a coal famine, which was a source of suffering to many. But for the time the miners seemed to obtain great advantages by the combination. Even those not in the combination, but connected with them in colliery work, obtained higher prices. Very quickly, however, the inevitable result was produced. Trade fell off. Poverty and depression were felt on all hands. The miners fully shared the economic misfortunes of the country.

But the trades union sentiment continued to grow. It had as a recommendation that its direct aim was to help those who were certainly the poorer classes. In an age of benevolent intentions that was enough to obtain support for it, regardless of the question to what extent the method adopted would accomplish the aim. With the increased political power of the masses, few cared to attack their cherished institutions. On all hands were those who, with the best possible motive, were willing to support them, even in face of opposition. Still more was it likely that they would help them forward in view of the popularity of the institutions. But a good motive could not cure a bad method.

The trade depression continued, at any rate, comparatively speaking, until about 1888. By that time money had become very plentiful. The Government found they could reduce the interest on the national debt. This was a benefit not so much in itself as in the effect it had on loanable capital and money generally. Money became easier to borrow. For a time, at least, there was comparatively abundant creation of capital. Besides this, the Government also decided to spend some millions on the improvement of the navy. The effect of this was to create a demand for the labour and material objects required for the purpose. No doubt the mass of the nation would have been more greatly benefited by the production of food, clothing, and houses for their own consumption. But the demand for labour and the higher prices accorded with the sentiments of the time. The higher prices induced speculation, besides leading the people to think that now they were getting better wages, and might work. Their working naturally produced to some extent the better real wages for them.

But the trade which was not altogether healthy (that is to say, it was partly speculative) was quickly hindered again. The coal-miners, who are remarkably cohesive and responsive to the will of the combination as expressed by that of its leaders, obtained large additions to their money wages. This was not all, however. With constantly increasing political power, and conditions still being bettered by improvements in the methods of production, the feeling in favour of combinations of workmen had grown apace. They might combine, and wealth still continue to be produced. In a sense they could afford the waste. On all hands, and in trades never before combined, trades unions were established. The artificial raising of prices naturally caused a falling off of demand. The fact that less wealth was produced affected the demand for one kind through the supply of another. The prosperity declined as quickly as it had arisen. Coal was a staple commodity, necessary not only for export, but also for the manufactures of the country. It fell in price to such an extent that a succession of contests was induced by the attempts of masters to obtain some reduction of the prices previously added. In 1892 a great lock-out took place in the Northumberland and Durham coalfield. Only after a long struggle and a great hindrance of wealth production was that settled. In 1893 a still more considerable stoppage occurred in the more midland counties, known as the Federation District. The numbers affected by it were still larger, and it continued for sixteen weeks, before a settlement was arrived at by means of government conciliation. After so protracted a stoppage of supply, it was only to be expected that for a short time at least the old prices could be given, although 40 per cent. above those of 1888. The settlement was, in fact, made on that basis as a temporary settlement: with an arrangement for the establishment of a Board of Conciliation to further consider the question.

The disorganisation of trade was such that in some districts the miners themselves appear to have suffered as much in the following year from the want of work and wages, as during the actual stoppage. The general depression was naturally more keenly felt afterwards than at the time. The reduction of 10 per cent. from the money wages of the miners did little to induce further demand. This reduction was in 1894. In that year, Scotland was the scene of a further struggle between coal-owners and miners. The depression and poverty brought about by these various interferences with trade, dating back to 1888, still continue at the time of writing. But the fixing of wages by combination instead of by competition, which is the root of the evil, apparently remains unquestioned.

No one seems to consider that combinations should cease to come between, and attempt to fix prices for, buyers and sellers of labour. The utmost that seems to be thought is that those who represent these combinations should be wise and moderate in their demands. Indeed, the spirit of interference between buyers and sellers of labour is causing the growth of the sentiment in favour of interfering between buyers and sellers of commodities. The advantages of free trade are being questioned, and protection advocated by a larger number than at one time would have been thought possible in England. It need hardly be said that as long as prosperity depends on the capacity and prudence of an individual or board of individuals to fix prices, and manage the business of others, trade depression and poverty will continue to exist.

Such, roughly, is the explanation of the economic history of England from the beginning of the nineteenth century to about the middle of the last decade. On one point England is ahead of other nations: that is in respect of free trade in commodities. But much remains to be done before the economic conditions are perfect. The first thing to be secured is free trade in labour. Improper taxation is an evil, but its amount can be estimated and allowed for. The loss of a strike is beyond calculation beforehand. Besides which there might be considerable cause of complaint if the government were to commence the reform of taxation at a time of depression resulting from other causes. For at such a time the prices could not easily so adjust themselves as to prevent absolute loss to those who, under the new system, must bear the burden of taxation.

As soon, however, as the nation has to some extent put itself to work steadily, a proper system of taxation ought in justice to be adopted. It will become all the more necessary, and on the other hand it can be applied without distress and loss by disorganisation. The measure should, for several reasons, be an imperial one, and not, as sometimes advocated, merely a power to local authorities to tax land in aid of local rates.

A better system of coinage might, perhaps without injury, be adopted immediately. But in justice to the holders of stocks of uncoined gold, and perhaps to avoid increasing the very evil to be remedied, some revival of prosperity might be awaited, rather than commence a new system at a time when there is so great a surplus of metal money as at present. On no account should bimetallism be adopted. As for the increased use of silver, that is not required for monetary purposes. It should be secured by a revival of prosperity, and the more extensive use of silver as a commodity. Nor is there any need to make any arrangements with other nations. Though of course a full discussion between the ablest financiers of all the civilized nations can do no injury, and should produce good.

The application of the conclusions previously set out to the conditions of other nations cannot here be undertaken at any great length. Nor does the writer pretend to be in possession of all the facts necessary for such an application. A few of the more obvious facts and their explanations may, however, be referred to.

The United States of America furnish a very good instance of the evil of interference with free trade in commodities. Few countries in recent years have carried out protectionist doctrines to such an extent. With such a country, and so able a nation, nothing but bad economic institutions could have produced anything like general poverty. But protection is not the only evil. The country is so much more like a continent—a rich continent—than a country, and its population proportionately so small, that free trade between the different states would in itself be sufficient to supply abundance of wealth for all the needs of the nation. But the taxation of imports has produced so great a revenue that the money has been squandered, merely to get rid of it. The system of taxation has permitted land to be held unused, or at high rents. Protection has allowed the formation of great rings and trusts. The workmen, instead of establishing concerns of their own to compete with the great capitalists, have made matters worse by spending their money in combinations on a tremendous scale, to still further hinder competition. In addition to all these evils, the owners of silver mines have been favoured at the expense of the nation by the purchase of a great quantity of silver not wanted for money purposes. It has practically been introduction into the currency. It is quite enough to produce poverty even in such a nation and such a country.

Australia and New Zealand are perhaps the great home of trade combinations. The hindrance to free trade in labour has for the most part been accompanied by the cognate hindrance to free trade in commodities. The natural outcome of all this is socialism. That also is not wanting. New Zealand some time ago adopted Mr. George's system of taxation. Some good was, without doubt, accomplished by it, but one reform is not sufficient when several different evils exist, requiring different remedies. The adoption of a good system of taxation will not abolish poverty if the competition of labourers is at the same time restricted or hindered. The mischief of socialism in New Zealand is enough to counterbalance the benefits of land taxation. The trade depressions and poverty, with the accompanying great financial disasters of Australia, find ample explanation in its trades unionism. In addition, however, protection, and reckless borrowing for works which government should not even have undertaken, have helped to the same result.

India has greatly suffered from the exactions of native princes in the past, and England's occupation has made little improvement in this respect. The borrowing of the government is an instance of further evil. Perhaps, above all, the depreciation of the currency,—not by debasing the coinage with light metal, but by admitting free coinage of the abundant supplies of silver,—has caused additional mischief.

In France and other European countries protection is the chief evil. The interference with free trade in commodities is general throughout Europe. Where, as in Russia, there is want of political freedom, this can hardly be laid upon the people themselves. But even Russia might be greatly benefited by a greater freedom of trade. In Germany and, indeed, in most other countries on the continent of Europe, socialism has a large following. Nor are trade combinations absent or lacking in influence in most of them. It may be stated generally that the very existence of a Socialist party, or group, or of a party calling itself a labour party, is sufficient indication of the existence of restrictions and economic evils.

The subject need not be further pursued. It is enough to have taken a few instances for the application of the theories put forward for the explanation of economic evils. These evils include all trade depressions, and poverty resulting from such trade depressions. Wherever there are men desiring employment, and unable to find it, a student of the science of political economy should be able to explain the reason. If a nation suffers poverty because the people are disinclined for work when it is offered to them, no further explanation is required. The rise and fall of nations is hardly a matter for discussion here. But bad economic institutions have, in most cases, much to do with the downfall of empires. The study of this question cannot be uninteresting to those who will pursue it.

It may be expedient, in view of the foregoing application of results, to make some remarks on the subject of the dynamics of the science. It is difficult to reconcile, or even understand, the meanings attached to the word dynamics by those who have used it in this connection. Possibly Professor Jevons meant by the statics of the science those influences which related only to the market, and which he discussed by reference to a single point of time. By dynamics he would then mean the ulterior influences outside the market, which have been referred to in the chapter on cost of production.

Mr. George means something different. All these influences he would include as the statics. They are the laws relating to the production and distribution. His problem is not the market, but poverty. He supposes a tendency to poverty. He seeks the impelling force which moves nations in that direction. He finds it in land monopoly. He thereupon gets the impression that progress must bring poverty; more wealth produced must increase rent; increased productive powers must reduce wages; all must cause poverty, because of land monopolisation. The dynamics of the science with him are the history of nations and institutions. This is erroneous. The science has to do with the supply of wealth. The rise and growth of institutions which hinder that supply are matters of economic history, not of economic science. The science, as such, points the institutions out once for all as injurious and unjust. The increase and improvement of methods and powers of production and distribution are matters of industrial history. Economic science only points out the conditions essential for making these improvements an unmixed blessing. The discovery and spread of the theories of the science are matters of the history of economics.

The science itself has nothing to do with long periods. Its dynamics relate to weeks, months, or at most a few years. Could but the truths of the science be flashed in a moment through the minds of all the people in this country, want of employment might cease, and the unemployed be at work in two or three weeks. Excepting the invalid, idle, and dissolute, that in itself would ensure the feeding of the nation. Such is the condition of supply. A few months would suffice to decently clothe all the people. The application of the science would in a year or two afford a respectable house for every family. But it would take a much longer time to give every family an active desire for a respectable house, decent clothing, and wholesome food. Their tastes would require more time to train than to supply. And, unfortunately, the truths of the science will not be flashed in a moment. Their teaching alone will take years or decades, rather than even months.

Strictly speaking, the inquiry ends here. With economic science the following chapter deals in a manner by no means necessary to its study. The doctrines have been stated, demonstrated, collected, and applied. Nothing remains to be done with regard to it. But to some it may not be uninteresting to give further consideration to the philosophy underlying the individualism here advocated, as opposed to the socialism which lies at the extreme pole from it. It may be, also, that without waste of time the ethical aspect of the conclusions of the science may be regarded from a somewhat more altruistic point of view.

CHAPTER XX

ETHICS AND PHILOSOPHY

FEW sciences have been more attacked in the name of religion and morality than has the science of economics. Most sciences have had to fight their way through misunderstanding and bigotry. It was hardly to be expected that this science could escape the same fate as others, for it has all along attacked established institutions and preconceived ideas. Moreover, with most ambitious men it is not pleasant to learn that they can do nothing better than seek out the natural path and follow that. Very many have ideas of paternalism in government by which they imagine they can set right all that is wrong, and put humanity into a groove of their own choosing. It is difficult for them to realize that the sum of human affairs is too large an undertaking for one man or a few to manage, or that every human being has a will of his own which must be allowed to have, at any rate, some free play. Most well-disposed persons have accordingly shown their good intentions by endeavouring to organize society on a model of their own. They have been told that the best thing they could do was to leave matters alone, and let every one do the best he could do for himself. But they have, figuratively speaking, lifted up their hands in pious horror at the hard-hearted indifference of the scientist and philosopher, as though he were an absolutely and wilfully cruel monster. The science has been called, with a touch of contempt, the dismal science,—not so much, perhaps, because it had to do with sordid gain, though that is one reason offered, but because it offered no brilliant schemes for taking from every man the trouble of looking after his own affairs, and gave no specific for making every man good in spite of himself.

On no ground, however, can the economist submit to have his science termed dismal. It does not, it is true, deal with the higher aspirations of the human soul. But it deals with what must ever be the foundation on which human welfare is built up. For when want and starvation are found beside abundance and luxury, injury is done to the highest interests of both rich and poor. To economic science alone can humanity look for direction as to how to avoid this undesirable condition, and no one need be ashamed even to grovel in the earth with a view to discovering what is the truth on this subject. As for its having no encouragement to offer to men burning to put matters right by their interference, perhaps a few words on the subject may not be inappropriate here.

A scientist need not plead guilty to heartlessness because he feels it his duty to insist on the acceptance of the unvarnished truth. The economist can only ascertain and announce the truth. Whether the world smiles or frowns on him, he can do no better service. Nor can he in any better way show his love for humanity. Yet because he has announced that free competition was the best method of meeting the struggle for existence, which, as long as the human race lasts, must ever continue, he has been denounced as soulless. It is true that free competition has not previously been offered exactly in the form here presented. But so far as the science has gone, that has always been its verdict; and the humanitarian world has generally received it coldly or not at all. Some have given credit to the Manchester school of free traders for their efforts for the repeal of the Corn Laws, but they do not include Cobden and his helpers amongst the social reformers of the century. That honour is reserved for a number of men who, with more or less pretence to scientific method (and the less the better), have taught ethics often regardless of philosophy.

The substantial contribution of the free traders to England's happiness has, however, at any rate, been felt if it has not been fully recognised. On the other hand, men with schemes of government from Plato onwards have received a sympathetic hearing. Their ideas, coming as they did from poetic minds, were enforced with great literary ability, and this added in no inconsiderable degree to their success. Whilst the analytic minds, who, following Aristotle, could accept nothing without proof, often failed to clothe their thoughts in language capable of attracting attention. Nor can it be hoped that this deficiency has been or will be remedied. Added to which it must be remembered that to follow an argument closely requires more mental exertion than many are willing to give.

For many years now there has been growing up a doctrine that Christianity and economic science are opposed to each other. The science is said to be too selfish. And socialism is held up as that which alone can accord with Christianity. The exact scheme of socialism which is to be adopted has not been agreed upon by its various advocates. That, however, is a matter of no importance. Political economy is not a scheme. It is *a science*. It seeks, states, and proves the truth. And whatever scheme may be offered, if it does not accord with the truth, it had better be rejected. Moreover, if the science has been properly interpreted, it points out the truth. And if Christianity does not agree with it, then Christianity is a lie. It is proposed, however, to show that no discrepancy exists between the two, and that neither in its origin nor in its doctrines has socialism anything to connect it with Christianity.

Apparently the only claim that socialism has to ally itself with Christianity is that it announces itself to be a scheme for promoting a universal brotherhood, and the due care of the weaker members of society. As an ethical ideal, no word can be raised against this object. But before accepting this scheme in its various forms at its own valuation, we must carefully look into its credentials, and see whether it offers what it professes to offer. The success of Christianity rests upon something more than its lofty ethical principles. The philosophy of Jesus Christ was as perfect as His morality was sublime, or His rule in the world to-day would not have been what it is. Now at this point Christianity and Socialism part company. To whatever extent the professed principles of Socialism may agree with those of Christianity, the moment the principles begin to be applied to human conditions, the two doctrines will be found to be diametrically opposed to each other.

Exactly what is meant by socialism, even its advocates do not appear ever to have explained. The word is used in a variety of senses, indicating that socialism is some scheme for improving the lot of humanity, more nearly equalising the distribution of wealth, or for uplifting the toiling millions. Now this, as a matter of intention and motive, is what very many persons would lay claim to. The number would include most candidates for public service, especially where the toiling millions have votes. The present author would even humbly desire to be enrolled under the list of Socialists of that description. But if socialism has no more definite meaning than this, it has no meaning at all worth consideration. The history of the expression Socialism, and of the theories to which it is attached, may afford some clue to its meaning. The word apparently started with Owen, an able money-maker full of schemes for uplifting those around him. But the idea expressed by it obtains its strength from more sources than one. Utopian schemes have not been confined to Sir Thomas More; St. Simon and Fourier had notions which J. S. Mill considered worthy of a place in connection with the science of economics. Communism in one form or another has had many advocates. But the community of goods which passes by the name of Socialism finds its chief economist in Marx. The foundation of his doctrine is Ricardo's error that wages are the amount essential for subsistence. From this the argument proceeds to speak of the exploiting of labour by capitalists who take the balance after paying subsistence wages. If the labourers were proprietary slaves, there would be some ground for this idea; but as the labourers who have the ability and character are free to become themselves exploiters, and to compete against the others, the notion is absurd. And in its place the wages of subsistence fallacy, on which the whole is based, was examined and disposed of. This error is the economic foundation or buttress of socialism.

Another source of the strength of the error is the philosophy of Auguste Comte. John Stuart Mill came under Comte's influence, and became more and more a Socialist as he grew older. He even defends Communism. It is doubtless quite true that a great number of professed Socialists have never heard of Comte; but that does not prove that the Socialism of the latter end of the nineteenth century exists independently of him. The truth appears to be this: Ricardo's error has developed into the socialism of Marx. Comte, by his writings, has influenced those who form what one may call the intellectual and literary section of the Socialists. At the same time, but quite independently of these influences, there has been growing up the ever-increasing influence of trade combinations.

The unconscious connection of socialism and trade combinations has already been referred to. They have, at any rate, this in common, that they make no pretence to respect individual liberty; the individual is ruthlessly sacrificed upon the altar of the community, whether the community be the members of a particular trade or of a whole nation, or whether it be, as with Comte, even more than that. Here, then, appears to be the origin of the socialism of the present time. It is to be found in the confluence of the course of those three distinct movements with some minor ones. The error of trade combination has been pointed out, and need not be further referred to. Ricardo's error, on which Marx built, has also been sufficiently noticed. Comte remains to be dealt with.

Now the prominent idea of Comte's teaching was the organization of society. With him society was an organism—not merely analogous to one. It was actually organic. The individual was but the organ of society. A single moment's thought should be enough to show the absurdity of such an idea. An organism has and uses its various organs for the good of the whole. Those organs are controlled by one mind and will; they are definite and fixed in number and position. If one is lost, another cannot take its place. With regard to some organs, their loss means loss of life altogether. Society is quite different. The individual acts for the satisfaction of his own desires, obeys his own mind and will, as far as he possibly can, and never thinks of putting the will of another before his own if he can avoid it. Moreover, there is free play to pass from one so-called function of society to another if the individual so desires.

It may readily be conceded that there is an

analogy between the organization of a living being and that of society. The analogy is found in the mutual assistance that the members of society render to each other. But it is not an analogy from which, in itself, any true conclusions can be drawn. We have only to take one step backwards in each case to find that on the very point on which we require similitude it is lacking. Asked why the members of society act after the manner of the organs of a living creature, the answer is, Because such actions best meet the desires of those members. Not the desires of society as a whole, but the desires of its members, cause the organization. In the other case, not the will of the organs, but that of the creature, determines their action. The organs have no will. This motive is the essential point, and if the motives are not the same, the analogy entirely fails for our present purpose.

Here, then, is the nature and signification of socialism. It sets itself in antithesis to individualism. It professes to seek the welfare of society, leaving to individualism the task of finding the true welfare of the persons composing society. Not a word further need be said to point out which is the correct method, or to satisfy the reader that Individualism can afford to be indifferent to the doctrine of Socialism. It will be remembered that the present inquiry commenced with an indication of the problem as that of finding how each individual could best be supplied with the wealth which was stated to be essential, and which was the object of the inquiry. Beyond that, and showing that the science had a sphere of its own, that no other science gave any indication that economists should endeavour to limit the welfare of individuals, it was unnecessary to go.

Socialism, on the other hand, is based on a theory diametrically opposed to the truth. Not only does it seek the welfare of society as opposed to the welfare of its members : it proceeds on the assumption that wealth production would be increased by taking away the incentive to its production. The whole theory depends on the notion that men work not to satisfy their own desires, but those of the community or society. The doctrine implies that if, instead of men being paid directly the market value of their efforts, they were required to give all their efforts to a common fund for the benefit of all, they would increase their efforts, and the nation would be richer. With such an error at the root of this teaching, true conclusions are impossible. And all this follows from Comte's philosophy. Socialism has its great support as a philosophic system in Comte's teaching.

How little socialism has in common with Christianity it will readily be seen. In the first place, Comte did not profess himself a Christian. He had something approaching contempt for the slaves of God. He wished to set up a worship of humanity with its temples, and a priesthood—the priesthood having a temporal power, only differing from those of past history in being, if possible, more despotic. The religion itself would have been greatly improved by an honest avowal of atheism. In the second place, his whole organization of society was quite unlike anything ever suggested by Christ or His apostles. To arrange as he did the whole of society into its various trades and professions, fixing—in the case of the priests at any rate—exactly the ages and salaries of the various grades, was certainly a pleasant amusement for a child. Most lads with a love of construction and ambitious ideas have mentally organized a colony or arranged a city in their younger days; but for a grown man of ability to imagine society can be brought into regimental array in that way is almost incredible. Furthermore, the positions assigned are in many cases hereditary, which is a system of slavery at least equal to that of the ancients.

That any professed Christian can ally himself with teaching of this kind can only be explained by concluding that he has not given sufficient consideration to the subject. So far from Christ wishing to organize society, it was the very thing He would not do. When the populace would have made Him king, He escaped from them. His kingdom was within, He told the Pharisees. So far from His putting society before the individual, it is to Him that mankind owes its appreciation of the individual and its knowledge of his worth. It was the one lost sheep, and not the ninety and nine, which received His sympathy. Moreover, He would not even give laws with regard to specific instances. He stated principles, and infused a true spirit into His disciples: and these were to be the guides of His followers in all ages. Subject to this, they were left each entirely to himself. This the apostles fully carried out in their writings. Nothing could be more truly in accordance with the spirit of individual liberty whilst teaching the highest and noblest brotherhood and charity. The communism of the early apostles is quite beside the question. It was for a definite purpose, the accomplishment of which was the foremost desire of each one of them.

Most of those into whose hands this book is likely to fall will readily concede that the true progress of humanity is towards Christianity. Now if socialism, as it is taught, means anything at all, that true progress is away from socialism and towards individualism.

The history of law as interpreted by philosophers points to a constantly progressing change, which we are told is a progress from status to contract. In the early stages of civilization persons occupy positions with regard to their personal relationship to others which are not the result of their choosing or agreement, but of their birth and circumstances. Their progress is to a condition in which each is free to make his own bargains with the rest of mankind, and to choose the best position he can obtain for himself. In the former case we may unmistakably see socialism in the only form possible to human beings. Property is held in common. The rule is a rule of persons. In the latter case individualism has asserted that all human beings should be equal in respect of their opportunities. The student of ethics may trace the same progress from socialism to individualism in the history of moral and religious teaching. In the early ages of society there are laws and regulations fixed for every detail. Mankind is bound round by rules and maxims, not without their object when framed, and occasionally of a beneficial nature, but out of which any nation must inevitably grow. In the later times, in morals as in laws, the principles underlying those laws and maxims which have proved themselves fit to survive are adopted as showing the desirable course. Human beings are set to move freely with these as their guide. This is but another instance of the progress of human beings from socialism to individualism.

It is true that socialism marks a stage removed from that of absolute savagery and fierce bestiality. In the latter case we may possibly have the entire absence of law or guidance. But it is a stage in the history of the species with which we are practically, and one might safely say entirely, unacquainted. We can conceive the possibility of it, but there is no good instance open to our examination. Our earliest knowledge of human institutions presents us with an organization in which, at least, there is the cohesion of tribesmen to each other. However savage they may occasionally be even amongst themselves, and whatever may be their code of right and wrong as regards others, they have at least the organization of a horde of savages. Moreover, in such cases there is usually a strong man amongst them, whom, under various names, they treat as chief and leader, and whose word is law. The progress of which we know anything is from this state to that in which not one nor many persons can decide the conduct of the whole, but in which principles of abstract right and justice are applied to the relations of each to one or all of the others. Briefly expressed, we may say that we can conceive that mankind first passes from the absence of rule and order to a rule of persons. We know that the race progresses from a rule of persons to a rule of principles.

Now the one central figure which marks the division of all we know of the origin and past history of our species from what we can forecast of its future destiny and progress is that of Jesus Christ. To Him and His teaching we owe the gradual abolition of the inequality of persons which made slavery possible. To Him more than to any one else we must ascribe the establishment of the authority of ethical principles as distinct from the persons placed in power. The philosophers of Greece are not to be forgotten, nor have they been forgotten by the writer in making this statement. In Jesus Christ there was something which inspired love, and banished the hatred engendered by the warring of tribes. Moreover, He not only laid down a code of ethics which was the highest the world has known : He taught that it was something under the outside action which must be changed, thus laying His finger on the springs of human action. He looked to human motive. From that point alone the action of the whole must be influenced. He taught that the internal desire was the cause of the external action. Out of the human heart proceeded human conduct. This is where He surpassed the philosophers of Greece. And this is the secret of His greater success in the conquest of mankind.

Socialism essentially belongs to the period which has been spoken of as that of the rule of persons.

Unless men are to be free, some must rule others. So much restraint as is necessary for the protection of others has already been conceded; but socialism goes further, and seeks to control the individual. Where that process will stop, or what its total sum of interference will amount to, cannot be predicted: nor is it a matter of concern. The essential feature is that if there is any control beyond what strict justice requires, the amount of it must be settled by persons and not by principles. Principles can only seek justice. It matters not that the persons deciding are the majority. The majority has no more right to despotism or to interfere with a man's true liberty than a single monarch has. The principles of justice are not to be submerged, even to gratify the majority. Besides which, even the majority is not always wise.

Moreover, the majority may profess to rule. But the majority has not a common interest or will, any more than the whole community has. To both there is a common interest that justice should be done. Beyond that there is no other interest. As for the common will, that is inevitably the will of one or a few. Men cannot think in unison. At best the majority requires to have its visible representatives. They, in effect, become the rulers whose thoughts guide those of others, or at least prescribe conduct for them. This is the essence of socialism. And if society could be organized anew to please these schemers, it must be on the model of the persons in power at the time. The national well-being would be in proportion to their wisdom and disinterestedness. If both were perfect and their knowledge infinite, the nation might be perfectly governed. Failing that, it could not.

All this, however, belongs to past ages. The community of property so dear to the hearts of Socialists is well known to the student of early institutions. The fixed and unalterable position of persons belongs to the same era. The minute regulation of the details of daily life is all characteristic of the dark days long since gone. In religion, in politics, in law, and in economics this is what we have struggled through and left behind. Now we are asked to go back to it. We are not told so plainly, but that is a trivial feature. The fact remains, nevertheless; and it would be a blessing to mankind if the advocates of Socialism would tell us definitely (providing they are able to see it so plainly) that they wish us to go back to the days of slavery. It is better to face the whole truth. But there is this, at any rate, in a name: that by means of a new name it is very possible to more or less effectually disguise an old acquaintance.

The human race will not, however, return, though its progress may be hindered. For nearly half a century the pendulum has swung backwards, but the forward course will assuredly be resumed in some place, and at some time—probably not a very distant time. Free competition will be accepted eventually by the world as the truest and most efficient method of supplying the wants of mankind. The only questions to be determined are when and where. On the latter depends the determination of the nation which shall next lead the van of human affairs, scattering the blessings of prosperity and commerce over its own people and the remainder of the world. On the former depends the answer to the question of how long the poor shall groan under a load of preventable distress and suffering, whilst the rich deteriorate through sheer super-abundance of goods. The one is a question of patriotism, the other of philanthropy.

After all, unrestricted competition is not so selfish a policy as many imagine. If it were selfish, it would be the best policy, as has already been shown. Moreover, the production of wealth is not the department in which altruism is required for human welfare. It is sufficient and much better that it be exercised in the matter of the consumption of wealth. Doubtless there are some who are able and specially competent in the matter of wealth production, and who can obtain for themselves a large share of wealth, who are nevertheless quite selfish with it. But it is useless to try to prevent their obtaining the wealth, except by allowing as far as possible the free play of the individual ability of others. These latter, in competing with them, benefit the rest. The policy of restriction and control results only in hindering those of second-rate ability from competing with those of the first-rate, and bringing them to compete with those of the third-rate. There can be but one result: namely, to separate by a constantly widening gulf the upper and lower classes. In that process the poorest are crushed to the very dust. Besides all this, many efficient wealth-producers are liberal givers. To constantly denounce and endeavour to injure them is a sure method of alienating the sympathies they may possess.

The doctrine of restriction, whether applied to governments or combinations, is of all things that which should lay no claim to unselfishness. Only by free commerce with each other can all the nations of earth become as one. The principle of protection by hostile tariffs, by which nations shut themselves up from each other, is as inconsistent with world-wide amity and friendship, or even with peace, as it is with good economics. This applies whether the principle of protection is in its extreme form or the modified form of List. Nations have no separate interests. The welfare of each is bound up in the welfare of all. The same applies to different classes in the same nation. The advocacy of seeking out distinct trade interests, and the setting up of barriers to protect them, in furtherance of the brotherhood of man, is, to say the least, unique. No good can come to those who have to carry on the wealth-producing work of a nation, or of the world, by setting up walls of division between different sections or classes of workers. Philosophically and ethically it is alike unsound.

More than all this, however, is true. Every reader must by this time have observed that the whole process of wealth production and distribution is a question of the balancing and weighing of two sides. The object of the whole is to balance certain essential desires possessed by the human race. But under the modern system of production and commerce, few produce what they require for themselves. Every one produces for others, and receives money as a measure of his share in production and consumption of wealth. The result is that each has the service he renders in this matter valued by the remainder of mankind, the persons to whom the service has ultimately been rendered.

It may be true that some have considerable capacity for getting their services valued more highly than their true utility, and that the benefits rendered by others are considerably under-valued. But even this statement can only be accepted on the showing of an individual who may be no wiser than the collective aggregate of those who, in fact, fix the valuation. At any rate, they can express their own desires better than he can express those desires for them. If the desires are not wholesome and beneficial, it is a matter for regret. But it is not within the power of even a sage to compel men to give up their desires and accept for their benefit the satisfaction of his desires.

If, on the other hand, it is not the badly chosen desires, but the ignorance of the people as to the true value of the services rendered, which enables a man to get himself overvalued, it is always open to any one to prove that to be the case by offering the same service at a lower rate. It is very certain that such a method of valuation is much more nearly perfect than could be the valuation of any one person or senate. The people themselves can better choose those things and pleasures which minister to the satisfaction of their desires, than any one could choose for them. Even though his knowledge of human nature, giving him skill to discern character and ability, and his personal disinterestedness should be alike perfect, the sage's best efforts could but be to find out their choice. That does not need a government or senate. It is done naturally by means of money. To place the nation at the disposal of such a government would be foolish, if it were possible.

If, then, mankind pays each man, as nearly as it can judge, according to the service he renders, it follows that, with equality of opportunity, he who receives most renders most service. He who receives least, in such conditions, does least service; so that the strong competitors, who get much, must have done much service to the weaker ones, and the weaker competitors, who get less, have done less service to the stronger ones. In other words, the true condition of mankind, as pointed out by economics, is one in which the strong labour for the weak, the weak giving such help as they can to the strong. It might fairly be suggested, providing the matter came within the present subject, that the burden of the altogether incapable should be put upon the strong, as it must be under the taxation which has been advocated. The result of such a plan must be that, in the endeavour to carry that burden, by absolutely giving what those incapable ones need, the strong must be constantly urged to a greater endeavour. The benefit of that endeavour will go to the weaker ones (who are not altogether incapable) in return for their help towards the support of the weakest. Such a method is a constantly impelling motive to the exertion of the strong, and that by the gratification of their own desires—a perpetual self-working arrangement for the strong to help the weak.

Moreover, it has sometimes been suggested that the perfection of distribution of work and wages would be that each should work according to his ability, and receive according to his needs, which is exactly what is meant by free competition. Each man's needs express themselves in his desires. In every well-balanced mind nature has proportioned desires to capacity. All other minds must strive to correct their want of balance. Under the best system, therefore, since needs are by nature proportioned to capacity, the wages supplying those needs will be proportioned to the work accomplished by that capacity, which, as already remarked, is free competition.

Surely if any science is to be called dismal, it is quite time the appellation should be shifted from that of economics, and put upon some other science. No suggestion is made, however, as to what science should receive it, or that any science or true knowledge can be dismal.

In speaking in this way, it is not, of course, meant that these results are properly attained under the system in vogue in the nineteenth century. Wherein that system is wrong, it has been to some extent pointed out. The science of economics is not, however, responsible for that, but rather the nostrums which affect to treat the science as dismal and heartless.

Nor is it forgotten that many men possess themselves of considerable wealth by mere speculation. But the possibility of speculation is, by the adoption of a truly natural system, reduced to the barest minimum. This would be seen in seeking and laying down the means of keeping value perfectly constant. It is the departure from a truly natural system which permits of the evils of speculation.

The system pointed out by economic science as the most beneficial for mankind is not only truly natural, but absolutely just. In every portion of the inquiry the natural system has been assiduously sought. What has been meant by a natural system has been that which was in accordance with perfect liberty to all; but, at the same time, that which was, as far as could be ascertained, perfectly just and equal between opposing interests. Justice, in fact, is equality; but it is a natural equality. An attempted equality which is not free and natural is a false equality. No person should be deprived of his liberty any more than of his limbs, provided that he accord to others rights equal to his own. Beyond this truest liberty and equality, human beings are so constituted, their interests are so bound up together, that each one, even in seeking his own interest (if he does it consistently with the foundation principles of liberty and equality), will find that he is at the same time practising real fraternity. Beyond this, if but consistently with it, he may still go, and find his own happiness in a Christian charity which is Divine. And this accords with the true science of wealth.

www.ingramcontent.com/pod-product-compliance
Lightning Source LLC
Chambersburg PA
CBHW030424300426
44112CB00009B/834